Cognitive therapy in clinical practice

Cognitive therapy is perhaps best known as one of the most effective methods for treating depression. Its applications, however, are much broader and it is being applied in an increasingly wide range of clinical situations: for example with anxious, hypochondriacal, or obsessional patients, with clients who have eating problems, with drug abusers and suicidal patients, and to overcome the psychological distress that may accompany physical ill health.

The contributors to *Cognitive Therapy in Clinical Practice* discuss the use of cognitive therapy in these and other contexts, giving examples of how cognitive therapists working with different groups of clients have applied the cognitive model in their field. They combine an overview of the current status of cognitive therapy in their domain with case studies that demonstrate its particular applications. Extracts from therapy sessions are given, enabling the reader to 'hear the voices' of the patients described, to empathise with their problems, and to get alongside the therapists as they seek to build a collaborative relationship with the clients.

Of interest to a wide range of students and practitioners in clinical psychology, behavioural psychotherapy, and psychiatry, the book should do much to stimulate therapists to try out the systematic application of cognitive techniques to an even wider range of client groups.

Cognitive therapy in clinical practice

An illustrative casebook

Edited by Jan Scott, J. Mark G. Williams, and Aaron T. Beck

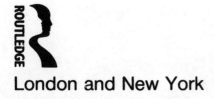

London and New York

First published 1989 by Routledge
11 New Fetter Lane, London EC4P 4EE
29 West 35th Street, New York, NY 10001

First published in paperback by
Routledge in 1991

Reprinted in 1992

© 1989 Jan Scott, J. Mark G. Williams, and Aaron T. Beck

Typeset by Photoprint, Torquay, Devon
Printed and bound in Great Britain by
Biddles Ltd, Guildford and King's Lynn

British Library Cataloguing in Publication Data
Cognitive therapy in clinical practice: an illustrative casebook.
  1. Medicine. Cognitive therapy
  I. Scott, Jan II. Williams, J. Mark G.
  III. Beck, Aaron T. (Aaron Temkin)
  616.8914

Library of Congress Cataloging in Publication Data
Also available

ISBN 0–415–06242–X

Contents

Contributors   vi

Foreword
Aaron T. Beck   vii

1 **Severely depressed in-patients**
Ivy M. Blackburn   1

2 **Panic disorder and agoraphobia**
Ruth L. Greenberg   25

3 **Obsessions and compulsions**
Paul M. Salkovskis   50

4 **Hypochondriasis**
Hilary M.C. Warwick and Paul M. Salkovskis   78

5 **Cancer patients**
Jan Scott   103

6 **Eating disorders**
Shelley Channon and Jane Wardle   127

7 **Drug abusers**
Stirling Moorey   157

8 **Offenders**
Amanda Cole   183

9 **Suicidal patients**
J. Mark G. Williams and Jonathan Wells   206

10 **The wider application of cognitive therapy:
the end of the beginning**
J. Mark G. Williams and Stirling Moorey   227

Index   251

Contributors

Aaron T. Beck, Center for Cognitive Therapy, 133 South 36 Street, Philadelphia, PA 19104, USA.

Ivy M. Blackburn, Medical Research Council, Brain Metabolism Unit, Royal Edinburgh Hospital, Morningside Park, Edinburgh EH10 5HF.

Shelley Channon, Psychology Department, Institute of Psychiatry, De Crespigny Park, Denmark Hill, London SE5 8AF.

Amanda Cole, 44 Church Road, Alphington, Exeter EX2 8SZ.

Ruth L. Greenberg, Center for Cognitive Therapy, 133 South 36 Street, Philadelphia, PA 19104, USA.

Stirling Moorey, Institute of Psychiatry, De Crespigny Park, Denmark Hill, London SE5 8AF.

Paul M. Salkovskis, University Department of Psychiatry, Warneford Hospital, Oxford OX3 7JX.

Jan Scott, University Department of Psychiatry, Royal Victoria Infirmary, Newcastle upon Tyne NE1 4LP.

Jane Wardle, Psychology Department, Institute of Psychiatry, De Crespigny Park, Denmark Hill, London SE5 8AF.

Hilary M.C. Warwick, University Department of Psychiatry, Warnford Hospital, Oxford OX3 7JX.

Jonathan Wells, Social Work Department, Fulbourn Hospital, Fulbourn, Cambridge CB1 5EF.

J. Mark G. Williams, Medical Research Council, Applied Psychology Unit, 15 Chaucer Road, Cambridge CB2 2EF.

Foreword

Aaron T. Beck

The success in cognitive therapy in treating a range of depressive disorders and in reducing the risk of relapse (Blackburn *et al.* 1987; Simons *et al.* 1986) has encouraged its application to clinical problems other than depression. This wider application is consistent with the cognitive model which, from the outset, was not intended to be confined to depression, but was applied to other behavioural and emotional disorders (Beck 1976; Beck *et al.* 1985). In many situations, people are subject to external events or bodily symptoms in which differences in cognitive interpretations lead to different patterns and intensity of affect and behaviour.

The extension of any therapeutic practice to a new problem area has to be taken in stages. Success in treating single cases is an essential first step. It allows us to say that a therapeutic strategy can sometimes work with this problem area. The addition of more single cases (a clinical series) will, if they also respond well, add plausibility to the claim that initial successes were not merely chance results. This is how all new therapy applications have had to start.

The efficacy of a therapy for a certain client group will ultimately be judged by a full outcome study in which a large number of similarly diagnosed patients are randomly assigned to groups, carefully assessed, and compared to patients in control conditions. But outcome studies are very expensive in time and money and cannot therefore be justified until there is a good prima facie case that a treatment will work.

The different problem areas discussed in the chapters in this book all broadly come into this initial stage, where the plausibility of applying cognitive therapy to new client groups is examined. We believe strongly that the cognitive model is relevant to these disorders and we need to listen carefully to experienced cognitive therapists to learn which aspects of cognitive therapy they have found most helpful.

The result is a volume containing examples of how cognitive therapists working in different settings with different groups of adult clients have applied the cognitive model in their domain. We have encouraged the authors to illustrate the way they work by using extended case material and to present frankly the difficulties of working with their clients. This they have done admirably, and readers will soon find themselves hearing the voices of the patients described, empathising with their problems, and getting alongside the therapists as they seek to build a collaborative relationship with the clients. Detailed consideration of case material of the sort we present in this book will always have a place in the teaching of therapeutic methods. Any psychotherapist, no matter how experienced, knows there is always more to learn about how to deal with the problems of their clients. One way of doing so is to hear cases presented by other therapists. This volume allows others to 'listen' to the cases we have presented.

In the first chapter, Ivy Blackburn discusses the problem of applying cognitive therapy (CT) to severely depressed in-patients. Blackburn's work in testing the efficacy of CT for depressed out-patients and GP patients is well known (Blackburn *et al*. 1981; Blackburn *et al*. 1987). It was the first test of CT efficacy outside of North America. But as she points out in her chapter, most outcome trials have used mild to moderately severe patients, the type of patients who are normally treated by GPs or as out-patients. In-patients are likely to have special problems, their symptoms being more extensive, severe, and disabling. Application of CT to this group has not only the difficulty of the patients' symptoms, but also of the ward milieu which is very different from the environment of the out-patient, and leads to different expectations in the patients.

The description of the patient Blackburn presents suggests that this person would have been excluded from outcome studies published to date because of the presence of psychotic symptoms. (The patient believed people were following her, that detectives were watching her. Colleagues at work, she thought, were disguised in order to watch her. She thought one of the nurses on the ward was a policewoman.) Assessment and cognitive formulation needed to be done with great care. Assessment took place over two sessions. No mention of cognitive therapy was made during session one and was held back in session two until the therapist felt that the patient was familiar with the style of cognitive therapy. The vocabulary of the therapist and the nature of the questions asked implicitly reflected the cognitive model, but the model was only explicitly produced when a good example presented itself in the normal course of therapy.

Therapy sessions were scheduled frequently during the 8-week admission. At times this was on a daily basis, and there was a total of twenty-six sessions while the patient was in hospital. No medication was used for the patient throughout her admission. Therapy continued on an out-patient basis for twice a week at the outset and for once a week for a further fifteen appointments. Despite the greater time commitment than is usually the case for out-patient depressives, if the outcome with severely depressed patients is as successful as with this patient, and if there is a reduced risk of relapse, cognitive therapy will have brought about a major improvement in quality of life for these patients as well as releasing further resources to help others.

In Chapter 2, Ruth Greenberg describes the way the cognitive model has been applied to patients with panic disorder and agoraphobia, who characteristically make catastrophic misinterpretations of bodily symptoms or mental experiences. The way these patients have difficulty in identifying thoughts as erroneous inferences, rather than as reality, is different from that often met in depression. For many depressed patients, thoughts such as 'I'm a failure' seem true (even within the therapy session). The result is that the patient finds it very difficult to see it as an 'idea' to be tested out. But many anxious patients *realise* when non-anxious (e.g. in a therapy session) that their thoughts are not realistic. Their problem is that when they next experience symptoms, this knowledge generally does not help. They will still believe, *at that moment*, that they are going to faint, go crazy, die, or lose control.

Greenberg shows how this problem can be overcome partly by persistent 'stripping away' of thoughts, images, and assumptions about being out of control; partly by behavioural experiments within the session (such as hyperventilation); and partly by identifying the core dysfunctional beliefs: their origin, development, and validity for the present. Greenberg's case example shows these procedures in action. One can see clearly, in her description of therapy, how at many points a psychodynamic therapist might have wished the course of therapy to proceed along other lines. But we also see how Greenberg's gentle but persistent investigation using the cognitive framework gains relatively quick access to some core issues for the patient (regarding his relationship with his mother) about which he was barely conscious prior to therapy.

The influence of early experience in setting up rigidly held beliefs is well illustrated in the case of an obsessional patient described by Paul Salkovskis in Chapter 3. This particular application of the cognitive model to obsessions and compulsions has been developed by Salkovskis in earlier papers (1985). The central aspect of Salkovskis's theory is that intrusive thoughts may be positive, negative, or neutral, depending on the evaluation made by the individual experiencing them. Because it is the evaluation/appraisal of intrusive thoughts by the individual which is responsible for their acquiring emotional properties, the aversiveness of mildly negative thoughts can be exacerbated by such appraisal processes. For example, while many people may have thoughts about not leaving sharp knives around the house when children are about, some individuals will appraise this thought very negatively. They will ruminate about the most negative possible consequences, worry about their own responsibility, or tell themselves what an awful person they are to be having such thoughts. Cognitive therapy is useful not only in facilitating behavioural approaches (assessment, preventing drop-outs, improving compliance, maximising effectiveness of exposure and response prevention), but also as a treatment in its own right, especially for people who fail to respond to behavioural methods.

Once again there is a need to concentrate a great deal of care and attention to the setting up of therapy in the initial sessions (compare Blackburn's similar comments). Engaging the obsessional patient is not easy and Salkovskis provides valuable hints on how best to achieve this. He does not push the patient to talk of their troubling thoughts. Rapport is established by discussing more peripheral issues. He illustrates an important advantage of the cognitive model – that a patient's poor motivation to comply with therapy can itself be analysed in cognitive terms. Until the relationship between therapist and patient is truly collaborative, little progress will be made on the central processes maintaining the disorder.

Cognitive treatment of panic disorder (Chapter 2) and of obsessional patients (Chapter 3) raises the issue of the relationship between intrusive thoughts that are normal and those that are abnormal and how their appraisal affects mood and behaviour. This is central also to clients suffering hypochondriasis and illness phobia described in Chapter 4 by Hilary Warwick and Paul Salkovskis. These authors focus on three main mechanisms that combine to increase anxious preoccupation with illness and misinterpretation of (often normal) variation in bodily functions: increased physiological arousal; selective attention to bodily sensations or appearance; behaviour aimed at avoiding stimuli associated with illness or at 'neutralising' the anxiety. Once again, the cognitive aspect of such avoidant behaviour is seen as a central factor in maintaining the disorder. Reassuring these patients does not help and it may even contribute to the maintenance of the disorder. How to proceed to engage the hypochondriacal patient in therapy without bland reassurance or combative argument about the origin of their symptoms is a major concern of Warwick and Salkovskis's chapter. The patient's own view of their problems is not directly challenged. Rather, a spirit of open-ended *enquiry* is fostered. Evidence is gathered. Collaboration is built up by the therapist finding some area of agreement with the patient, some issue closely connected to the distress the patient feels.

Warwick and Salkovskis illustrate engaging a patient in therapy who had an apparently unshakeable belief of permanent damage having been done to her throat by an experiment carried out while undergoing a tonsillectomy many years before. A second illustration, of treating a patient who feared she had cancer, shows the importance of not questioning the veracity of the symptoms, but rather exploring alternative explanations of them. A third case illustrates a patient who feared he had contracted AIDS. It is particularly interesting in that the patient's occupation had brought him into contact with high-risk groups. Some health professionals might therefore describe his anxiety as 'reasonable', and as unsuitable for cognitive therapy. Far from it. Warwick and Salkovskis are able to make a point clearly which holds for cognitive therapy in general. Because the therapy explicitly deals with reality, rather than obscuring it with bland reassurance, positive self-talk, or investigation of complex psychodynamics, it has a good chance of being accepted by the patient as reasonable in their wish to get to the bottom of their symptoms.

Cognitive therapy has always been concerned with confronting reality rather than simply substituting positive for negative, distorted thinking. But what if the reality is itself *bad*? This question is confronted head on in Chapter 5. In most people's minds, few things could be worse than having cancer, and one would expect that extensive emotional disturbance would accompany such a condition. This is indeed often the case, as Jan Scott points out in this chapter. Yet depression and anxiety accompanying cancer are often either unrecognised, or, if recognised, go untreated because they are seen as a 'natural' response.

In her chapter, Jan Scott gives reasons why the emotional disturbance associated with severe physical illness deserves attention in its own right. First, treating the emotions may enhance the physical outcome. Second, the quality of the (sometimes shortened) life that is left for the patients may be considerably enhanced by working with them to gain as much control as possible over their illness: the physical pain, the loss of self-image related to disfigurement, changes in role if work has to stop, the grieving for the former 'well' self.

Scott illustrates these points with a case description of a 37-year-old woman, referred following diagnosis and treatment for carcinoma of the breast. On preliminary assessment she was hopeless, depressed, anxious, irritable, withdrawn, and restless. Her Beck Depression Inventory score was 27 (severely depressed). Scott outlines the goals of therapy: learning to recognise stress-provoking situations and thoughts; learning to cope with stress and altering maladaptive coping strategies; examining and improving social and family relationships; and reducing anxiety related to health. These goals were achieved (the Beck score fell gradually over ten sessions to very low levels) by careful monitoring of automatic thoughts and images, making underlying assumptions explicit (especially the belief that in order to be liked she should not manifest any weakness in the face of stress, and that she could not be happy unless she was independent of others).

Here we see how cognitive therapy can help patients with a severe physical illness. It may be 'understandable' to be frustrated, anxious, and sad about their disability. But depression is not mere 'sadness'. It is rather a deep emptiness, a wishing to withdraw, a not thinking *anything* is worthwhile, based on unwarranted assumptions about the world, the self, and the future. Of course, one can understand a person being profoundly sad if they have cancer; but they need not be left with the belief that it is their fault, that nobody loves them because they are unlovable, that to be weak is shameful.

In Chapter 6 Shelley Channon and Jane Wardle discuss the application of cognitive therapy to anorexia nervosa and bulimia nervosa. The treatment draws together a wide range of techniques including anxiety reduction and self-management principles as well as modification of dysfunctional attitudes. Because of the nature of eating disorders, with starving and vomiting being central features of the disorder, there is more emphasis on behavioural techniques than is the case with cognitive therapy with other problems. Through the description of a single case, Carol, Channon and Wardle take us through medical assessment, psychological assessment, devising a treatment plan and developing motivation for its implementation (especially by making the rationale of the treatment clear and explicit and by providing relevant factual information). Treatment then focuses on weight restoration, on specific aspects of eating behaviour including binge eating, and vomiting and laxative abuse where these occur. From an early point in treatment, therapists focus on identifying and modifying dysfunctional thoughts. Since these often arise in very precisely defined circumstances of eating, the therapist can set up an experiment in which a small amount of 'fattening food' (such as chocolate) is to be eaten during the therapy session. The patients then record their thoughts before the food is presented, when it is presented (before eating), during eating, and after eating. Modifying maladaptive aspects of these thoughts becomes an important factor alongside behavioural intervention.

Cognitive therapy with drug abusers poses many severe challenges for the therapist. Yet, as Stirling Moorey indicates (Chapter 7), the cognitive model has grown in popularity over the last 10 years since it appears to provide the best currently available way of integrating diverse approaches within therapy into a single rational package. As Moorey points out, cognitions stand at the interface between physiological, affective, and social process; thought, beliefs, and expectancies are all concepts which can be readily understood by the patient and other professionals.

Moorey considers a range of therapeutic strategies, placing them within the context of the physical aspects of addiction and its management. The different aspects of therapy are tackled in turn: engagement, problem definition and cue analysis, problem solving and cue modification, identifying and challenging underlying assumptions, and redefining maladaptive roles. As with cognitive therapy for obsessional and hypochrondriacal patients, the problems in engaging the client are legion. Moorey indicates the importance of trying as far as possible to mesh the therapy strategies to the individual's temperament. Without such attempts a therapeutic relationship will be much harder to establish. An important consideration here is the very complex motivations which patients have. As Moorey comments, it is not possible to talk of people being motivated or unmotivated to give up drugs. Fluctuation in commitment is normal and must be expected. Prochaska and DiClemente's (1983) cyclical model of recovery and relapse is commended as a helpful framework.

Listing advantages and disadvantages of giving up addictions may be one way to proceed, and Moorey gives examples of such procedures. The emphasis on specific description is continued throughout the subsequent therapy sessions – especially in cue analysis, but also in problem solving, modifying situational and emotional factors by monitoring thoughts during exposure, predicting high-risk situations and coping with them if they cannot be prevented. Dealing with underlying assumptions is an important aspect of reducing risk of relapse and is closely linked with an addict's self-schema.

Many of the problems found in cognitive therapy with drug abusers arise also in cognitive therapy with offenders. Amanda Cole (Chapter 8) describes how motivation for therapy may be very mixed in those who have offended. But consistent with the suggestions of Moorey in relation to drug abusers, this should not be taken to preclude therapy. She also describes behaviour within therapy similar to patterns described by Moorey: apparent predisposition to repeat the same vicious circle of (in this case) offending, despite punishment, despite confrontation, or despite insightful 'therapeutic' observation from professionals or others.

There is a need for careful analysis of the thoughts and images associated with the specific situation in which the offence has taken place, similar to the careful analysis which is done for clients with eating disorders (Chapter 6) and addictive behaviours (Chapter 7). The cognitions thus elicited are the 'raw material' for cognitive therapy. Cole shows how they can be used to formulate hypotheses, conceptualise the case, decide on the need for therapy, and determine which technique will be most appropriate. She uses imagery to elicit thoughts associated with offence situations, showing how it reveals a wide range of interpretation by the clients of their own feelings and of other people's attitudes and reactions. Thus offenders have beliefs such as 'Women wear tight jeans to turn men on' or 'The woman who pays attention when I expose myself is showing how it excites her'.

In a case description, Cole illustrates offender–therapist collaboration in analysing the problems associated with a recidivist exhibitionist, deciding on treatment strategies and implementing these by testing and modifying hypotheses. A major goal of therapy was not only to analyse and cope with the offence behaviour itself but also to cope with the client's dependency on therapy itself. He had stopped offending during previous therapy attempts, only to start again afterwards. Maintenance of treatment gains was to be a goal defined at the outset of treatment rather than left to the final few sessions.

Therapy was not a smooth progression from 'problem' to 'solution'. It is rare for clients undergoing any psychotherapy to experience a smooth recovery process, and cognitive therapy is no exception. The clinical course of recovery in any individual is variable. However, if the therapist has adopted an empirical approach at the outset, then problems will be anticipated and can aid therapy by contributing to the testing of hypotheses about the maintenance of the disorder. The case described by Amanda Cole is a good example of how such an approach *uses* the difficulties that arise in the course of therapy to enhance rather than undermine therapeutic progress.

During the course of cognitive therapy with any of the client groups discussed in this book, suicidal thoughts may arise. This is especially true in relation to depression, but the risks are also significantly increased in other disorders, particularly eating disorders and addictive behavioural patterns. Mark Williams and Jonathan Wells (Chapter 9) draw on their experience in dealing with depressed patients who are also suicidal and in counselling patients after they have attempted suicide, to describe therapy for suicidal patients. They point to the evidence which shows that depression by itself is often insufficient to produce thoughts of suicide. It is when depression combines with hopelessness and despair about the future that suicidal behaviour is most likely. Such hopelessness and despair may be associated with many different problems other than primary depression. Therapists must therefore be vigilant for expressions of hopelessness. These may be disguised beneath such comments as 'Sometimes I just don't know why I bother'.

Later in their chapter Williams and Wells describe a therapy session in which the thought 'Nothing has changed' is being evaluated. The thought that 'nothing has changed' crops up time and again in the minds of people when they are suicidal. As far as patients are concerned, it often provides all they need in the way of evidence that they may as well 'end it all'.

It is worth emphasising some other points made by Williams and Wells in their chapter. First, the importance of assessing the extent to which suicidal wishes are motivated by a desire to *communicate* something to somebody, and to what extent by a desire to *escape*. For most patients these motivations are mixed, but they are not necessarily conscious of either. Second, if expressions of hopelessness are taken to signal suicidal intent, then bringing such ideas out in the open is essential. As they indicate, there is no evidence that discussion of suicide promotes suicidal behaviour. Third, if suicidal ideas are being expressed, the therapist needs to assess the probability that the patient will act on these thoughts. Williams and Wells describe the factors that will need to be taken into account, especially assessment of the stability of the life situation and the person's impulsivity. They give details of cases to illustrate three approaches which supplement usual cognitive therapy techniques, listing reasons for living versus dying: targeting specific hopeless thoughts for reality testing; using time projection to encourage a patient to visualise some concrete future possibilities.

This overview of the clinical presentations should give the reader the flavour of each of the chapters. We hope that this will induce the reader to explore the topics in depth. We do not attempt to summarise the main themes in this Foreword or to speculate at this point on the next steps for cognitive therapy. We shall leave this job to the final chapter. This book will have fulfilled its aim if it excites further enthusiasm for therapists to try out the systematic application of cognitive techniques with a wider range of client groups.

ATB

References

Beck, A.T. (1976) *Cognitive Therapy and the Emotional Disorders*, New York: International Universities Press.

Beck, A.T., Emery, E., and Greenberg, R.L. (1985) *Anxiety Disorders and Phobias: A Cognitive Perspective*, New York: Basic.

Blackburn, I.M., Bishop, S., Glen, I.M., Whalley, L.J., and Christie, J.E. (1981) 'The efficacy of cognitive therapy in depression: a treatment trial using cognitive therapy and pharmacotherapy, each alone and in combination', *British Journal of Psychiatry* 139: 181–9.

Blackburn, I.M., Eunson, K.M., and Bishop, S. (1987) 'A two-year naturalistic follow-up of depressed patients treated with cognitive therapy, pharmacotherapy and a combination of both', *Journal of Affective Disorders* 10: 67–75.

Prochaska, J.O. and DiClemente, C.C. (1983) 'Stages and processes of self-change of smoking: toward an integrative model of change', *Journal of Consulting and Clinical Psychology* 51: 390–5.

Salkovskis, P.M. (1985) 'Obsessional–compulsive problems: a cognitive–behavioural analysis', *Behaviour, Research and Therapy* 25: 571–83.

Simons, A.D., Murphy, G.E., Levine, J.E., and Wetzel, R.D. (1986) 'Cognitive therapy and pharmacotherapy for depression', *Archives of General Psychiatry* 43: 43–8.

Chapter one

Severely depressed in-patients

Ivy M. Blackburn

Introduction

Cognitive therapy (CT) of depression (Beck *et al.* 1979) was described as a method of treatment for out-patients with mild to moderate depressions. All published controlled studies of efficacy have so far included only out-patients, usually satisfying research diagnostic critieria for major or definite depression (Spitzer *et al.* 1978; Feighner *et al.* 1972), unipolar subtype. Seven studies have compared CT with antidepressant medication, each alone or in combination (Rush *et al.* 1977; Beck *et al.* 1979; Blackburn *et al.* 1981; Rush and Watkins 1981; Murphy *et al.* 1984; Teasdale *et al.* 1984; Beck *et al.* 1985). The results of these treatment trials have all confirmed the efficacy of CT in the treatment of depression, CT being found equivalent or superior to antidepressant medication. Other studies have compared CT with behaviour therapy in the treatment of depressed self-referred students and media-recruited depressed individuals. These studies (Shaw 1977; Taylor and Marshall 1977; Zeiss *et al.* 1979; Wilson *et al.* 1983) have found CT superior or equivalent to behaviour therapy and superior to waiting-list controls. Various other studies (e.g. McLean and Hakstian 1979; Shipley and Fazio 1973) have used behaviour therapy with a strong cognitive component in depressed out-patients or depressed students, and found cognitive behaviour therapy to be an effective treatment, superior to psychodynamic or supportive psychotherapy.

Thus, the efficacy of CT, as described by Beck *et al.* (1979), or of other types of short-term therapies which are primarily cognitive in orientation, has been relatively well established in the treatment of depressed out-patients. Questions which are often posed are: 'How effective is the same treatment method in the more severely depressed in-patients?' and 'Can cognitive therapy be applied to in-patients?' There are, unfortunately, no published studies to date which could begin to answer these questions, but they are undoubtedly important practical questions. In this chapter, I will discuss some of the problems involved in the treatment of severely depressed in-patients and describe a case study as illustration.

1

Cognitive therapy with in-patients

Why do cognitive therapy with in-patients?

Since the majority of depressed patients in Britain are treated primarily by their general practitioners and, secondly, as out-patients in psychiatric clinics (Goldberg and Huxley 1980), depressed patients who become in-patients have specific characteristics which distinguish them from the majority of depressed patients. In general, depressed patients who become in-patients in the National Health Service may have one or several of the following characteristics: psychotic features, that is delusions and hallucinations; high suicidal risk and/or suicidal behaviour; severe impairment with gross retardation or agitation, anorexia, and sleep disturbance; the need for electroconvulsive therapy (ECT) because of past history of response to ECT or because of current severity of illness; failure to respond to out-patient treatment and long duration of index episode of illness.

Severely depressed in-patients are almost invariably treated by physical methods of treatment, medication, and/or ECT, with little or no psychotherapeutic input. There are, however, several arguments for the usefulness of a psychotherapeutic approach such as CT in these patients because of, rather than in spite of, the chronic and severe illness characteristics described above.

1. Depressed in-patients may often exhibit hopelessness regarding their prospect for improvement. They are likely to have been depressed for a long time and to have already been treated with two or three different antidepressant drugs. They may have, naturally, become sceptical about outcome of further treatment. CT offers an alternative approach which has face validity and may revive some hope in treatment in general. CT techniques can also be used to increase compliance with drug regimens when a combined treatment is being considered.

2. The long months of illness or the recurrent nature of the illness, in addition to fostering hopelessness, also creates a sense of lack of control which is increased by the medicalisation of the illness. The patient may often voice the implicit message given by the physician: 'Something is wrong with my biochemistry – there is nothing I can do about it.' By its methodology which stresses coping techniques and empirical verification, CT increases a sense of control which is in itself beneficial. A problem may arise about the apparent double or inconsistent message which is being given to the patient when he is receiving both CT and pharmacotherapy. This will be considered later in this chapter.

3. Many behavioural problems accompany severe depressive illness,

either as primary symptoms of depression or secondary to the chronic nature of the illness. These are inactivity, apathy, increased dependence, lack of self-assertion and indecision. Such problems can be dealt with effectively through cognitive and behavioural methods of treatment.

4. The alternative of introducing depressed in-patients to CT after the treatment of their acute episode with physical methods of treatment may decrease the credibility of the therapy as a method of treatment for depression. The patient, who is already nearly recovered, is likely to be less involved in the treatment and less motivated to comply with the tasks which are an integral part of the therapy.

5. The promising results on the effectiveness of CT in the prevention of relapse (Simons *et al.* 1986; Blackburn, *et al.* 1987) may indicate that CT, at least as an adjunct to pharmacotherapy, is essential for depressed in-patients who have a history of frequent relapses. CT, in these cases, is often best considered as an additional treatment, in combination with medication, but, in my experience, it can also be effective on its own.

Specific problems relating to cognitive therapy with in-patients

Besides the general difficulties encountered in doing CT with severely depressed patients, the ward setting itself imposes constraints and conditions which are not operative in the case of out-patients. First of all, the environment is very restricted in terms of whom the patient interacts with, in terms of potential activities which are available, and in terms of expectations from staff and relatives and of the demands which are consequently put upon the individual. Second, hospital units and wards, in particular in a teaching hospital, are staffed by multidisciplinary teams within which widely different orientations are often represented. Unless good liaison is established, the patient may become totally disoriented. For example, the patient may be expected to attend psychodynamically oriented group therapy in the morning, have 1 hour of CT in the afternoon, talk to ward nurses who may take an excessively supportive role, be interviewed by medical students for teaching purposes, and take medication before going to bed if a combined treatment is being administered. The therapist in charge of the cognitive treatment must, therefore, be in constant liaison with the rest of the staff to inform them about the current stage of therapy and the problems which are being discussed and to get feedback in turn about ward behaviour or other problems. For example, the therapist should attend daily ward staff meetings to discuss the events of the previous day, set common goals, ensure a consistency of approach, and set a certain degree of demarcation for the role of different staff members who are involved with the patient. Third, a necessary deviation from standard out-patient practice is the setting of more frequent appointments. In my experience, daily sessions are indicated at the beginning of the therapy, even if they are short (half-hour) sessions. This is particularly important if the patient is receiving only CT, as otherwise that person might feel that not enough care or attention is being given relative to patients who receive regular medication.

Finally, although the explanation which is given to an in-patient regarding CT does not differ from that given to an out-patient, this requires particular care in the case of patients who may have been treated with only antidepressant medication for a long time before coming into hospital or who may, indeed, be continuing on a different or higher dose of medication while in hospital. Different rationales are called for if a switch from drugs to CT is being offered, or if both treatments in combination are proposed. In the former case, the risks are that patients feel desperate and see CT as the end of the road – 'If this fails nothing else will work'; or they may feel angry and think that their time has been wasted so far, that they 'should have been given cognitive therapy before'. A helpful introduction to CT in such a case, after an initial interview for suitability (see later), may be: 'Mrs Smith, now that you are here in hospital, we can perhaps think of an alternative treatment approach. You have been taking these tablets for a little while now and, though they have helped a bit, there is still some way to go. We could try one of several other types of medication. However, it may be useful to take a rest from pills at this point and try a different treatment which does not involve taking medication. The treatment I have in mind is cognitive therapy. It involves talking about problems and learning some new skills to cope with them. If this treatment does not suit you after we've tried it for a little while, we will think of alternatives. Does that sound OK with you?' The therapist would then continue in the manner recommended by Beck *et al.* (1979: 72–4) to explain CT and socialise the patient to CT.

When a combined treatment is being envisaged, the introduction may be: 'Mrs Smith, now that you are here in hospital, we can see whether discussing your problems on a regular basis and learning ways to deal with them, as well as continuing to take the tablets, may help you better. There are many reasons why people become depressed and often we are not sure what these are for each individual. Sometimes, medication alone can help, but sometimes we find that combining medication with a therapy that helps people to work on their problems can be more helpful. Both treatments are equally important and work together. Let me tell you about cognitive therapy. . . .' And again the usual explanation and socialisation would then ensue.

The following case study will try and elucidate these points further, as well as describe the course of therapy.

Case example (Anne)

Short case history and presentation

Anne was a 58-year-old single woman who was admitted to hospital after a referral by her general practitioner. Her *presenting complaint* was 'people talking about my secret affair with a gentleman'; 'people following me'; 'CID people watching me'; 'disappointed in and suspicious of everybody'. She had felt depressed and suspicious for a year, having been passed over at work for promotion to a higher rank among the office secretaries. She was having difficulties learning new computing skills and felt that the other typists thought her 'lazy' and ignored or shouted at her. Her suspicions had worsened over the last two or three weeks. She thought that people at work were people in disguise in order to watch her and that one of the nurses on the ward was a policewoman. She also complained of a flat mood, being unable to feel and to cry. She looked depressed and agitated.

On *mental state* examination, she reported sleep disturbance with early, middle, and late insomnia, low mood, guilt, inability to concentrate, loss of interest, somatic and psychic anxiety, loss of appetite, loss of weight, loss of energy and fatigability (score of 27 on the seventeen-item Hamilton Rating Scale for Depression, HRSD, Hamilton 1960). When the research diagnostic criteria (RDC, Spitzer *et al.* 1978) were checked after a diagnostic interview on the Present State Examination (PSE, Wing *et al.* 1974), the diagnosis was Major Depressive Disorder, psychotic, endogenous, recurrent unipolar depression. A previous episode of depression, thirty years before, had been treated on an in-patient basis with ECT and sodium amytal.

Personal history was unremarkable. Anne lived with her father who was a healthy octogenarian. Her mother had died in her seventies, nine years previously, and a younger sibling had died in childhood when Anne was 10 years old. Her work history was stable; she had gone to college for secretarial training after school and had worked steadily since, her last job having been in the same office for twenty-five years. Her physical health was good and she had some good friends and a number of interests.

Ward decision: Anne was prescribed only amylobarbitone 60 mg nocte, and within three days on the ward her paranoid delusions became only intermittent and she appeared to have good insight. It was felt that with her marked improvement and the fluctuation of delusional beliefs, ECT was not indicated at the time and that she would be assessed for suitability for CT. If CT was not suitable, she would be treated with amitriptyline. The reasons for considering CT were: in addition to the pattern of endogenous symptoms and the paranoid ideas and delusions, the patient expressed a number of negative views about herself; she herself expressed a preference for psychotherapy and an unwillingness to take medication;

5

she could participate in an on-going research project on neuroendocrine changes during recovery with different treatments, including non-pharmacological treatment.

Assessment of suitability for cognitive therapy

Two main aims were set for this first interview: to assess whether the patient used some psychological terms in describing her problems and concerns, and to arrive at a cognitive conceptualisation of the case. It is advisable to keep a broad outlook and not to focus on any one area in order to obtain a general picture at this point. I find that the first interview is a very important session both for the patient and the therapist and I will, therefore, describe this interview in some detail. This interview sets the tone for the patient and should set landmarks for the therapist.

After an introduction and enquiry about how she was feeling, the questions were targeted at finding out how Anne understood her illness and how she expressed her current concerns:

T: I would like to spend an hour with you, Anne, to talk about the things that have been bothering you, the problems that you've been having. Is this all right with you?

P: Yes. Will you be able to help me?

T: We may be able to work things out together. Let's see how it goes. You can let me know if you think it's not helping.

P: All right, I can try.

T: What has been bothering you most before you came into hospital?

P: It's all my fault. I'm to blame for everything. I don't have any confidence in myself any more. I don't want to do anything.

T: When did all this start?

Note that the therapist does not pursue further the specific points raised by the patient and does not attempt any modification technique at this point.

Anne then described how she dated her problems back to three years previously when she was off work because of a surgical operation. When she went back to the office, she found that she had more responsibility, having to learn word processing on a new machine and her boss preparing for retirement. A new person was brought in to be in charge instead of Anne.

T: How did that make you feel?

P: This shook my confidence. People would be wondering why I did not get the job. I must be inferior.

T: That's what you *thought*, but what were your *feelings*, can you remember?

P: Oh . . . sad and disappointed. I was still weak because of the operation. I cried a lot.

Quite early on, the therapist begins to emphasise the differentiation between thoughts and feelings and how they are connected.

T: Did this last long?
P: I got better by the summer, but I had no respect for the new boss. She would come back from her lunch at 3.45 p.m. I thought the *standards* would drop. I had to show her the way and there was a lot of friction.
T: What sort of friction?
P: It was because of the word processor. The younger girls wanted to work on it all the time. Then I was moved to a different group. I felt like a battery hen. I was uncertain. I did not know what was going to happen to me.
T: What did you think could happen to you?
P: I don't know. Why was I moved to another room after twenty-five years?
T: Did you have any idea yourself about why you were moved?
P: I was not as quick on the word processor. When I went on it, one girl used to shout at me. The other one did not speak to me.
T: What did that girl shout at you?
P: She was difficult and created a bad atmosphere. She had to be the centre of attention.
T: Did she shout anything specific?
P: She called me a 'hard-faced, frustrated old maid'.
T: How did you cope with that?
P: I don't like disagreements. It makes me feel terrible. I was trying to be loyal to the new boss, Mrs T. The girls were complaining about her to the staff office.
T: OK. Let me try and summarise what you've been telling me so far, to see whether I got all the points. You feel that things have not gone well for you since your operation three years ago. There were changes in the office, a new person was put in charge, and not you; new word-processing machines were brought in and you felt that the younger members of staff were getting more time than you on the machines and that they were rude to you at times. You felt sad and disappointed and you thought that other people would think that you are inferior. You also worried about the standards dropping. Is this right, Anne?
P: Yes, but I kept hoping things would get better.

At this stage, the points which have emerged are concerned with standards, pride in job, difficulty adapting to new work methods, hurt by feeling of displacement and being passed over; concern about what others think of her.

7

T: It's now a year later, isn't it? Did things get better?

P: Oh no! Everything went from bad to worse. Two jobs were advertised one grade up from me and I applied. There were lots of applicants; most were not even from our own department.

T: What happened?

P: I did not get the job. The interview was unfair. They kept talking about my weakest point, the word processor.

T: How did that make you *feel*?

P: Terrible disappointment.

Anne went on to describe how she was then moved to a different group in the office and, a few months later, was moved again to another group, where she had to work on the word processor without any help.

P: People must have thought: 'Why is she being moved about? She is incompetent.' I was so upset that I could not go to work for one day. I went to see my GP. I felt like my balloon had burst. I could not sleep. I had nightmares about people putting me to death. I cried all the time.

T: Did you get some help from the GP?

P: He gave me Mogadon [sleeping pills].

T: Did that help?

P: Well, I went back to work. A little later, I got a presentation from the staff for twenty-five years' service.

T: Did that make you feel good?

P: I thought they just felt sorry for me. I was on the same salary, but I felt like a junior. I was unhappy and bored. I had written to the staff officer about the word processor. He wrote back saying I could not be given special treatment.

T: Were you unhappy and bored *all the time*?

This is an attempt to test whether the patient can perceive an overgeneralisation.

P: I decided to start doing other things – I joined an evening language class and a choir.

T: Did that help?

P: A bit. I went back to the GP. He said, 'What I can't cure I must endure.' I felt so frustrated. I thought that it must be my fault.

T: We are now nearly at just a few months ago. Is that right? Did anything else happen at work?

P: More disagreements and problems. I lost faith in people. I felt sick.

T: Did you do anything about it?

P: No. I thought, 'I must be strong enough to cope on my own; I should not need pills. Because of my faith, I should have had more strength.'

T: OK, Anne, I can see that you have been having a really tough time at work. I can also see that you have been battling for a long time, on your own. Are you always so hard on yourself?

P: You know, telling you about all that happened in this way makes me think how unwell I've been for a long time and that I should have come for help sooner.

T: Have you found something else to blame yourself for there, Anne? [*I smile and Anne smiles back with full understanding of what the smile implies.*] OK, we have talked for a good hour. Let's stop here and we'll continue tomorrow. I understand that there have been other problems?

P: Yes.

T: We'll talk some more tomorrow to get a full picture and we will decide then how to proceed. If you can, I'd like you to fill in some of these forms for me. They are self-explanatory. If you have any difficulties, I'll help you with them tomorrow. [*Self-ratings were done on repeated occasions and will be reported on in a later session.*] Is there anything I've said that you are not clear about and that grated on you in some way?

Beginning of cognitive formulation of case

At this point, I have decided that it may be possible to attempt CT with this patient. My conceptualisation, which will need checking and refining in future interviews, is that Anne's depression has developed over a long time in the context of events at work: changes and displacement. She expresses a negative view of herself and blames herself for lack of 'strength' and inability to 'cope'. She also expresses a negative view of the world which she sees as 'unfair' and full of 'trouble-making' people. She appears to operate under high standards, to be demanding of herself, and possibly to need constant proof of respect and affection from others. She expresses a preference to work out problems rather than take pills and she talks about her difficulties in psychological terms. Though she complains of feeling flat emotionally, she showed a lot of emotion during the interview, crying a great deal, but also responding to slight humour from me. A beginning of rapport had been established.

Because of the severity of the case, this interview is slower than it might have been with an out-patient. No explanation of CT has been given yet and the second session to complete assessment and for history taking is to take place the next day.

Session 2 (continuation of assessment for suitability for cognitive therapy)

In this session, which was six days after admission, Anne expressed more delusional ideas than she had the previous day: 'I feel that people are out to catch me, to put me to death, to make me insane'; 'people want to put me away in prison, because I'm spreading rumours'; and 'people may be doing things to me in the night, giving me ECT'.

The events that she related in this interview coincided in time with the problems which were happening at work. She had been very involved in her church activities and suddenly found that she was being supplanted by a younger woman, as convener of a committee and as Sunday school teacher. She suspected the younger woman of being a close friend of one of the church elders who was showing favouritism by putting her in charge of many things. They had scenes and the young woman's brother had threatened her.

The therapist does not attempt any specific cognitive therapy at this stage, as this would be premature. At this stage, the therapist is still attempting to formulate the case and is content with familiarising the patient with the style of CT. Instead, a lot of empathy is shown about how bad she must have been feeling and similarities are drawn between the work and the church situation by inductive questioning.

T: Did you feel that what was happening reflected on you?
P: Nobody wanted me any more. I'm no good.
T: Are there any similarities between this situation and what we were talking about yesterday?
P: Yes, I see that now. I was being treated as a reject.
T: How did this make you feel?
P: I felt it was so unfair. I might just as well give up.
T: Did you feel so bad, that you felt that life was not worth living?
P: Well . . . It crossed my mind. I wouldn't do anything though. My faith would not allow me to and I would be too afraid to do anything. And then there's my father. Couldn't do that to him.

The risk of suicide was not considered to be high.

T: Did you discuss any of these problems with your friends?
P: With two of my friends. People at church could see what was happening. Everybody was talking about it. Probably laughing at me.
T: Did your two friends think like you, that you were no good and that nobody wanted you?
P: Well no, they blamed her. She has made a lot of enemies.
T: OK, Anne. This is a good example, isn't it? It shows how different people can see the same events in quite different ways and understand what's happening quite differently. Changes were happening at work and in your church and you interpreted these as meaning that other people did not like you, that they laughed at you, and that you were no good. It may be that when we discuss these things some more there may be different explanations which are more valid and less hurtful. This is what cognitive therapy is about. You have just explained very

well, haven't you, how thinking certain thoughts, interpreting things in a certain way led to unpleasant feelings, depression, suspiciousness, for example. Your interpretations are just interpretations – in fact they differ from your friends'. Interpretations are not reality, because many different things can colour our perspective of things and events. Let me give you an example which is more straightforward. [The usual example comes from Beck *et al.* (1979: 147–8). It's about the different interpretations which can be reached if one hears a noise in the house at night and the different emotions and behaviours which ensue.] Do you see what I mean?

P: Yes, but do you think I've been making up all these things?

T: No; unpleasant events have really been happening in your life, but you've put the worst possible meaning on them. I understand how this could happen, but your interpretations may be exaggerated and they certainly have made you feel very bad, haven't they? *You and I* must look again at what's been happening and examine other possible interpretations and other things that you might try. Is this OK with you?

P: OK.

T: Is there anything I've said which is not clear to you? You've often thought recently that people were laughing at you or criticising you; did you think that about anything I've said?

This last question was important in this case because of the known suspiciousness and paranoid ideas.

She had not felt that the therapist had laughed at her or criticised her and thought that, on the contrary, the therapist had been very understanding.

T: How are you feeling now?

The interview ended with an enquiry into how Anne was spending her time on the ward and on suggestions for activities. She was given *Coping with Depression* (Beck and Greenberg 1974) to read and an activity schedule to rate her activities for Mastery and Pleasure. The activity schedule was used to check on the diurnal variation in mood, which was one of the problems that ward staff commented on.

The decision was now reached that the patient was suitable for CT. Good rapport had been established and the concerns and difficulties could be understood in terms of how the patient viewed herself and her circumstances. No change was made in the formulation at this point.

Progress of therapy

Session 3

The next day was given to discussing CT further and to making up a list of problems to work on. Anne liked the booklet *Coping with Depression* and thought that the examples given were applicable to her. The list of problems we reached was: work problems, church activities, and a third one relating to home. She felt that she was giving up too much of her life for her old father. She decided to discuss this last item, as it was the least difficult of the three, while being quite important.

We made a detailed list of how she spent a typical week and the conclusions were that she did try to do too much on the whole. Every lunch hour, she would rush home to prepare lunch for her father and rush back to work. She prepared meals every evening and sometimes went out afterwards. Though she had a wide circle of friends, she rarely saw them because her father did not like to be left alone and often passed unpleasant comments if she was slightly late in coming back. Weekends were spent mostly on housework and church activities.

Definite conclusions were reached about changes she could make to lighten the load of housework and how to plan some of the things she liked doing. This part of the discussion involved making lists and looking at possible options. Since Anne was an in-patient, the discussion was not to lead to immediate application and testing. However, she then expressed the attitudes and the feelings which prompted her to behave in this way. It seemed that Anne felt guilty if she rested or did something she enjoyed: 'I should be doing something useful.' A discussion ensued about 'shoulds' which occurred often in her conversation.

It might be considered early in the course of therapy to tackle what appears to be a basic attitude, but it was felt that this was a more general problem involving a typical systematic error, arbitrary rules, and that tackling it at this point would help the other problem areas by generalisation.

T: You say that you *should* be doing something useful at all times?

P: Yes, if not I think that I'm being lazy.

T: Now when you say 'should', this to me indicates that there is some sort of law or rule which you mustn't break. Is there such a law, civil or moral, which says that you should be doing something 'useful' all the time?

P: Uh . . . uh.

T: Well, is it the same as 'you should not kill' or 'steal', for example? Even killing is allowed, of course, under certain circumstances, for example wars.

P: Well, it's not the same, but that's what I think.

T: Right, you mean it's a rule that you've made up for yourself, an arbitrary one? Would something bad happen if you broke that rule?

P: I would be lazy.

T: Even if you break the rule only on occasions?

P: It may become a habit.

T: Yes, that would be unhelpful if you did nothing useful *all* day *all* of the time. But does it make you feel good to be on the go all day, even if you're dead tired?

P: No, actually I get depressed when I'm very tired.

T: So, that's a rule that is harmful at times? Would it be more helpful if your rule was a bit more flexible?

P: How do you mean?

T: Well, if you allowed yourself a little time to relax, maybe read or listen to music or watch TV, do you think it might do you some good? Make you feel better, enjoy the work a bit more?

P: Probably.

T: So, are we agreeing that relaxing is 'useful'? Maybe, Anne, you've been defining 'useful' in a very narrow way. Washing, ironing, cleaning, cooking, etc., are useful; and relaxing or doing something enjoyable are *also* useful. Maybe it doesn't need to be black and white – either you're working all the time or you don't work at all. Maybe you can do both and feel better for it. What do you think?

P: I never thought of it that way. Maybe you're right. I'll have to try.

T: OK. But it may be difficult. You've been a slave-driver to yourself for a long time now. You're going to have to work hard at it, to allow yourself time off. What we'll do is plan things together so that you can try a new schedule. This will be for when you get home though. Now, I'd like to talk about your activities on the ward. I see from the form that you filled in yesterday that the mornings are still pretty bad for you and that you haven't found very much to do.

We then planned specific things for the next day. Anne was still waking up early, at 4 a.m., so that she felt tired, weepy, and lethargic in the morning. She was in the habit of sitting about in her dressing-gown until lunch-time. She usually had visitors in the afternoon, and in the evening she tried to watch TV or join in a card game, or help with a jig-saw puzzle.

Assignments If she woke up early, to get up and talk to the night nurse (she was still having frightening dreams). To dress soon after breakfast, take a walk round the grounds or go down to the shops at the hospital gate if anybody else was going.

The hospital notes at this stage comment on diurnal variation and that 'there are intermittent times when she believes with almost delusional intensity that she is going to be cornered or taken away to jail'. If she had not improved by the end of the week, physical methods of treatment would have been considered.

Session 4 (three days later)

Anne's mood was improved. She was enjoying her walks and helping other

13

patients on the ward. The whole session was devoted to discussing one of her central problems, the importance of what other people thought of her – at work and in the church. The main points were: Could she expect to be liked by everybody in these two large institutions? Did she like everybody? If she didn't particularly like X, should X be depressed? Were there people who liked her? What about her friends? How long had she had these friends? If she was such an unlikeable person, how come she had kept these same friends for so long? What were her main reasons for going to work or going to church? Was it to obtain love and respect?

The aim of this type of questioning was to facilitate reasoning, to help the patient see the two situations in a different perspective, and to alleviate the painful emotions associated with them. It would have been valueless to try and reach the same aim in a didactic way: first, the therapist would not have been able to guess what the patient really thought and therefore might have made irrelevant points; second, the patient might have taken advice as implied criticism; and third, the patient herself would have have no training in applying her own reasoning and thus have lost an opportunity to learn.

Assignment Aimed at strengthening the conclusions of this discussion. To write down in two columns all the reasons

1 Why it is important if somebody thinks badly of me.
2 Why it is not important.

Session 5 (next day – half an hour)

Review of homework. All the arguments were well rehearsed. Her conclusion was: 'I feel if I do my best and my conscience is clear, it does not matter what other people think.' She had also narrowed down her concern about what people in general thought of her to 'people who are in a supervisory or commanding position'.

The discussion was, therefore, directed at these classes of people. In her experience, were people in a supervisory or commanding position always right? Could she relate any instances of blatant unfairness or wrong decisions or actions? If she is criticised by such people, what can she do about it? Would discussions with them help pin-point things, so that she could either defend her position or change her way of doing things if the discussion revealed that they had a valid point?

Assignment Continue activity scheduling and rating of Mastery and Pleasure (see Beck *et al*. 1979: 128–31).

Session 6 (next day)

The focus was on her thought 'I am inferior, I can't do things', as her current concerns were about what would happen when she left hospital. She was still suspicious at times on the ward, but no longer concerned about what people would say at work or in the church. The hospital notes reported her as saying: 'Let them say and do whatever they want.' She had managed to go to her church the previous Sunday and was happy that she had not cried and everything had gone well.

The discussion, in the form of inductive questions, was aimed at eliciting what we called assets and liabilities about herself: what did she consider herself good at and were there things that she thought she *should* be able to do and could not do? Anne wrote down, with prompts, what she could do: gardening, cook, bake, knit, sew and embroider, appreciate music, sing (by ear), type, spell well, read bad writing, like poetry, walk long distances, cycle, use audio equipment, understand two foreign languages, paint, sketch a little, get on well with children. Her liabilities were: can't play a musical instrument, can't read music, don't like to talk in front of people, don't do shorthand, can't drive, not very good at maths or bookkeeping, can't swim, can't paint pictures.

After making this list, it was obvious to Anne that she had more assets than liabilities.

T: How important is it that you can't do these things here, on this side of the paper: read music, paint, swim, etc.

P: It would be nice if I could do these things.

T: Yes, but does it make you inferior because you can't?

P: Some people may think so.

T: Do you know people who cannot do many of the things that you've listed here as your assets?

P: Many.

T: Do you think of them as inferior, then?

P: Of course not.

T: Do other people think of them as inferior?

P: I don't think so.

T: Is it likely, then, that people don't think of you as inferior because you can't do certain things?

P: I suppose so.

T: Maybe, Anne, it is you who judge yourself in that way. Maybe you expect yourself to be good at everything. Is this another one of your *shoulds*?

P: Yes, I am a perfectionist. I expect everything to be perfect and I put people on a pedestal. Then I get disappointed.

T: Yes, I think that's been one of the basic problems – these high expectations. We'll have to talk about this again at a later date. What we can start doing, meanwhile, is to record some of the thoughts you have, especially in the morning when you wake up early, which make you feel bad, tearful or anxious or afraid.

Table 1.1 Examples of dysfunctional thought forms collected over the course of therapy

Situation	Emotion	Automatic thoughts	Rational response	Outcome
Wakened up thinking of how I usually enjoyed all the Christmas preparations and music, etc., and how near Christmas is	Flat, low (100%)	I won't be able to cope with the Christmas preparations (90%)	I managed to write a letter last week. I have about 100 cards to write. I'll ring my father and ask him to bring some cards and we could start on that tonight. I'll see how I get on. It's better to withhold judgement about whether I can cope or whether I will enjoy myself until I try (50%)	Hopeful (20%) low (30%)
Another patient talking of her experience with the police	Uncertain (50%)	Was I really followed by CID or not? (40%)	In my discussion with the doctor, we both thought I hadn't done anything wrong (100%) So it must have been my illness, as other things that I thought were true were not so either (100%)	No longer uncertain (0%)
Woke up and kept thinking of office situation	Disturbed, anxious, low (70%)	What mess am I going to have to go to? (70%)	I'm crystal ball gazing. It may not be a mess. However, if it is less well organised than before, it will be the	Anxious (20%)

			Responsibility of the supervisor. I can only do my work as well as I can and let other people worry about their work (100%)	Disappointed (20%)
Went into town on shopping trip	Churned up inside and disappointed (75%)	I can't even cope with a little excursion. I had been feeling so well this morning and now I feel so tired and upset. I thought I had more energy than this. I have only been out for half an hour (75%)	This is the first time that you've been in town and it's another test which proves you're not ready to cope with the hurly-burly of town yet. You've been in quiet surroundings for some time. I'm still comparing my progress with a fully fit person instead of how much progress I've made in the past 2–3 weeks	
Thinking of visit to hospital	Disappointed (75%)	Dr B is working hard with me – and I'm not pulling my weight. Should be further on. Am I keeping myself back because of stubborn refusal to appreciate myself more? (75%)	I'm being hard on myself again. Read *Feeling Good* and part of 'Learning to endorse yourself'.* Decided to make a chart of mastery and pleasure for a day or so to try to monitor how much I really do and get pleasure out of. It is a simple exercise but it might help me to start to appreciate more (75%)	Hopeful (75%)

* See Burns 1980.

It was considered premature in this case to discuss perfectionist attitudes at this point and appropriate to start monitoring and challenging automatic thoughts in a systematic way. The patient's perfectionist attitude appeared more basic than the 'I should do something useful at all times' discussed earlier. Challenging basic attitudes at an early point in therapy may alienate the patient and make her feel threatened and insecure. Towards the end of treatment, the therapeutic bond is stronger and often the attitude has been weakened by dealing with the automatic thoughts which it fosters.

An explanation followed about how to fill in the dysfunctional thought forms. These forms were not used earlier on, because the assignments were primarily behavioural or related directly to rehearsing what we had discussed in the sessions. At this point, Anne understood the process of CT well. Her mood was better, though fluctuating. Her sleep was still disturbed in the morning and her only medication was still amylobarbitone 60 mg nocte.

Assignment Thought forms and distraction in the morning (reading and talking to nurses).

Sessions 7–26

These sessions continued mostly on a daily basis, with breaks at the weekend when the patient often spent time at home. Special behavioural assignments were set up during these weekend breaks. A great deal of time was spent on discussion of the daily records of thoughts which Anne filled in diligently. At first, the rational column was completed in the session and later Anne could do the modifying of the automatic thoughts herself. Table 1.1 gives examples which are extracted from several of the forms which were completed on carbonised sheets, so that both patient and therapist could keep copies for their files.

Anne had become very proficient at challenging her automatic thoughts, as she could remember the discussion we had in the sessions and could reproduce appropriate responses which she found elevated her mood on the whole. She had started reading *Feeling Good* (Burns 1980) and enjoyed re-reading certain parts of the book which she felt applied to her.

Dysfunctional attitudes These were not difficult to elicit in Anne's case as she herself often summarised her attitudes to prompts like: 'What does that indicate?' We also developed a sort of game which involved underlining or repeating the words she used very often. These were 'unfair', 'should', 'full potential', and 'standards'. She herself had mentioned the word (or, rather, the neologism) 'perfectionistic'. We reviewed the themes which had emerged through the sessions and these related to being liked, to coping, and to achieving. When asked about what there was in common in the work and church situations which hurt her the most, she said: 'The loss of status, it's so unfair.'

T: Yes, our discussions seem to show that. Also, you remember the words we noted that you used a lot. 'Unfair' was one of them and there were others: should, standard, etc. It sounds as if you have been operating under a rule which says: 'If I work up to my full potential, I will be liked and rewarded. If I am not, either I am no good or people are being unfair.' Does that sound right to you?

P: Yes, that's been the trouble. It's also because I put some people on a pedestal. It's as if they can do no wrong. And when they do, I feel terribly disappointed.

T: Do you then feel they are letting you down personally? Do you personalise it?

P: I feel let down and insecure. I feel I can't have faith in anybody.

T: You feel that they *should* not come off the pedestal you've put them on?

P: *Laughs.*

T: Did they ask to be put on a pedestal?

P: No. It's silly, isn't it?

T: Well, it's not silly, but it's not helpful. It's as if you're setting yourself up to be disappointed. It's related to these high standards and expectations, isn't it?

P: Yes. But what can I do about it? I'm too old to change now.

T: Is this true? Have you changed your ways of thinking about anything recently? It's the same about these attitudes. You remember the work we did before on allowing yourself time to relax without feeling guilty?

P: Yes, I'm much better at that now. I plan my time better and I don't feel bad about it.

T: That's good. It means that change is possible, isn't it? You told me that you've been reading the chapter in *Feeling Good* about perfectionism; did that help?

P: Yes, quite a lot.

T: Maybe you could do an exercise for next time specifically about this attitude: 'If I work up to my full potential, I will be liked and rewarded. If I am not, either I'm no good or people are being unfair.'

Assignment What are the advantages and disadvantages of holding such a belief?

In later sessions, the inconsistencies in the belief were also examined: how does one work to one's full potential? How does one know when one has reached one's full potential? Are there other ways of being liked? Do different individuals have different criteria for liking and disliking, for deciding what's good and what's not good? Fairness is desirable, but is it reasonable to expect it at all times? Can people do something which you think is unfair, but that they would not think is unfair, because they are using different criteria? As can be seen from the next section and Figure 1.1, this patient did not have high dysfunctional attitudes, as measured by the Dysfunctional Attitude Scale (DAS, Weissman 1979). This was reflected in what transpired during treatment. Her basic dysfunctional attitudes were circumscribed and apparent from the very beginning of therapy. Dealing with the automatic thoughts weakened the strength of the schemata so that their modification proceeded quickly and smoothly.

Outcome

The patient was discharged from the ward after eight weeks in hospital and twenty-six sessions of CT. She still had intermittent depressed mood, some diurnal variation, and early morning wakening. She continued to attend as an out-patient twice a week at the outset, then once a week for a further fifteen appointments. Apart from consolidating what had already been covered in previous sessions, a new problem arose. This was trying to reach a decision about early retirement or staying on for a further two years. This was discussed in terms of the advantages and disadvantages of each alternative and rehearsing in imagination what her life-style would be if she continued working or stopped working. We also did a series of role plays and role reversals to rehearse assertive behaviour in her interviews with her employers.

   In fact, early retirement was accepted on advantageous terms. Anne was able to increase her leisure activities and enjoy things that she had not had time to do while working. She has remained well since discharge three years ago.

Ratings

The scores obtained on various rating scales over the eight weeks of in-patient treatment are shown in Figure 1.1.

   The Hamilton Rating Scale for Depression (HRSD, Hamilton 1960), seventeen-item version, was administered weekly by the consultant in charge who was not, in any way, involved in the treatment. The score at admission was 27, which is considered severe, and came down steadily to a non-depressed level (score 6), just before discharge. The increase in HRSD score at week five coincided with a disappointment for the patient. She had been on pass the day before and had gone to a concert. She had to leave the concert hall after half an hour, because the music appeared too loud and noisy, although it was her favourite music. Her head felt 'like

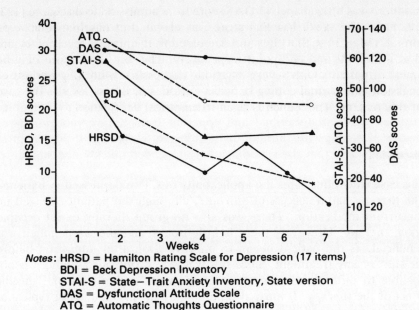

Notes: HRSD = Hamilton Rating Scale for Depression (17 items)
BDI = Beck Depression Inventory
STAI-S = State–Trait Anxiety Inventory, State version
DAS = Dysfunctional Attitude Scale
ATQ = Automatic Thoughts Questionnaire

Figure 1.1 Ratings over the course of in-patient treatment

bursting' and she felt sick. Her thoughts were 'I'm not able to cope with this. It was silly to come' and 'I can't see myself getting better'.

Self-rating questionnaires were administered three times, at the beginning of treatment, and in the fourth and seventh weeks. The Beck Depression Inventory (BDI, Beck *et al.* 1961), a measure of self-rated depression, showed a decrease in score in parallel with the HRSD, consecutive scores being 22 (moderate), 13, and 9 (not depressed). The State–Trait Anxiety Inventory, State version (STAI–S, Spielberger *et al.* 1970), also showed a decrease from 57 to 34 and 36 consecutively. Blackburn *et al.* (1986) reported a mean score of 56.7 in a group of depressed patients and a mean score of 37 for recovered depressed patients. The two cognitive scales, the Dysfunctional Attitude Scale (DAS, Weissman 1979) and the Automatic Thoughts Questionnaire (ATQ, Hollon and Kendall 1980), on the other hand, indicated low scores at baseline relative to depressed patients. The mean scores of 147.7 on the DAS and 82.5 on the ATQ reported by Blackburn *et al.* (1986) for their depressed group are typical of scores reported in other studies. The corresponding scores for this patient were 122 on the DAS and 64 on the ATQ. This DAS score is more typical of the normal controls (M = 114.4, SD 24.3) in the Blackburn *et al.* (1986) study. It is, therefore, not surprising

21

that there was little change in DAS score from admission to discharge (122, 119, 115). The ATQ baseline score was elevated at baseline relative to normals (M = 34.9, SD 13.4) and decreased to the normal levels of 44 and 43 at mid-point and end-point respectively. The low DAS score may be typical of patients with severe psychotic depression, with long periods of remission and normal coping between episodes of illness, as was the case for this patient. This hunch is open to empirical verification.

Discussion

This case study illustrates the applicability of CT to depressed in-patients. The therapy had a successful outcome, although the patient received no concurrent medication. There was also no group therapy or set occupational therapy. However, there is little doubt that the ward milieu was beneficial, as the patient began to improve soon after admission before the start of any treatment. Since this was not a controlled study, it is not possible to differentiate the effect of the ward milieu from the specific effect of the therapy. It must also be noted that this case is not typical of in-patient treatment, because, in my experience, most in-patients who receive CT are also on antidepressant medication. It was, however, decided to describe a case which was treated with CT alone to demonstrate the feasibility of this approach in a severely depressed in-patient. The combination of CT with ECT is probably not advisable, as the disruptive effect of ECT on memory would interfere with the continuity of successive sessions.

This case study has also demonstrated that, although the specific methodology of cognitive therapy is similar for in-patients and out-patients, there are important differences in the style of delivery of the treatment. The sessions are more frequent, there are more sessions, but the pacing of each session is slower. Other differences involve the need to keep other members of the ward staff fully informed of progress in therapy, for the therapist to gather information about the behaviour of the patient on the ward from the rest of the staff and to try and keep the approach of different members of staff as consistent as possible.

In many instances, CT, alone or in combination with other treatments, is not suitable for severely depressed in-patients. Although it is difficult to specify objectively the conditions which would determine the unsuitability of certain patients, it is possible to give impressionistic guidelines derived from experience:

1. Patients with an extensive delusional system, often including delusions of guilt, poverty, and hypochondriasis, do not appear to respond to CT.
2. Patients who present with no insight, that is, who do not think that

they are depressed or ill, or who attribute their illness to physical causes, do not benefit from a psychological approach.

3. Patients who are too severely affected to be able to establish a rapport with the therapist or who are unwilling or unable to collaborate in a problem-solving approach are not suitable.

4. In a previous study (Blackburn *et al.* 1981), we found that out-patients with chronic depressions of many years' duration, on the whole, do not respond to CT alone or in combination with medication. Fennell and Teasdale (1982) reported very modest results in a report of CT with five treatment-resistant patients who had been continuously depressed for 18 months, 3, 7, 8, and 16 years respectively, with only short remission periods. However, it is possible that a combined treatment approach, over a much longer period, may be the most valuable approach for this notoriously difficult group of patients. More controlled research is urgently needed in this area.

References

Beck, A.T. and Greenberg, R.L. (1974) *Coping with Depression*. New York: Institute for Rational Living.

Beck, A.T., Hollon, S.D., Young, J.E., Bedrosian, R.C., and Budenz, D. (1985) 'Treatment of depression with cognitive therapy and amitriptyline', *Archives of General Psychiatry* 42: 142–8.

Beck, A.T., Rush, A.J., Shaw, B.F., and Emery, G. (1979) *Cognitive Therapy of Depression: A Treatment Manual*, New York: Guilford Press.

Beck, A.T., Ward, C.H., Mendelson, M., Mock, J.E., and Erbaugh, J.K. (1961) 'An inventory for measuring depression', *Archives of General Psychiatry* 4: 561–71.

Blackburn, I.M., Bishop, S., Glen, I.M., Whalley, L.J., and Christie, J.E. (1981) 'The efficacy of cognitive therapy in depression: a treatment trial using cognitive therapy and pharmacotherapy, each alone and in combination', *British Journal of Psychiatry* 139: 181–9.

Blackburn, I.M., Eunson, K.M., and Bishop, S. (1987) 'A two-year naturalistic follow-up of depressed patients treated with cognitive therapy, pharmacotherapy and a combination of both', *Journal of Affective Disorders*, 10: 67–75.

Blackburn, I.M., Jones, S., and Lewin, R.J.P. (1986) 'Cognitive style in depression', *British Journal of Clinical Psychology* 25: 241–51.

Burns, D. (1980) *Feeling Good: The New Mood Therapy*, New York: William Morrow.

Feighner, J.P., Robins, E., Guze, S.B., Woodruff, R.W., Winokur, G., and Munoz, R. (1972) 'Diagnostic criteria for use in psychiatric research', *Archives of General Psychiatry* 26: 57–63.

Fennell, M.J.V. and Teasdale, J.D. (1982) 'Cognitive therapy with chronic, drug-refractory depressed out-patients: a note of caution', *Cognitive Therapy and Research* 6: 455–9.

Goldberg, D. and Huxley, P. (1980) 'Mental illness in the community', London: Tavistock Publications.

Hamilton, M. (1960) 'A rating scale for depression', *Journal of Neurology, Neurosurgery and Psychiatry* 23: 59–61.

Hollon, S.D. and Kendall, P.C. (1980) 'Cognitive self-statements in depression: development of an Automatic Thoughts Questionnaire', *Cognitive Therapy and Research* 42: 383–95.

McLean, P.D. and Hakstian, A.R. (1979) 'Clinical depression: comparative efficacy of out-patient treatments', *Journal of Consulting and Clinical Psychology* 47: 818–36.

Murphy, G.E., Simons, A.D., Wetzel, R.D., and Lustman, P.J. (1984) 'Cognitive therapy and pharmacotherapy, singly and together in the treatment of depression', *Archives of General Psychiatry* 41: 33–41.

Rush, A.J., Beck, A.T., Kovacs, M., and Hollon, S.D. (1977) 'Comparative efficacy of cognitive therapy versus pharmacotherapy in out-patient depression', *Cognitive Therapy and Research* 1: 17–37.

Rush, A.J. and Watkins, J.T. (1981) 'Group versus individual cognitive therapy: a pilot study', *Cognitive Therapy and Research* 5: 95–103.

Shaw, B.F. (1977) 'Comparison of cognitive therapy and behaviour therapy in the treatment of depression', *Journal of Consulting and Clinical Psychology* 45: 543–51.

Shipley, C.R. and Fazio, A.F. (1973) 'Pilot study of a treatment for psychological depression', *Journal of Abnormal Psychology* 82: 372–6.

Simons, A.D., Murphy, G.E., Levine, J.E., and Wetzel, R.D. (1986) 'Cognitive therapy and pharmacotherapy for depression. Sustained improvement over one year', *Archives of General Psychiatry* 43: 43–8.

Spielberger, C.D., Gorsuch, R.L., and Lushene, R.E. (1970) *Manual for the State–Trait Anxiety Inventory*, Palo Alto, CA: Consulting Psychologists Press.

Spitzer, R.L., Endicott, J., and Robins, E. (1978) *Research Diagnostic Criteria (RDC) for a Selected Group of Functional Disorders*, 3rd edn, New York State: Psychiatric Institute, Biometrics Research.

Taylor, F.G. and Marshall, W.L. (1977) 'Experimental analysis of cognitive–behavioural therapy for depression', *Cognitive Therapy and Research* 1: 59–72.

Teasdale, J.D., Fennell, M.J.V., Hibbert, G.A. and Amies, P.L. (1984) 'Cognitive therapy for major depressive disorder in primary care', *British Journal of Psychiatry* 144: 400–6.

Weissman, A.N. (1979) 'The dysfunction attitude scale: a validation study', *Dissertation Abstracts International* 40: 1389–90.

Wilson, P.H., Goldin, J.C., and Charbonneau-Powis, M. (1983) 'Comparative efficacy of behavioural and cognitive treatments of depression', *Cognitive Therapy and Research* 7: 111–24.

Wing, J.K., Cooper, J.E., and Sartorius, N. (1974) *The Description and Classification of Psychiatric Symptoms*, London: Cambridge University Press.

Zeiss, A.M., Lewisohn, P.M., and Munoz, R.F. (1979) 'Non-specific improvement effects in depression using interpersonal, cognitive and pleasant events focused treatments', *Journal of Consulting and Clinical Psychology* 47: 427–39.

Chapter two

Panic disorder and agoraphobia

Ruth L. Greenberg

'Fear has big eyes', says a Russian proverb. Cognitive therapists agree. Beck (1976) argued that exaggerated thoughts of danger are a central feature of the anxiety disorders; at our Center for Cognitive Therapy in Philadelphia we routinely observe, in patients with anxiety, both inflated appraisals of risk and a big-eyed hypervigilance for potential sources of future harm. Nowhere are these features more apparent than in panic disorder and agoraphobia.

Cognitive treatment of panic disorder and agoraphobia: a brief synopsis

Beck and Emery (1985) described a model of anxiety in which an 'emergency response system' is activated by the organism's perception of danger. The system evolved to abet survival, in the face of actual physical danger, by preparing the organism for aggression or escape (fight, flight) or inhibiting it from sudden movement (faint, freeze). But the 'emergency response' may itself alarm the individual, as it generates disturbing body sensations and transient cognitive dysfunctions that may themselves be perceived as sources of danger: racing heart, feelings of dizziness or weakness, a sense of unreality, other discomforts. When the emergency response is activated, as in a panic attack, fear and anxiety accelerate rapidly, and rational thinking is undermined. The terrifying experience tends to increase apprehensiveness, predisposing the sufferer to experience more symptoms. A vicious spiral of fearful expectations and frightening symptoms is established.

According to the Beck–Emery model, distorted perceptions of danger play an important part in this spiral. In a vulnerable 'mode', patients tend to overestimate danger and underestimate their capacity for coping. The distorted appraisals may affect their responses to psychosocial stress and also to internal experiences, such as the sensations that come into play with the emergency response system. In the case of panic disorder, anxiety-related sensations (such as lightheadedness, rapid heartbeat, breathlessness, choking feelings), as well as other physical and emotional changes the person cannot easily explain, tend to become the target of misinterpretations. When feared sensations occur, thoughts and images of catastrophe are triggered: 'What if my throat closes up completely? I might choke to death!' 'The world looks blurred and funny. I must be going crazy!' And dysfunctional coping strategies may be invoked: 'Chest pain – maybe a heart attack this time! Better not be alone.' The thoughts and images (states the model) tend to increase anxiety, accelerating the vicious spiral of fear and symptoms. Further, the belief that symptoms foretell catastrophe contributes to phobic dependency and avoidance.

Identifying the catastrophic misinterpretations of symptoms is our initial focus in treating panic disorder and agoraphobia. In the first session, we elicit a description of the sensations, thoughts, images, emotions, and impulses that typically occur during the panic attack. We 'socialise' the patient to the idea that thoughts and beliefs can be contributing to the panic attacks, and we try to 'normalise' anxiety – help the patient see anxiety responses as part of the body's normal repertoire. For 'homework', the patient makes further observations about thoughts and images during periods of anxiety and panic.

We use these data to define the mistaken ideas the patient holds about specific symptoms and about panic generally. The Panic Belief Questionnaire (Figure 2.1) compiles forty-two of these beliefs into a scale which we are now administering to panic patients. The beliefs seem to contain a number of basic themes: *vulnerability* ('I am vulnerable to harm'), *escalation* ('Symptoms will escalate into something worse'), and *copelessness* ('I can't control symptoms or cope with the problem on my own') (see Beck and Greenberg 1988). Our therapists have used the scale as a diagnostic device, to help clarify the patient's dysfunctional assumptions about panic and anxiety.

With the key beliefs defined, we set out to help the patient test their validity. Whenever possible, we attempt to reproduce the feared sensations in the consulting room; our goal is to develop an alternative, non-catastrophic view of symptoms. Often, the first method chosen is the hyperventilation technique of Clark *et al*. (1985; see also Salkovskis *et al*. 1986). Briefly, the procedure involves having the patient breathe rapidly and deeply for a period of two minutes, observe the effects of overbreathing, and assess the similarity of the resulting sensations to those of a panic attack. If the similarity is strong, the patient is guided towards the conclusion that hyperventilation is contributing to symptoms; they are then taught a breathing technique ('control breathing') that controls hyperventilation. When patients observe that a simple, non-pathological process can produce feared sensations, they tend to correct their attribution of symptoms to impending medical or psychological catastrophe.

If hyperventilation fails, we attempt to evoke sensations by other methods – having patients focus on frightening mental images, jog in place,

Figure 2.1 Panic Belief Questionnaire

Name: _____ Date: _____

Please rate how strongly you believe each statement on a scale from 1 to 6, as follows:

> 1 = Totally disagree
> 2 = Disagree very much
> 3 = Disagree slightly
> 4 = Agree slightly
> 5 = Agree very much
> 6 = Totally agree

_____ 1. Having a bad panic attack in a situation means I will definitely have one there again.

_____ 2. Having panic attacks means I'm weak, defective, or inferior.

_____ 3. If people see me having a panic attack, they'll lose respect for me.

_____ 4. I'll have disabling panic attacks for the rest of my life.

_____ 5. Exerting myself physically during a panic attack could cause me to have a heart attack and die.

_____ 6. If I have panic attacks, it means there's something terribly wrong with me.

_____ 7. I'm only safe if I can control every situation I'm in.

_____ 8. I'll never be able to forget about panic attacks and enjoy myself.

_____ 9. If I have to wait in line or sit still, there's a good chance I'll lose control, scream, faint, or start crying.

_____ 10. There's something wrong with me that the doctors haven't found yet.

_____ 11. I must be watchful or something terrible will happen.

_____ 12. If I lose my fear of panic attacks, I might overlook other symptoms that are dangerous.

_____ 13. If my children (or others close to me) see me having panic attacks, they'll become fearful and insecure.

_____ 14. I have to keep checking how my body is reacting or I might have a panic attack.

_____ 15. Crying too much could cause a heart attack.

_____ 16. I have to escape the situation when I start having symptoms or something terrible could happen.

_____ 17. There's only so much anxiety my heart can take.

_____ 18. There's only so much anxiety my nervous system can take.

_____ 19. Anxiety can lead to loss of control and doing something awful or embarrassing.

_____ 20. My emotions (anxiety, anger, sadness, or loneliness) could become so strong I wouldn't be able to tolerate them.

_____ 21. Panicking while driving or while stuck in traffic is likely to cause an accident.

_____ 22. A panic attack can give me a heart attack.

_____ 23. A panic attack can kill me.

_____ 24. A panic attack can drive me insane.

_____ 25. A little anxiety means I'll be as bad as I was at my worst.

_____ 26. I could experience terrible emotion that never ends.

_____ 27. Expressing anger is likely to lead to losing control or provoking a fight.

_____ 28. I could lose control of my anxiety and become trapped in my own mind.

_____ 29. It could be dangerous to carry on my usual activities during a panic attack.

_____ 30. I must be near my companion to be protected from panic.

_____ 31. I can't deal with panicky feelings on my own.

_____ 32. I must be able to reach my 'support system' at all times or a catastrophe could happen.

_____ 33. I can't do things that other adults can do – e.g. wait in line, sit in a traffic jam, give a speech, travel away from home.

_____ 34. The only thing that can take away anxiety is alcohol or tranquillisers.

Figure 2.1 *(continued)*

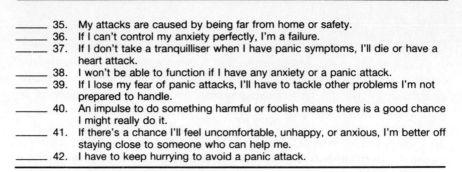

_____ 35. My attacks are caused by being far from home or safety.

_____ 36. If I can't control my anxiety perfectly, I'm a failure.

_____ 37. If I don't take a tranquilliser when I have panic symptoms, I'll die or have a heart attack.

_____ 38. I won't be able to function if I have any anxiety or a panic attack.

_____ 39. If I lose my fear of panic attacks, I'll have to tackle other problems I'm not prepared to handle.

_____ 40. An impulse to do something harmful or foolish means there is a good chance I might really do it.

_____ 41. If there's a chance I'll feel uncomfortable, unhappy, or anxious, I'm better off staying close to someone who can help me.

_____ 42. I have to keep hurrying to avoid a panic attack.

or stare at disturbing visual patterns, for example. We teach a variety of coping strategies (reading 'flash cards' that contain the non-catastrophic view of sensations; refocusing attention; taking a walk) and encourage patients to practise using these techniques both during spontaneous panics and during planned exposure to feared situations. When patients have mastered coping techniques and have grasped the idea that symptoms are neither dangerous nor entirely uncontrollable, we urge them gradually to let go of techniques and simply allow themselves to experience symptoms.

As the fear of symptoms diminishes, we focus increasingly on the patient's reactions to 'background' stressors, such as family and work interactions, again applying a cognitive model. Not infrequently, we find similarities between patients' attitudes towards symptoms and their outlook on other problems (e.g. 'This means I'm defective and can't handle things'; 'Problems always get worse and they last for ever'). For further details see Beck and Greenberg (in press).

A many layered fear of internal experience: the case of John

I often think of these symptom-focused methods as a way of peeling off an outer layer of somatic preoccupation, in order to expose underlying issues and ultimately reveal the pungent core of the onion. As long as visions of death, heart attack, or insanity dance in patients' eyes, it is hard to direct their attention to longstanding problems. A climate of crisis and urgency prevails.

John's treatment is an example of the onion principle. A bright, loquacious, psychologically minded, 30-year-old computer specialist, John entered treatment with frequent panic attacks, episodic bouts of depressed mood, and considerable phobic avoidance. He had been agoraphobic for ten years. Only with terror could he drive long distances, ride in a car with others, remain alone, eat in restaurants, or attend theatre or sports events

– despite previous behavioural treatment. He feared that the panic he experienced in these situations would lead to heart attack; thus he must not be away from help.

John felt childlike and helpless in relation to his phobias and panic symptoms, but also in regard to other 'layers' of his problem, such as dealing with his wife, his parents, and a hostile colleague. His intense emotional reaction to family and work conflicts contributed to his panic attacks, but it was his fear of the meaning and potential consequences of the attacks that preoccupied him and kept him phobic and dependent.

It became clear, when we examined the attacks closely, that John feared the experience of intense affect. He believed his sadness and loneliness signified a terrible flaw within himself, but also that experiencing these emotions could lead to heart attack and death. Feeling unable to care for himself, dependent on people who angered and disappointed him, led to even more self-doubt and resentment. We had to deal, then, with several layers: his fear of the physical effects of panic, his fear of affect, his reactions to family and significant others, and eventually, his view of himself as inadequate and incompetent. I pulled out my paring knife and set to work.

In the first session, John grasped the cognitive model of panic and agreed that for homework he would log his attacks and related 'automatic thoughts'. That assignment produced an unexpected 'Aha!' Sitting in his car, in his own driveway, he had had a severe attack. When symptoms began, he realised he had been picturing himself becoming anxious on a long drive to the country he was expected to take the next evening, to attend a reception at which his company was to display new products. 'So it's the *thoughts* that make me panic – not the places!' Although he had worked through exposure hierarchies in his previous treatment, John had not realised that all his phobias had this element in common: frightening thoughts, frightening images. The feeling of having an overwhelming number of problems and deficiencies began to ease.

In our second session (an edited transcript appears below), I was determined to pry loose the idea that panic symptoms might lead to heart attack, and brought to the task my favourite tool, the overbreathing demonstration (Clark *et al.* 1985). John's response to the demonstration was actually rather weak, in the sense that he observed only a modest similarity between the effects of overbreathing and an actual panic attack. But asking him to identify *differences* between his sensations in the session and a panic attack did enable him to articulate a key belief: that intense emotions could lead to heart attack. The demonstration also provided an opportunity to disconfirm a negative prediction about a physical sensation (in this case, brought on by overbreathing): 'I could faint!'

In my mind, what distinguished this session was the doggedness with which I had to stick to my agenda of disconfirming John's belief that he was physically endangered by symptoms. John wanted so much to talk about his feelings of emotional isolation! However, I was sure that would bite off more layers than we could chew in a single hour. In later sessions, we took on his loneliness, his marital difficulties, his feelings of incompetence, and his fear of expressing anger. By the tenth session, a large segment of which I also reproduce below, we had begun to discuss his fear of taking on adult responsibility. In this session, emotion-laden memories emerged, and a schema was articulated: 'I don't deserve mother's love'.

Throughout our sixteen-week course of treatment and following it, John was expected to expose himself continuously to feared situations, using the techniques and understandings he had gleaned in the early weeks of treatment, and remaining alert to new 'automatic thoughts' on which he might hone his thought-testing skills. To overcome his fear of riding with others, he (ingeniously) took up golf. To remember to assert himself to his sulky, aggressive colleague, he made self-instructional 'flash cards' similar to those we had used to cope with panic symptoms. Once he had acquired the idea of self-help and a new perspective on basic issues, he was able to help himself with diverse problems.

Occasional booster sessions and phone calls have been sufficient to nudge John through periodic impasses. But I will save the most enlightening of these for a postscript.

Second session

John: Today was a panicky day for me, especially when I started coming down here.

Ruth: Especially then.

John: I think it is just talking out my feelings that is difficult to do.

Ruth: So you think something about that brings on the panic symptoms?

John: Well, I started making some mental notes like that panic for me is almost a substitute for saying what's on my mind to people, getting into the emotional. Because sometimes when panic comes on I get to that crescendo! All of a sudden I feel like I want to cry. Like a sadness comes over me, and when I get to the point where it really starts to peak, then I think, 'Why am I coming here? Why am I doing this to myself?' Then I was saying, 'You know, you're really not weak', because I feel weak. In a way you are strong, because somebody who had this, a normal person who had this come on them all of a sudden, probably wouldn't keep going, you know.

Ruth: And you are here. Which shows that you did do it.

John: Right. I didn't give in to it, although it was push and shove all the way.

Ruth: I would like to come back in a minute to this number eight attack you had today, and then there are some things I had in mind to do with you, but what I would like to do first is get a sense of how the week has been in general. Is that agreeable? Generally, then, how has the week been for you?

John: After I left here last week, I felt really good, and I had a difficult thing to do Friday night – go to this reception that was in the middle of this remote area, it was at a state park, it was night and it was dark, and I had to drive. So, I was saying to myself, you know, you are probably going to get this heightened sense of anxiety, and just remember that it is not that you are going to have some type of heart attack. Your system is just going to ready itself, because it is going to sense a dangerous thing if you give it that type of input. So, that really helped. I still got anxiety when I got to the place, the parking lot. I had to park all the way farthest from the building, of course. That was my luck! And I got out. I felt really weak, you know. And I said, this is an illusion, just stay with it. And in my mind, you don't know how far away you are.

Ruth: How far away you are from what?

John: You know, safety, comfort zone, that type of thing. And as I got into the place, I just told myself, just stay with it, and then it did pass. It just started to diminish and I could finally relax and start looking at the exhibits. Whereas the first few minutes I was there it was like, 'I'm going to shoot through this thing and go'. That was kind of the way I felt when I came down here today.

Ruth: On the way here today?

John: Yeah, on the way down. To a certain point now, even though I'm sitting here talking, relaxed, I'm still panicky. Maybe my panic's gone down to a five and I was at an eight at one point.

Ruth: I want to hear very exactly what you experienced at this eight level. In fact, what led up to the eight. But I do want to say something to you, which is, I understand what you are saying about wanting to be able to express your emotions, and I think that is an important thing we need to work on. Today, I would like to focus on the panic itself, and perhaps next week we can move in a little more closely on this question of expressing yourself. OK. So, I think the thing to do to start is to tell me about this attack that you had.

John: OK, we will start out from this morning. When I woke up this morning, I felt a little on edge and I thought – what came into my mind was: 'Probably because I'm going to the therapist today'. So, during the course of the day, driving into work, being at work, I was just in a nervous state. Not in extreme panic, but just in a nervous state. A feeling of, like, 'I don't know if I want to stay here or if I want to go'.

Ruth: You had automatic thoughts like 'I don't know if I want to go or stay at work'?

John: Right. But I just said, 'This is it, I'm just going to ride this thing through', and then I started to – I was having some problems with my bowels, which happens when I get nervous. Then I would forget about it for a while, then it would start to come back, and then I started looking at the clock and it was 12 o'clock and I thought, 'Gee, I gotta get rolling here'.

Ruth: At this point were you aware that it was something about the session that was upsetting you?

John: Yeah, that's what I thought. That it's difficult. To me it's almost physical – it's the mental equivalent of having an operation. I'm getting basically looked into – my mind, my thoughts, my feelings – and bringing lots of feelings out.

Ruth: What is upsetting about that?

John: Well, when I look over things, I see I've also had depression. You know, they must be second cousins, anxiety and depression – one feeds the other. And I started thinking, why was I depressed? You know, I have been using a mental flashlight, going in. But every time you go in and look at these things, it's painful.

Ruth: So, looking at yourself is painful?

John: Yeah, right.

Ruth: What is painful about it? Is there something you are afraid of finding?

John: Yeah, some inadequacies, probably, that I have that, you know, I may be semi-aware of.

Ruth: So the idea you have is that this process may make you aware of inadequacies that you have?

John: Yeah, right.

Ruth: That's an automatic thought. Do you realise that?

John: Right, that's –

Ruth: Something about this is going to bring out inadequacies that you are not aware of now.

John: Exactly.

Ruth: Well, I'm sure we will have an opportunity to come back to that. So now –

John: The anxiety is almost a safety valve for not getting into the emotional outpouring – which I don't know why I'm scared of. I feel like I want to cry and logically you would say well, you know, just cry and see what happens from there. But to me the crying would only be leading into physical consequences.

Ruth: If you cry, what would be the physical consequences?

John: I don't know what they would be. But I guess what I told you last week about having a heart attack.

Ruth: So, if you cry you might have a heart attack?

John: Right, yeah.

Ruth: Now, when the anxiety got acute today, what was that like?

John: Torture, extreme torture. Because I felt scared, really scared. The thing that comes to mind is like wanting your daddy or mommy to be there to help you. You're going through something alone, like, I would equate it to a child having to go to a hospital in an emergency. And you don't really know what is wrong with you and you're just really scared that something could happen, that you could die.

Ruth: Is that the thought that you had, that 'I could die', when it was very bad?

John: Yeah. I was trying to repress it at the same time.

Ruth: Yeah, but you had the thought, I could die? What made you think you could die?

John: I guess the physical sensations, you know.

Ruth: And what were they?

John: Fright. Fright was the one. It's like a paralysing feeling that comes over you. And that's, you know –

Ruth: Is the fright a physical sensation? Could you describe it more in physical terms?

John: Physically, it was basically just hyperventilation type of symptoms. Butterflies in my stomach.

Ruth: What are the hyperventilation symptoms?

John: Increased breathing – I noticed I was breathing more. Discomfort, some faintness.

Ruth: Discomfort, faintness, and increased breathing? OK, and butterflies and a paralysing feeling.

John: Yeah. The fear was more mental than physical, though. It was just like, 'What could happen?'

Ruth: Tell me everything you know about what you thought could happen.

John: In a way I thought, 'I'm not going to be able to continue. I want to turn around. I could get faint. I don't want to make a fool out of myself.' That type of thing came into my head.

Ruth: While you were driving?

John: Right. 'Maybe I'm pushing it. Maybe I'm doing more than I should. Probably a lot of people just come down here with somebody else, or maybe it would be better if I had my wife with me.' And I was also saying. 'I did it before. This can't be as hard as it was the first time.'

Ruth: You mean you were able to talk back to yourself to some extent? Reassure yourself. And that's how you got through it.

John: Right. I said to myself, 'It's going to get to an extreme and then it is probably going to level out.' And it did get to an extreme and then it kind of levelled out. Yeah. I'm thinking, 'How worse can it get? I've been doing this for so long.'

Ruth: Uh-huh. You have some familiarity with it. Now what did you think would happen that would make a fool of you?

John: That I would have to get out, or have to call somebody on the phone and say I'm in real danger.

Ruth: What would lead you to that point? What would happen?

John: There was a past experience where I remember doing that – calling my father and having him come to where I was at and get me because I was so shaky. Another thing was times when I have had the panic so bad that I did go to a hospital. So the thought is, 'Because I got help before, I would have to get help again.'

Ruth: Is that what you think? That there is a point at which you should go to a hospital or you shouldn't be by yourself or you should ask for help?

John: Yeah. That's what I am thinking.

Ruth: How much do you believe that now?

John: Well, at this moment, it seems a little bit more far-fetched than it did when I was in the car.

Ruth: So, on a scale of 1 to 100 how much do you believe that you could die from these symptoms?

John: Right now, I would say, it would be really an outside chance of that happening.

Ruth: 1 to 2 per cent?

John: Yeah, I guess so.

Ruth: And on the way down here, when you were at a panic level of eight, how much did you believe it?

John: Well, then I believed it more and I was thinking, 'Why is this happening? I'm a good boy. I've been doing all my homework. I've been reading my books. I think I understand it and yet it is still happening.'

Ruth: So you thought you should be over it in one session?

John: I guess so. Well, that plus the fact that I've had it for a few years now. That when these things came at me as strong as they come, that I would recognise the fact that I've never really been physically damaged by it. I've never gone off the deep end mentally. Turned from anxiety to schizophrenia.

Ruth: So what came to your mind was, why is it happening to you? Would you say you felt anxious having that thought, or confused? What was your reaction?

John: When I get to the point where I'm about an eight, I don't even want to have thoughts. I try to just –

Ruth: You try to block them out.

John: Yeah.

Ruth: But if I asked you at that moment, how strongly do you believe you could die from these symptoms, what would you say?

John: It would probably be about 10 per cent, I guess.

Ruth: Even then, it's not very much, yet you were very frightened.

John: I guess so, because, you know, it's funny, you can have anxiety and laughter at the same time. Because when I saw you when I came in, I was in a very good mood. Maybe when I'm panicky I should think about something else, like have a sexual fantasy or something.

Ruth: Have you ever tried that?

John: Semi, yeah I did, semi.

Ruth: How did it work?

John: I want to experiment more with it.

Ruth: I want you to experiment with that. And maybe we will make that part of the homework. I think it is a pretty good idea. But, I want to try something else first. You mention these paralysing sensations and hyperventilation symptoms. What do you think is the relationship between your breathing and these other feelings that you have? Have you ever thought about that?

John: Well, no. My impression is that if you are anxious, that your breathing is going to pick up because of that, and the symptoms.

Ruth: So they just all pick up as a result of anxiety?

John: Right.

Ruth: What I would like to try is to explore what that relationship is, just to see what we can find out about your symptoms from it. Are you willing to do that?

John: Yeah.

Ruth: Well, what I would like you to do is spend two minutes or as much of that time as you can breathing very fast and deep. And I'll set the pattern for you. And we just want to see what your reaction to that is. OK?

John: OK.

Ruth: All right. Now what I'm going to ask you to do is something like this. [*Breathes quickly and deeply through mouth.*]

John: OK.

Ruth: Think you could do that?

John: Yeah.

Ruth: OK. Now if you should find that this is very disturbing –

John: I thought you were going to say, 'If you should faint, I'll get the smelling salts!'

Ruth: Do you think you might faint?

John: No.

Ruth: If you should feel very uncomfortable, there is a way of removing any troubling sensations that you have. [*Demonstrates how to breathe into paper bag.*] OK, so suppose you start. And I'll start with you. [*Starts overbreathing.*] That's good. That's very good. Get it even deeper if you can. Really forcing air out and taking a lot in. Very good. That's about half a minute.

John: Oh, God, really, now that does make me feel faint.

Ruth: It makes you feel faint?

John: And lightheaded.

Ruth: OK, well that's good. Can you do it a little bit longer?

John: I could. It's uncomfortable but . . . OK. [*Overbreathing.*] This definitely makes me feel dizzy.

Ruth: You are definitely dizzy?

John: Yeah.

Ruth: Is this anything like –

John: From like here up, you know.

Ruth: From here up dizzy. Is it anything like what you felt today when you were panicky?

John: No, I wouldn't say so.

Ruth: Not like it. Can you keep it up a little longer? You are getting pretty well into this two minutes. I would like to see how far we get . . . Almost done.

John: My throat's getting dry.

Ruth: Your throat's dry? OK, let's give it another ten good seconds. . . . OK, you can stop.

John: OK. [*Stops.*]

Ruth: I would like you to close your eyes now and try to observe what you are experiencing. . . . Now open them and see if you can mark this checklist to show what you felt.

John: Well, weakness. [*Marking the checklist.*] Numbness of extremities. Heart racing – moderate. Slight sweating, drowsiness, stinging, apprehension. What's this? Urinate? Yeah, I have to urinate. It was making me anxious.

Ruth: Moderately anxious?

John: Yeah. Heart pounding? – between moderate and severe. Definitely faint. Tension? Yeah, I had that. Tingling? – slight. Pins and needles? – I'm kind of getting that now. Dizziness, tight muscles, breathlessness . . . I was experiencing those. And I was getting fear.

Ruth: Fear?

John: That's not a sensation, it's a feeling.

Ruth: What was going through your mind? What thoughts?

John: Like a fear that I could faint, maybe.

Ruth: 'I could faint?'

John: Yeah.

Ruth: How much did you believe you could faint at the time?

John: Well, it would depend on how hard I was going to push myself. At one point, you probably noticed, like towards the end, I started breathing harder than I was, because at that point I thought, 'No, it's not going to happen, I won't faint', and then I started to get into it. I wanted to really push it.

Ruth: So at some point you thought it pretty strongly?

John: And I started breathing, like maybe the last half minute or so, I started going stronger, saying come on, let me see if I can do it because I don't think I can at this point now.

Ruth: And in fact you didn't faint. How strongly, at the strongest point of when you thought you could faint, how strongly did you believe it? What did you think the chances were?

John: I thought it was probably about maybe 15 to 20 per cent. . . . Because I thought, you know, I've had times that I've felt faint without fainting.

Ruth: So just 15 to 20 per cent. Now at the time when you had this feeling of fear, what images were in your mind? Were you picturing anything? Were you imagining anything?

John: Outside before I came or just now?

Ruth: Either time.

John: Just like, if I did, would help be able to get to me?

Ruth: If you did faint? Here?

John: Yeah, or outside. That's the kind of feeling I get. 'Can I get to help?' or 'Can help get to me?' Like, 'I'm all alone here, could I get to . . .' and then I start thinking who I could get to. And, 'Gosh, if I died, what would happen? I wouldn't even be able to get to do . . .' and then, 'What is it? What is it that I want to get to do?' And I think, 'I could die. Well, who would care? People would just be indifferent to it.' Then I think, 'I can't let this happen to me now. I have got to get out and do things.' And then the thought comes over me is, 'Well, when you try to get out and do things, that is when this thing is coming over you.'

Ruth: So you have thoughts that you are going to die, and about how people wouldn't care. How much do you believe that?

John: I guess not that much because I don't keep dwelling on that.

Ruth: But you do have the thoughts that people don't care?

John: Yeah.

Ruth: And they come up at these times? Do you think they might be connected to your wanting to call your father?

John: Oh, sure, sure. Or help. That type of reaching out. You know, getting to someone. Yeah.

Ruth: But the sequence is, at first you think you're going to die or you are going to faint – something bad is going to happen to you physically. Did you see it in kind of a picture in your mind? Your dying?

John: No. I don't picture that so much as something that is behind the dying. Maybe there is something that is even worse than dying.

Ruth: And what do you think that is?

John: I guess like some type of abandonment. Like dying without a purpose, maybe. Without having really rectified things, made amends for things that I did that were wrong, resolved things – maybe with my parents. Without having developed closer relationships with not only myself but the people who are near and dear to me. Those types of things.

Ruth: OK, so again we see there are two components here. One is – just like we said in the beginning – there is a component of thinking you are going to die, thinking your symptoms are dangerous. But there is another component of feeling people don't care. Or that there is some obstacle to your emotional relationships with people. And again I think we need to deal with these things separately. And right now, I want to focus on this idea that you could die. If that's OK with you?

John: Oh, yeah. But the only thing that I could really die of, in my mind, is a heart attack. I can't die of really anything else.

Ruth: OK, but the idea is that in the panic attack you might be having a heart attack.

John: I am, but then when I examine my chest, then I say, well, I'm not getting extreme pain in my chest, you know.

Ruth: So you already have a coping skill that we want to build up, we want to vitaminise. But getting back to the basic idea, this frightening idea that you are having a heart attack or something you could die of.

John: You know what it is? It's basically the fear itself I guess. That this fear is so strong that's coming on me, that my system is not going to be able to handle this fear.

Ruth: Your system?

John: Yeah. The fear is building up and I don't know how far it is going. It's coming at me and that is what is going to do it to me if anything. This fear. It's the fear itself!

Ruth: There is a limit to how much fear your body can tolerate and still survive. That's what you think?

John: Yeah. And I'm caged at the same time. I'm caged because it's like . . . what comes to mind is like a rat being in a cage and not being able to get out and a fire is getting close to him. I don't know whether to keep going, or to turn around. But with me, turning around and going back, I could get just as much panic out of that because now I'm a failure.

Ruth: So the caged feeling is part of it, too. Now, going back to this feeling that you experience when you overbreathed, how similar is that to how you feel during a panic attack? What if you were to rate it on a scale of 0 to 100?

John: I think the symptoms are somewhat similar because I do start to have a weak feeling. Probably I don't feel as faint as I did doing that.

Ruth: This makes you more faint?

John: Yeah. And the fear is not as much doing this as being in a situation.

Ruth: Why do you think that is?

John: It could be because I'm here with you. That could be one reason that it's better here.

Ruth: But again, if you were going to give it a rating overall, how similar is it?

John: It's maybe 30 per cent. In some areas I think the symptoms are more extreme, as far as the faintness and the numbness.

Ruth: What do you make of the fact that you can get those symptoms from breathing rapidly and deeply?

John: I was asking myself, I was wondering if other people get the same type of breathing rapidly like that? Like do they get a tingling in their arms or extremities? I guess if you are hyperventilating you are taking in more oxygen than your system can dispense with.

Ruth: Actually, it's blowing off the carbon dioxide that creates those symptoms. But there is an answer to your question and that is that it's a well-known effect of overbreathing to get those symptoms.

John: Right. I think that's why they have pregnant women concentrate on doing these breathing exercises so they won't get into this hyperventilation type of thing.

Ruth: So what do you make of that? If you can get those sensations from doing what we did, how does that affect your belief that you'll have a heart attack or that they are lethal symptoms?

John: In a way it diminishes it because having done the hyperventilating here, it's not that extreme really when I am in the anxiety attacks. Actually, all during the week I believe that I'm not going to have a heart attack – while sipping lemonade and talking about it, I believe I'm not. But being on the battle lines is another thing. This big voice, the fear, it's powerful. Rahh! [*Growls threateningly.*] And this little voice is telling him, 'Be logical.' It's like this big guy against this little guy, you know. It's like Goliath and David. That type of thing.

Ruth: But we are going to try to reverse the David and Goliath. Again, you expressed the idea even in the session that you could faint. That there was a limit to how much of *this* you could tolerate without something bad happening.

John: I did think that . . . up until the point when it hit me with its hardest shot. But the fact that I could still keep going, then I saw it didn't have the power over me that I thought.

Ruth: When I first had you breathe quickly, you thought you would faint. And then, in fact, it turned out you didn't faint, and you pushed yourself to see if you would faint and, in fact, you didn't faint. What does that do to the belief that there is a limit to how much of these sensations you can tolerate?

John: That helps very much. It probably would help even if I fainted.

Ruth: Well, you are very unlikely to faint as a result of this.

John: Well, even if I did, so what? Because usually people who faint come back to after a couple of minutes.

Ruth: Right, but the point was that you thought there was a limit, and that you couldn't keep going. And actually you kept it up for the full two minutes and nothing happened, except that you did produce these sensations. So what I'm pointing to is your idea that there is a limit to how much fear your body can tolerate. And this is an idea I would like to question. And maybe we will focus in on that.

John: Is there? I wonder, is there?

Ruth: Do you know anyone who has been in a war? Who has been very, very scared, repeatedly?

John: No. But I would imagine that a lot of people have, right, been in a war and been in very frightening situations, very fearful situations, and you know, it didn't kill them. I imagine that once the fear gets to a certain level, I just can't tolerate it for any continuous length of time. I think, 'If it got any more intense, I don't know what I would do with it. I don't know how to handle this thing that is happening to me.'

Ruth: OK, well I think the thing for us to do now is to focus on ways to handle it. Because there are ways of handling it. One of them has to do with the breathing and that is what I want to focus on today. Another one you came up with yourself, which is changing the fantasy to something pleasant. Or even just focusing on what's around you. But the key thing you have to understand, and I think you will begin to understand that as we go into it, is that your body would take over and help to bring your body rhythms back to normal, all by itself. Physiologically the mechanisms would adjust themselves on their own.

John: OK. That is what I was going to ask you. If you are experiencing this intense fear, at a certain point does the intensity get to the point where it basically dissipates itself, regardless of what you do?

Ruth: It will stop. Your breathing muscles will be tired –

John: Because you almost feel like you have to do something. You *have* to do something.

Ruth: That's well said. I think there is something that you can do that can calm you somewhat and can regulate it somewhat.

John: A tranquilliser, right?

Ruth: No, not a tranquilliser, although that would do it too. What I am going to show you would do it in a more useful way, I think. But the key thing to understand is you really don't *have* to do anything. This is just to give you a tool. You don't have to do it because your body would regulate the fear response just like it regulates everything else on its own. I mean, you don't have to think about your digestive processes – you don't have to worry about getting the right enzyme down to digest your Wheaties!

John: Exactly.

Ruth: However, this is what I want to show you. Maybe the best way to do it is to just have you overbreathe for a minute, or thirty seconds, just to get started up a little bit. OK, can you do that?

John: OK, ready. [*Starting to overbreathe.*] You don't have to do it, no sense both of us getting anxious.

Ruth: OK, thanks. . . . OK, that's thirty seconds. Now just close your mouth and breathe through your nose. Breathe slowly and regularly. Breathe to the count of four, slowly, and then breathe out to the count of four, slowly. I'll count it for you on your next breath. Try to relax. Settle back. Now in, two–three–four. Slow it down even more. [*Continues to teach control breathing.*] You want to tell me how are feeling?

John: Well, when I was doing it I just noticed that my head was getting lightheaded, all through here, it was a dizzy feeling.

Ruth: So after thirty seconds you were lightheaded. And then what happened when we went into this close-mouthed, slow, relaxed breathing?

John: Well, it was . . . I could just feel the level of this coming down.

Ruth: So it did calm you?

John: Yeah. It did have a calming effect.

Ruth: What do you make of that?

John: Well, I should use that breathing, you know. But sometimes I don't want to break out of the panic. I want to see why this is happening, because this fear is some type of illusion for something else.

Ruth: So it seems useful then to experience this panic. You have a mixed mind about it?

John: Until it gets to the point of eight, I guess, and that's when you know –

Ruth: And then you want to shut it out completely?

John: Then it gets a little too frightening to handle, and I guess at that point that's when I can start using these tools to get back to a manageable level.

Tenth session

John: . . . Responsibility – I was thinking about it on the way down here, and getting anxious. You give up so many things when you take on responsibility. You have to give up the crutch of being able to give it to somebody else.

Ruth: You have some resistance maybe to seeing yourself as a responsible person.

John: Yeah. Like there is a lot of stuff that comes with it. Like when you get it you have to – you know, suffering comes with it. It involves a stick-to-it-iveness type of thing, like staying with something. It involves dealing effectively with situations and feelings. It's like, it's almost like – what came into my head was my wife when she was in labour, saying, 'I can't do it. I can't do it.' And that's like what I'm afraid of, that I will get responsibility and then think, 'Oh God, I can't do it, I can't do it.' You know, the fear of failure.

Ruth: Well, I think the thing to do is to try to be concrete about what you think you can do and can't do.

John: Yeah, like not to take on more responsibility than I need to, and not feel responsible for things that are out of my control. That's another thing that I become involved in.

Ruth: So, that's pretty interesting. We started a few weeks ago with the idea that you *can't* handle responsibility and maybe you have gone a little bit past that to the idea, 'Well, maybe I can handle it, but maybe if I do I'll try to take *too* much responsibility.'

John: Right. I wrote down these different thoughts, like 'I can't handle the responsibilities of a perfect person'. I think when I take responsibility on it's almost like I have to take it on as a perfect person would and not feel this or not feel that – like Dr Spock or something. I have to take it on in that respect.

Ruth: Taking responsibility to you means that you are not supposed to have any feelings?

John: Yeah. That's a little distorted but that's it. Responsibility is like – it's hard to start thinking about it sometimes, it's like a key issue. Because once you abandon responsibility then you invite anxiety in its place.

Ruth: That's an interesting way of looking at it. But I think we would be doing better, you and I, if we stuck to the specifics.

John: OK, good.

Ruth: So suppose you tell me about what happened today, on the way down here.

John: Well, when I was going down, I stopped and got a soda and some crackers to eat because I really didn't have a chance to get lunch. I was going over this responsibility thing and I could feel anxiety coming on with thinking about responsibility. You know, giving up things, you have to give up this and you have to give up that. And then I had, like, an overload of feeling. Like what do you do if you overload? And, well, the overload could go into anxiety, I thought. And so I wrote down [*recording automatic thoughts*], 'How do I deal with torment?' And the answer to that seemed to be, 'Get out of torment by staying with it. If you try to get out of it, it stays with you.' So, that's what I was doing. Instead of fleeing anxiety or the feelings of anxiety, I was staying with it. That's really the key responsibility, maybe not doing anything but just staying with it, just staying with the moment, a little further, another block, another block, mentally as well as physically travelling, you know, just stay with it.

Ruth: Just following through rather than running away from it. Is that it?

John: Right. Because earlier this morning when I was driving, I put a thought down that came to my mind because I was thinking, thinking, thinking, and it was like a curse word, 'Don't "F" with the unconscious.' That came into my head. And I guess because of the reading [in psychoanalysis] that I'm doing, it was like 'Stop screwing around, stop meddling with things you shouldn't be meddling with because they are going to explode in your face'. Then I was thinking, 'Well, what's the worst that can happen there? What's the worst that I could find out about within my unconscious? It can't be something that is going to kill me, it can't threaten my life.'

Ruth: What were you doing that you thought was meddling with the unconscious?

John: Well, I was reading about the Oedipus complex. I was thinking that makes a lot of sense to me. In fact, that's what I was really getting angry about when I was driving down here – I realised that I really had some angry feelings towards my mother. I didn't think that she cared about me enough the times that I needed her. I really needed her and I didn't think that she cared about me. And that's really – I was distraught over that.

Ruth: You had this angry thought about your mother?

John: Yeah. I feel real bad about it. I might start to cry about it. Because it's like you feel like you have these ill feelings, yet you are not supposed to have ill feelings against your mother.

Ruth: What kind of person would have those feelings about his mother?

John: I don't know. I just have this feeling that society would think something must be wrong with a person who had bad feelings about their mother.

Ruth: So that is an assumption that you have. Society would think badly of you if you had angry feelings towards you mother?

John: Yeah. But it's really me who is feeling bad about it. I'm just saying, it's a 'can't win' situation. You have bad feelings about, let's say your mom, she doesn't care about you, but at the same time, you try to prevent yourself from having these bad feelings.

Ruth: Right. You have the feelings but you are angry at yourself for having the feelings.

John: . . . And I had the thought that if I'm taking on responsibility, that means having to resolve some things with my mother. How could I resolve that? The feeling of always wanting her to care about me. And deal with the fact that I really can't come to her as a child any more but as an adult. I guess in the back of your mind that's why you feel like you are helpless and anxious, because you feel like you are just a kid and if you could take your problems to your mother, everything will be OK. She will take them from you. So, you can't do that.

Ruth: And *have* you been able to do that?

John: Well, what I have been doing is putting distance between my parents and myself. If I don't have to be in their company, then I feel like maybe I can resolve it.

Ruth: So, as a practical matter you have just been staying away from them. But there's a thought that if you *are* close to them, they will take away your problems? And at the same time you have a sense of resentment against your mother for not having been there in the past.

John: Yeah, there is.

Ruth: So, that's contradictory. What do you make of that?

John: Maybe I think that she would come through this time. One time I was at the supermarket. I was working, I was about 14 or 15. My dad was away and I came home and I was really nervous and upset, and I think I was doing that to give her another chance. I keep giving her another chance. And when I see her I want her to be real affectionate, give me a hug or something. This way she'll get another chance to make up for it.

Ruth: And does she make up for it?

John: Not like I want her to.

Ruth: What is it that you want?

John: That she would be very warm, and hug me and say I'm glad that you are my son. All the things that I never really got, you know.

Ruth: What does it mean to you that you never got those things?

John: Well, the one part of it you want to say is that I never got it because I didn't deserve it, that's the one part.

Ruth: That's what you think?

John: Yeah, that I didn't get it because I didn't deserve it. Now the second part of it could be I didn't get it, not through any fault of my own, but because of her own problems.

Ruth: Such as?

John: Well, the other thing I thought about was she had a son who died. He was 17, and I was like 3 years old. That just pains me to talk about. [*Begins to cry.*] But then when I try to think of it, I can sympathise with her because I think of my dog dying and not wanting to have another dog. So that she probably wanted to insulate herself from getting too involved with me. Because if she did and then something happened to me she would really be devastated.

Ruth: Was she warmer to your sister?

John: I don't really think I can say that. No. I think she just clammed up.

Ruth: She clammed up after this boy died?

John: Yeah. And it's funny. She always talked about him as if he was her idol, perfect.

Ruth: And what did you make of that?

John: That if I was like him, then it wouldn't be that way, So I must have taken the responsibility for things I shouldn't.

Ruth: How have you done that?

John: In this instance? Always trying to be somebody I'm not. And then I guess feeling guilty because I think of it as a no-win situation. That's what I do. Because he's haunted me. It's like competing with somebody who is not there. You know, it's just like when somebody dies, you never see the bad part of them then, you only see the good part.

Ruth: How do you know she treated this brother better than you?

John: I only know about that from things that she would say. How he was this and how he was that. But, if you look at my mom's life after that, she seems to have gone into deprivation, into atonement.

Ruth: Let's backtrack about what you seem to have thought about yourself as a result – that your mother is cold to you because you weren't as good as your brother who died.

John: I never thought of it really this way at all. I had no memory of his death. But I probably do have a memory of this going on and my reaction to it.

Ruth: Your mother talking about him all the time?

John: Yeah. It definitely related back to me. Somehow I was not as good as him. So I think I tried different ways. I probably tried by being bad to get attention, then maybe good to get attention. I wanted to get a reaction out of her.

Ruth: And how did she react?

John: I think she distanced herself.

Ruth: You have been trying for years to be very, very good. And how is that working?

John: Well, that has just created other situations. Anxiety for one.

Ruth: But it hasn't radically changed the way she relates to you. No matter what you do she is still cold to you. So how much does it matter whether you live according to her rules or not? Let's go back to this idea that your not being as good as this boy is the reason she is so cold to you. The fact is you don't know how she related to your brother.

John: Right. It could have been similar.

Ruth: Has she ever been warm to anybody that you know? Anyone in your family? Children in the neighbourhood?

John: Not especially. I think she is warmer to my wife than she is to me. It's like when we are leaving the house or coming, she will kiss my wife but she won't kiss me. Stuff like that.

Ruth: Did you ask her why not?

John: No.

Ruth: Well, does she kiss other men? Does she kiss your father?

John: Definitely not.

Ruth: Is it possible that that is just her nature? She is generally not very warm, not very sexual, depressed, dwells in the past?

John: Yeah . . .

Ruth: And if you were to ask her how you compare to this brother, what do you think she would say?

John: She would probably be a lot kinder to me than I would think, than I probably presume. But probably she would point out a lot of similarities and stuff. I'd probably find out it's my imagination.

Ruth: Yes. I think you have to think about what this would be like for anybody. A person who dies, you know, you are not involved in any petty hassles with them any more, you just tend to remember the best of what they had to offer. You forget the details.

John: I can definitely see that, but I don't think when I was 5, 6, 7, and 8, that I could think like that. That's probably what the problem was.

Ruth: It sounds like a lot of the problem was that you saw her doing this, and you didn't know how to interpret it. But now you have a chance to start to test the belief. I mean is there any sign, for example, that she *does* approve of you?

John: I don't know. But whenever she says anything like 'You need a haircut', I say that's really supercritical. Maybe it comes out more critical to me than she means it.

Ruth: So she criticises you and you take that as evidence that she doesn't approve of you? Is there anything on the other side? Does she do anything that could be interpreted as caring?

John: Oh, yeah, yeah.

Ruth: What does she do?

John: She overprotects me.

Ruth: For example.

John: 'Don't do this because you are going to get a cold.' Just the other night she was there. I'm in a hurry to get out. She says, 'Do you lock your doors when you go out?' In other words, she always seems like she is concerned about my welfare.

Ruth: So, would she do that if she didn't care about you? If you were a worthless good-for-nothing?

John: No. I understand it really. Even though she doesn't want to get intimately involved because of losing her son, at the same time, she did love me because she wanted nothing to happen to me.

Ruth: Yeah. That's –

John: Just like anybody. Like you could get divorced, and you would like to have a relationship but you don't want to fall right back into it – the same thing.

Ruth: Yeah, but I think you can take it even farther. You don't know that she was any more intimate with your brother. You may just be picking up a lot of idealisation in retrospect. You don't really know that she was any warmer.

John: Right. Because she is like that with my sister and she was older when our brother died, so she would have noticed a big difference.

Ruth: So it may be that your mother just has this kind of restricted ability to express emotion. It may be that, with her, you have to read between the lines. It's as though 'Lock your doors at night', that's a code word for 'I love you and I care about you and I value you and I'm glad you're my son'.

John: Yeah, right, that is.

Ruth: But you have to be old enough to decode it.

John: Yeah, exactly. I understand that. I'm surprised really that that came out about my brother. I wasn't conscious of it.

Ruth: You weren't conscious of it but you are conscious of having some need that wasn't met with your mother. You were conscious that you had felt for a long time like you are just not up to snuff.

John: Right.

Ruth: Just hearing this over and over again.

John: Right. I remember going to the cemetery every Sunday to revere him. He became just almost like a saint.

Ruth: OK, let's see what we have learned here. You have a fear that you are incapable, that you can't take on responsibility. And then you begin to see that you have taken on *too much* responsibility. You've taken on the responsibility for trying to live up to saintly standards.

John: Right.

Ruth: It may be that being a responsible adult may actually *decrease* the demands on you! It might be that just leading an ordinary life as an adult and managing decisions and not running excessively for help, that might be easier for you than what you have been trying to do. Because what you have been trying to do apparently is –

John: Is live up to great expectations.

Ruth: Live up to great expectations. Get your mother to give some sign of warmth she may be incapable of producing. In other words, trying to do the impossible. But there is also this idea that it is a terrible thing to have angry feelings towards her. How much do you believe that?

John: Well, you know. I have given myself good reason to have angry feelings towards her, you know. Like a child definitely gets angry if you are not affectionate to him.

Ruth: OK, so the child in you is very, very angry, but there is the parent in you who says that is terrible, terrible, you shouldn't have that awful feeling. You're a bad boy. Now the question is: What are the rational responses to these thoughts?

John: That you were right to feel angry about that as a child, but it's time to give it up. Now it's time to look at it – like what we are doing, try to analyse it, be objective about it, see the different sides of it. How you felt, how she felt. Recognise that it is not something that just goes away overnight, but if you can recognise it, then you can deal with it.

Ruth: Yeah, I would say that's fair.

John: But realistically I recognise that there are a lot of people walking around who have very mixed feelings about their parents. In fact, I don't know anybody who doesn't. They have good features and they have bad features – when you get older, you do see their limitations. But hopefully you can put it in place and realise few people are perfect people or perfect parents and really good in all aspects of being adult.

Postscript

John was markedly improved at the end of our regular sessions, but soon after he suffered a severe panic, driving towards a bridge with his wife *en route* to a week's vacation at the beach. He called me from his car phone: he could not cross the bridge.

John's automatic thoughts, while circling before the bridge, weeping, were an amalgam of fears he had expressed previously: 'I'll fall apart [emotionally] on the bridge.' 'I'm all alone. No one loves me.' 'I'll be far away from my parents; what if I need medical help?' And finally, 'I have to feel closer to my wife before I attempt these things.' Together, we developed some 'rational responses': 'I've *already* 'fallen apart' – at least I'm pretty upset. What worse can happen?' 'I'm not really in medical danger – anyway, there are hospitals at the beach.'

The matters of love and closeness were harder to test. To gather some evidence on the point, I asked to speak to his wife. Yes, she was trying to be supportive (though a little frustrated with the length of the trip). Yes, she would hug and kiss him and tell him she loved him. 'Put John back on now', I said; and to John, 'Doesn't that mean someone loves you?' 'But it's not enough!' said John.

'But that's as good as love gets!' said I.

'But I don't think she feels what I feel – I'm all alone!'

'How *can* she feel it? Your body is racked with fear and anxiety, and she is calm. Still, she's been frightened before, and she can understand what you feel. Check it out.' He did, and she confirmed this.

'But I have to feel close to her before I go over.'

'That will never happen – you'll only feel close after you cross. Call me when you do!'

Half an hour after this dialogue, a triumphant John called from the other side of the bridge – feeling euphoric, close to his wife, and very appreciative of cognitive therapy!

References

Beck, A.T. (1976) *Cognitive Therapy and the Emotional Disorders*, New York: International Universities Press.

Beck, A.T. and Emery, G.D., with Greenberg, R.L. (1985) *Anxiety Disorders and Phobias: A Cognitive Perspective*, New York: Basic.

Beck, A.T. and Greenberg, R.L. (1988) 'Cognitive therapy of panic disorders', *American Psychiatric Association Annual Review of Psychiatry* 7.

Clark, D.M., Salkovskis, P.M., and Chalkley, A.J. (1985) 'Respiratory control as a treatment for panic attacks', *Journal of Behaviour Therapy and Experimental Psychiatry* 16: 23–30.

Salkovskis, P.M., Jones, D.R.O., and Clark, D.M. (1986) 'Respiratory control in the treatment of panic attacks: replication and extension with concurrent measurement of behaviour and pCO_2', *British Journal of Psychiatry* 148: 526–32.

Chapter three

Obsessions and compulsions
Paul M. Salkovskis

Introduction

Obsessional disorders are characterised by the occurrence of *intrusive and upsetting thoughts* which the patient usually regards as senseless, and which are accompanied by the urge to 'put right' or *neutralise*. Compulsive, overt behaviour such as repetitive washing or checking is the most obvious form of neutralising, but neutralising may also take the form of cognitive behaviours, such as thinking a 'good thought' whenever an obsessional intrusion occurs. Neutralising behaviour, either cognitive or overt, usually occurs repetitively and is often identified as the principal problem leading to the patient seeking treatment. For example, a patient was referred because of repetitive hand washing. On interview, he reported that two years previously he had read about a toddler dying after drinking from a bottle of domestic bleach. Since that time, he had been troubled by the thought that he had become contaminated by bleach and could harm others as a result. This led him to wash his hands repeatedly, taking up to an hour at a time, several times every day. When he tried to stop, he had the thought, 'What if I missed some bleach and touched my baby son?' When this thought occurred, he had a terrifying image of his son's face, horribly distorted, and his wife reproaching him for his carelessness and the death of their child. He would then have the thought, 'I can't risk it, just for the sake of washing for five minutes.'

This sequence of a thought leading to distress or discomfort, then to disturbed behaviour, further upsetting thoughts and more distress and disturbed behaviour in a vicious spiral is characteristic of obsessional problems. Similar observations have led to the formulation of cognitive models and treatment of other anxiety disorders (see Beck 1976; Greenberg, this volume; Warwick and Salkovskis, this volume). However, the treatment of choice for obsessive–compulsive disorder is behaviour therapy; little attention has been paid to cognitive approaches to treatment. A brief inspection of the literature suggests that this is because behaviour therapy is so successful that cognitive approaches have not been considered necessary. However, more careful examination of reports of outcome studies reveals important shortcomings. While success rates of up to 85 per cent (median 75 per cent) have been reported (Foa and Goldstein 1978; Marks 1987), these figures may not reflect the typical outcome of out-patient treatment in routine clinical practice. Almost all of the outcome studies have been carried out in carefully selected research populations, and in centres of excellence, using a team of highly trained staff in an intensive in-patient setting. Even in this context, 25 per cent of patients screened as suitable refuse treatment when it is explained; a further 12 per cent drop out when treatment starts. Longer-term relapse rates are unknown; there is certainly some evidence that relapses do occur (Espie 1986). These figures lead to the conclusion that, in a research setting, true success rates are less than 50 per cent of the patients who seek treatment and are judged to be suitable. Furthermore, behavioural treatment is associated with high levels of distress, sometimes making treatment a prolonged and difficult matter. For some patients distress may be so intolerable as to lead to refusal to proceed with further exposure, or even withdrawal from treatment. Exposure programmes have been developed so that flooding with 24-hour response prevention is used (Foa and Goldstein 1978); it is difficult to envisage more intensive exposure. Most authors now agree that the most substantial gains lie in developing techniques intended to alter the beliefs which give rise to difficulties in exposure treatments and the obsessions themselves (Foa *et al.* 1983; Rachman 1983).

Thus, the major problem which has yet to be adequately dealt with is patients who *do not respond to exposure treatment*. Foa *et al.* (1983) have identified the major problems; these are patients who refuse or drop out of treatment, patients who are convinced that their worries are sensible (described as 'overvalued ideas'), patients with severe concurrent depression and patients with obsessions *without* accompanying compulsive behaviour.

Cognitive therapy could therefore be useful in three major areas: in developing techniques which can be used to allow behaviour therapy to be carried out, to make behaviour therapy more effective when it is carried out, and as a treatment in its own right, particularly for patients who are known not to respond to behavioural techniques ('treatment failures'). This chapter briefly describes the behavioural model upon which exposure treatment of obsessions is based and goes on to describe the cognitive–behavioural hypothesis of the nature of obsessive–compulsive disorder, including some discussion of the relationship between cognitive and behavioural treatments. The assessment and treatment techniques which are based on the cognitive–behavioural hypothesis are discussed and illustrated by clinical examples.

The behavioural model

The behavioural model of obsessive–compulsive disorder proposes that the occurrence of compulsive behaviour serves to maintain obsessional problems. The main points of the behavioural model are detailed in Table 3.1 below:

Table 3.1 Behavioural model of obsessive–compulsive disorder

(1) *Obsessions are conditioned stimuli* It is assumed that obsessions are conditioned anxiety stimuli which have been resistant to extinction (habituation).

(2) *Anxiety relief reinforces compulsive behaviour* Behaviours which terminate the anxiety or discomfort associated with obsessional thoughts are reinforced by the reduction of discomfort, so that these behaviours become increasingly likely to follow obsessions.

(3) *Avoidance behaviours* There are a range of behaviours which are developed over a longer period, and which have the effect of reducing the occurrence of obsessional thoughts; where extensive, these avoidance behaviours can resemble that observed in agoraphobia.

Practical implications Avoidance behaviours prevent and compulsive behaviours terminate exposure to feared stimuli, producing short-term relief of anxiety but preventing exposure and extinction of anxiety.

It is evident from this outline of the model that there are two principal ways in which compulsive behaviour could maintain obsessional problems. Reduction in anxiety which follows the performance of obsessional rituals may reinforce the obsession, and the occurrence of compulsive behaviour serves to *terminate* exposure to the obsessional thought and thereby prevents habituation.

Cognitive hypotheses of obsessive–compulsive disorder

There are two principal ways in which a cognitive formulation could be applied to obsessive–compulsive disorder: either as an alternative explanation of the existing behavioural paradigm, or as a more comprehensive view which encompasses and expands the behavioural model. The first of these is similar to the cognitive explanation of other behavioural procedures in the treatment of anxiety; it could be said that obsessional behaviour maintains fears by preventing *reappraisal* from taking place. An example is the patient who was upset by the thought that he might harm his children through contamination unless he washes his hands in a particular way. He washes, experiences considerable relief, and his children do not come to harm. This experience is repeated many times, and he concludes that he has been successful in protecting his children from harm. Thus, the washing prevents him from discovering the true facts: only by being exposed to contamination and not washing will he discover that his fears are groundless. Note that this formulation leads to conclusions which are mostly identical to those of the behavioural model. The principal addition to existing techniques is to be found in the way that this view predicts that exposure would be most effective when it has the greatest information value, i.e. it is carried out in a way which maximises information which is inconsistent with feared disasters. An example of exposure used in this way is outlined on pp. 69–70.

This slight extension of the behavioural model, whilst having the advantage of simplicity, does not fully rescue the older behavioural model from the problems which are revealed by research findings. For instance, there is evidence in some patients that anxiety can increase as a consequence of obsessional thoughts (Beech and Liddell 1974). Discomfort evoked by obsessional stimuli is substantially reduced by the presence of the therapist in patients with checking rituals but not in patients with contamination and washing rituals (Rachman *et al.* 1976; Roper and Rachman 1975; Roper *et al.* 1973). The inability of the behavioural model to account fully for the phenomenology of obsessive–compulsive disorder and the limitations of the therapeutic applications of behaviour therapy described earlier in this chapter highlighted the need for a cognitive hypothesis on which treatment of obsessions could be based (Salkovskis 1985).

The cognitive hypothesis of obsessions proposes that intrusive thoughts are a normal phenomenon (Rachman and de Silva 1978; Salkovskis and Harrison 1984). Intrusive thoughts do not automatically have affective connotations, but acquire emotional properties as a result of appraisal. That is, intrusive thoughts can take positive, negative, or neutral affect depending on the evaluation made by the individual experiencing them (Salkovskis 1985). Intrusive thoughts are adaptive and functional in that they are crucial to a variety of human activities, including creativity and problem solving. Intrusive thoughts persist to the extent to which they have implications for *intentional behaviour* on the part of the person experiencing them (Salkovskis 1985, 1988). If an intrusive thought has no implications for further deliberate thought and/or action (such as mental problem solving) it will not persist. On the other hand, if an intrusive thought *does* have implications for intentional behaviour, then further processing will take place. A cognitive system which works in this way has several advantages; in particular, it allows the selection of important ideas from the welter of cognitive activity, and ensures that ideas most relevant to current concerns (positive or negative) will persist.

The cognitive hypothesis of the development of obsessional disorders

A more unfortunate implication is that particular types of intrusive thought will interact with beliefs of responsibility in 'oversocialised' individuals. These are the people described by Rachman and Hodgson (1980) as being 'of tender conscience', and therefore especially sensitive to ways in which

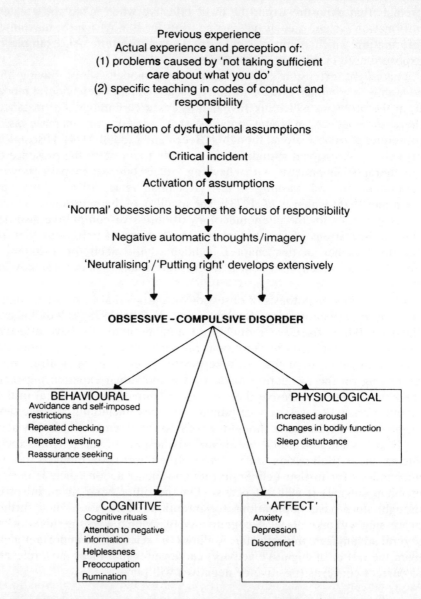

Previous experience
Actual experience and perception of:
(1) problems caused by 'not taking sufficient
care about what you do'
(2) specific teaching in codes of conduct and
responsibility
↓
Formation of dysfunctional assumptions
↓
Critical incident
↓
Activation of assumptions
↓
'Normal' obsessions become the focus of responsibility
↓
Negative automatic thoughts/imagery
↓
'Neutralising'/'Putting right' develops extensively

↓   ↓   ↓

OBSESSIVE – COMPULSIVE DISORDER

BEHAVIOURAL
Avoidance and self-imposed
restrictions
Repeated checking
Repeated washing
Reassurance seeking

PHYSIOLOGICAL
Increased arousal
Changes in bodily function
Sleep disturbance

COGNITIVE
Cognitive rituals
Attention to negative
information
Helplessness
Preoccupation
Rumination

'AFFECT'
Anxiety
Depression
Discomfort

Source: Reproduced from Salkovskis and Warwick 1988.

Figure 3.1 Cognitive–behavioural model of the development of obsessive–
compulsive disorder

intrusive thoughts might infringe upon their strict moral beliefs, and as being particularly likely to attempt to feel obliged to try to correct any infringements. Thus, the interaction of intrusive thoughts and strict beliefs can result in the characteristic pattern of thoughts and neutralising behaviour which develop into obsessional disorders (Salkovskis 1985). In particular, beliefs overemphasising responsibility for possible adverse consequences of one's thoughts and actions are likely to interact with thoughts of harm and lead to the taking of precautions or corrective action ('neutralising') (an example was given on p. 50). Neutralising can therefore be either overt or covert behaviour, provided it is intentional and initiated as a result of the negative evaluation of an intrusive thought (see also the section below on obsessions without overt compulsive behaviour, p. 72). Figure 3.1 shows the way in which the cognitive hypothesis accounts for the development of obsessive–compulsive disorder.

For example, Mr Johnstone was an obsessional patient who was troubled by the thought that he had offered activities to the devil. (His treatment is described in detail on pp. 63 ff. below.) He described aspects of his strict Roman Catholic upbringing in the following way: 'I was brought up in a convent school; we used to put at the top of our essays JMJ (Jesus, Mary & Joseph). By putting that there, you offered your work as a form of prayer or worship. You could do the essay without this, the pure act, but this offering made it different. Your whole life can become a prayer. So, when you sin, you can make this evil act a prayer to the devil by your attitude or offering. You are not just sinning, but you are committing a far worse sin.'

He went on to describe how, as a young child, he was extensively warned about the dangers of impure thoughts, and of the awful punishment which would follow from 'sin by thought'; the punishment could, however, be averted, by adopting a contrite attitude of mind. During his late teens he rebelled against these ideas, and behaved very much as he wanted. He was troubled a great deal by guilt; as he settled down, he began to believe that he had offered his 'wild living' to the devil. As this thought grew, he began to have another thought – that he would offer everyday activities to the devil. This thought increasingly occurred at times when he was in a state that he believed to be sinful, such as when he was angry or thinking 'lustful thoughts'. He tried to neutralise these thoughts ('put them right') by making 'a firm purpose of amendment', by saying prayers in ritualised ways, and by depriving himself of things he would enjoy (such as food, watching television). He became increasingly preoccupied with the idea of offering things to the devil.

This example illustrates the way in which an apparently innocuous attitude (that everyday activities can be transformed by an associated intention or thoughts into intrinsically good or bad acts) can lead to difficulties when intrusive thoughts occur which seem to run counter to the individual's particular beliefs. Similar and related beliefs led the patient to attempt to resist the occurrence of the thoughts and, when this did not succeed, to neutralise them. This increase in neutralising was associated with a progressive worsening of the patient's distress.

The role of cognitive and behavioural factors in the maintenance of obsessional disorders

Thus, the patient's attitudes and beliefs (particularly those concerning responsibility, blame, and blamelessness) lead the patient to negative appraisals of their intrusive thoughts. When this appraisal (which manifests in the content of negative automatic thoughts) includes a major element of both threat and responsibility for future harm, the patient will show a propensity to attempt some kind of corrective action. Such attempts to neutralise the implications of one's own thoughts will prevent reappraisal of the true risks, and have the effect of further amplifying pre-existing beliefs about responsibility. When issues of responsibility hinge on the occurrence of intrusive thoughts and the possible harm associated with not reacting to them, the effect of the neutralising behaviour will be to focus attention more closely on the subject of the original intrusion. This can take patients into seemingly never-ending sequences of intrusion–appraisal of responsibility–neutralising–intrusion–appraisal . . . and so on. That is, the effort towards neutralising leads to increasing preoccupation with the intrusion and its appraisal. The importance of responsibility in the ideation of obsessional patients clarifies several previously inexplicable aspects of their behaviour, particularly the way in which obsessions are not troublesome where it is possible for the patient to spread or pass on responsibility. This could be accomplished by avoidance (getting others to carry out tasks such as locking or checking) and by the seeking of reassurance. Reassurance seeking spreads responsibility by making another person aware of the details of the patient's recent actions or thoughts (usually someone in a position of repsonsibility, such as the therapist) (Warwick and Salkovskis 1985). Treatment is focused on aspects of the maintaining factors identified here and in Salkovskis (1985); on reducing avoidance behaviour and increasing exposure to problem situations and thoughts; on the modification of attitudes concerning responsibility; on modification of the appraisal of intrusive thoughts; on preventing neutralising which follows the appraisal of responsibility; and on increasing exposure to responsibility, by direct exposure and stopping reassurance seeking.

Applications of the cognitive model

Cognitive techniques can be used with obsessional patients in a wide range of ways. These include procedures designed to facilitate the behavioural approach to treatment (exposure and response prevention) as well as techniques more specifically intended to change the thoughts and beliefs which are directly involved in the production of distress in obsessional patients. The first category includes strategies which (1) facilitate assessment; (2) prevent treatment drop-outs; (3) improve compliance; (4) maximise the effectiveness of exposure and response prevention. In general, these techniques work by reducing the degree of distress experienced by patients, with the same amount of exposure, or even increasing exposure. The second category involves the use of techniques intended to allow the patients to modify negative evaluations of the obsessional thoughts, and to bring about more general changes in beliefs concerning responsibility. In practice, the most effective approach to the treatment of obsessional patients involves a combination of both cognitive and behavioural strategies (Salkovskis and Warwick 1988). Behavioural techniques are a particularly efficient way to bring about belief changes; designing and conducting behavioural interventions integrated with cognitive elements (for instance, as behavioural experiments as described on p. 70) can shorten and enhance treatment. Furthermore, cognitive techniques can considerably simplify the often difficult process of engaging the patient in behavioural treatment and ensuring compliance (see p. 63; Salkovskis and Warwick 1985).

General style of treatment

The general style of therapy is particularly important with obsessional patients. Obsessionals sometimes become argumentative, particularly if they are seeking reassurance from the therapist. If this happens, therapy seldom proceeds well, particularly as the patient ceases to process information fully from the therapist, and instead begins to look for defects in the information they are being given. This can usually be avoided by being less didactic and using a high proportion of questions, so that the information which is used to alter beliefs is provided by the patients themselves in answer to the therapist's questions. Whenever the sessions are in danger of becoming combative (i.e. when the patient and therapist begin to show signs of arguing), the therapist needs to *summarise* the discussion so far, ending by agreeing that the patient could be right in their assertions, and that the object is to *find out* the real situation rather than taking anything for granted. For instance, if the patient really believes that one further wash would make all the difference, this must be considered seriously as a strong possibility. What is the evidence from past experience? Has the patient ever believed that before? What happened? How could we find out whether it might be so on this occasion? Therapy utilises summaries by both therapist and patient as a way of clarifying the discussion from time to time.

As in cognitive therapy in general, *reframing* is used in order to enhance the collaborative relationship. Homework is presented as an exercise in finding out what will happen rather than simply exercises in mastering a series of therapist-devised tasks. Early in treatment, emphasis is placed on the idea that, whatever the outcome of homework, the exercise will have been a useful one. Patients are told, 'From time to time, people find the homework that has been set can be difficult. Sometimes, it is so difficult that it isn't completed. If that ever happens, then that's really important information, because it tells us a great deal about the kind of problems which you have. It would be particularly helpful if you could make careful notes on your homework sheet about what happened, what thoughts went through your mind and anything else which seemed important about the situation.'

Assessment factors

The cognitive hypothesis has implications for both the *implementation* and the *focus* of assessment. These two factors are examined in turn.

Problems encountered in implementing assessment

When attempting to assess obsessional problems one often encounters difficulties not found amongst other emotional disorders; often simply demonstrating an awareness of these problems in a matter-of-fact way is sufficient to change the patient's belief in the acceptability of their thoughts. The message which is conveyed is: 'OK, yes, I understand your worries about this. These are obsessional thoughts, I've dealt with them before lots of times, and they are not even slightly shocking to me. It's common both to have the thoughts and the worries associated with them. Let's sit down together, talk about them and get going with helping you deal with your problems.'

Content

By definition, the content of obsessional thoughts is unacceptable and often repugnant to the patient. Obsessional patients often believe that the thoughts reveal that they are unpleasant people; sometimes, that others (including their therapist) would criticise or reject them, or believe them to be insane. These beliefs are usually associated with considerable reluctance to describe their thoughts. Similarly, the thoughts may concern socially embarrassing subjects (e.g. contamination by faeces, urine, or seminal fluid). Obsessionals have often been described as being 'of tender conscience'; the difficulty they may experience in describing their worries to a total stranger is apparent.

Effects of discussion

Some patients have obsessional fears that talking about the obsession may make it worse or more real, or even make them act out the thoughts.

More specific concerns

Patients may have specific fears, such as the obsession being a sign of schizophrenia (implying immediate hospitalisation against their will). When the thoughts or impulses concern violence or other illegal or morally repugnant acts, patients often worry that the therapist will have them arrested.

Embarrassment

Patients with very severe problems (especially when extensive compulsive behaviour is involved) can be ashamed by the extent to which their obsessions are out of control, particularly as most patients regard obsessional thoughts as intrinsically senseless.

Chronicity

In chronic cases, the assessment and formulation is made more difficult by the habitual ('overlearned') nature of the behaviours. Compulsive behaviour and avoidance in such instances can become so extensive that the patient may have ceased to be aware of the underlying pattern of thinking and voluntary behaviours which pre-empt and mask obsessional thoughts, impulses, and images.

Cognitive techniques can be effectively employed to deal with these difficulties. The focus of these techniques is identification of cognitions which are making the assessment difficult, then helping the patient to find alternative responses. For example, a 37-year-old married woman with two children (3 and 7 years old) was referred. She complained of upsetting thoughts, the content of which she would not discuss with the referring psychiatrist. When she attended for assessment, she immediately apologised for wasting the therapist's time, and began to cry.

P: I shouldn't really be wasting your time.
T: It sounds like you had a really upsetting thought just now.
P: Yes.
T: What went through your mind right then?
P: I thought that I must be a very bad patient because I can't tell you about my problems.
T: Well, it's interesting you should say that, because it seems to me that you have just told me one of your problems; I mean that you have a problem talking about your difficulties.

P: Yes, but that's not my *real* problem.

T: Well, it sounds to me like it's a real problem. Also, if you can solve the problem about talking about the difficulties that would mean that we could start to deal with your *real* problem?

P: I see what you mean.

T: OK, but my guess is that you might be able to tell me about the kind of thoughts you have when you try to talk about your problem. That would seem like a really good place to start.

P: [*Laughs.*] You're right.

This brief initial interaction establishes a rapport with the patient, a focus on cognitive factors and how they affect the patient. Most important, it explicitly takes the pressure off the patient with respect to the need to disclose immediately the details of the problem. During the next few minutes, the therapist needs to build up the rapport already established.

T: I understand that it is often very difficult to discuss your problems with a complete stranger. In fact, it is actually a bit unusual if someone finds it easy. So, it's difficult for you; are there any questions you want to ask me which might help you feel a little easier?

and/or:

T: Could you tell me a bit about the difficulties which you have with talking about your problem?

P: I'm worried about what you might do, who you might tell.

T: You're worried about how I might react when you tell me your problem?

P: Yes. I worry that you might think I'm a terrible mother.

T: You worry that I might think you're a terrible mother . . . because of the thoughts you have?

P: Yes.

T: It might be helpful for you to know that you're not the first person who has said that to me. In fact, I very often see people who have that worry; so far, it's never even crossed my mind that any of the people concerned were terrible mothers. Usually, I think that they might be unhappy, and troubled by upsetting thoughts.

P: Other people have worries like this?

T: Well, I can't say for sure that your worries are exactly the same because I don't know much about yours, but they sound similar. For instance, it sounds a bit like someone I saw recently who had thoughts that she might lose control of herself and hurt her children; sometimes, she thought she might even *want* to hurt them. She was so upset about it, and that's a really important clue as to what's going on. If she *really* wanted to hurt her children, do you think that she would have been upset?

P: No, I'd never thought of that, no.

T: Right, but supposing she didn't want to have the thoughts and fought them off; what would happen then?

P: I don't know.

T: OK, will you try a little experiment for me? You remember the waiting room?

P: Yes.

T: Right. Just for a minute, I want you to do your best *not* to think about the waiting room. Try really hard, close your eyes, that's right. [*Pause*] What happened?

P: I couldn't get the waiting room *out* of my mind.

T: Right. Do you begin to see what I mean?

P: You're showing me that these thoughts can come because you *don't* want them?

T: Right.

Note here that the therapist is doing several things; he is beginning the process of educating the patient into a model of how intrusive thoughts work even before he has details of the content of the thinking. The particular intention is to account for the discomfort experienced in a less threatening way. Notice that the illustration used did not initially refer to the patient's obsessional thoughts, but used other thoughts as a close analogy. Having gained an initial impression as to the likely content of the patient's obsession, *the therapist provides a similar example* from his own experience, thus reinforcing the idea that this is a familiar problem. In this example, the interview developed further in the following way after an example of harming obsessions had been outlined:

T: Supposing you did tell me about your thoughts; what is the worst thing which could happen?

P: You might take my children away from me.

T: Because of the thoughts?

P: Yes.

T: Right. From what you've told me so far, that seems very unlikely. I have never even considered it when people have upsetting thoughts of the type I described. Are your thoughts very different from the ones we just talked about?

After the interaction above, the patient disclosed that she had thoughts of strangling her children. It may sometimes be useful to engage the patient in more discussion of hypothetical examples and further clarify the nature of obsession.

It can also be helpful to discuss other examples of people horrified by their thoughts, explaining that the nature of obsessions is such that only a religious person would be *upset* by blasphemous thoughts, a meticulous person by thoughts of contamination, a gentle person by thoughts of violence, and so on. A further useful strategy would be to ask the patient how they thought a truly violent person would react to thoughts of harming others; usually patients will decide that an evil person would be pleased by violent thoughts. A further helpful piece of information is to discuss the incidence of what appear to be obsessional thoughts in the normal population (Rachman and de Silva 1978; Salkovskis and Harrison 1984). Demonstrating that intrusive thoughts are a frequently experienced but seldom discussed phenomenon can relieve worries about the intrinsic abnormality of the problem.

Note that many of these interventions not only facilitate assessment, but can form the basis of the rationale for subsequent treatment. In some milder cases, these discussions with some further brief instruction in response prevention can be suffcient to resolve the obsessional problem.

Broadening the cognitive focus of assessment

The focus in routine assessment of obsessive–compulsive disorder is on the form and content of the obsession itself, and on discovering factors which may be maintaining the obsession and associated discomfort (see Salkovskis and Kirk 1989 for a full account of behavioural assessment). These maintaining factors include mood and behaviours which the patient uses to prevent them from being exposed to their obsession (avoidant behaviours) and/or behaviours which terminate exposure once it has occurred. The cognitive model indicates that a variety of other factors need to be assessed. These are:

1. The extent to which the patient makes specific evaluations (negative automatic thoughts) of their intrusive thoughts and the meaning of these; e.g. when a violent thought occurs, then having the negative automatic thought, 'If I have that thought it may mean that deep down I want to be violent, and could be if I am not vigilant'.
2. Behaviours which have the effect of reducing or passing on actual responsibility to others; e.g. asking others to carry out specific tasks.
3. Questioning others (seeking reassurance) in a way which ensures that responsibility for harm is reduced.
4. The occurrence of covert neutralising and avoidance (mental ritualising and avoidance); e.g. when the thought of someone dying occurs, trying to think of the same person alive.
5. Attitudes concerning responsibility; e.g. 'Having a thought about doing something is as bad as carrying out the action'; 'sin by thought'.

The transcript of the therapy session with Mr Johnstone (pp. 63 ff.) illustrates the way this type of assessment is developed, using techniques such as the downward arrow to gain access to the patient's fears.

Treatment

Engagement and ensuring compliance

As outlined in the section on style of treatment, problems can arise when the patient's view of the nature of their difficulties is not fully consistent with the therapist's perception of the problem. Where this situation occurs, it usually leads to problems with engaging the patient in treatment as a collaborative effort, and can lead to the situation where a patient reluctantly goes along with parts of the programme, but feels unable to comply fully with the more stressful or threatening components. A cognitive analysis of this situation will usually lead to the conclusion that the patient is not convinced by the therapist's formulation of their problem; e.g. they may be unsure whether the basis of their problem truly lies with anxiety or is actually with contamination. The patient will have such reservations because they are unconvinced by the available evidence. This is dealt with in two principal ways: first, the therapist makes explicit the two alternatives which could account for their distress (*that their worries occur as a result of anxiety*, or *that their worries are the result of an actual and realistic danger*), then elicits from the patient the evidence for each perspective; for convenience, these are placed in two columns (see Salkovskis and Warwick 1985 and 1988 for some examples of this). Having elicited the evidence, each item is discussed and the belief rated. Finally, belief in each of the two possibilities is rated. As far as possible, the therapist ensures that they are not engaged in discussing the original intrusive thought or directly involved in providing reassurance.

Sometimes this still leaves a major element of doubt, which is rather more difficult to dispel. This situation often arises once treatment has already begun and shown some signs of progression, and can lead to a halt in further progress. In the following example, the earlier stages of treatment had dealt only with one aspect of the obsession. Mr Johnstone was a 29-year-old married civil servant, referred with religious obsessions. At the time of referral, the obsessions involved having the thought 'I am going to offer what I am doing to the devil'; when this thought occurred, he would make a 'firm purpose of amendment' then ritualise, usually by repeating prayers 'until I am satisfied' and denying himself some pleasure later in the day. He initially responded well to exposure with response prevention, but improvement began to slow down within six sessions, and further progress ceased. He reported that he was able to stop ritualising in some instances but not others. The transcript below is taken from session ten.

T: You have doubts as to whether the thoughts are true or whether they are obsessions.

P: The main problem I had with previous treatment was that I was given techniques to change the direction of my thoughts when I was ritualising and I thought I could be killing my conscience by learning a trick. I worry about the harm that I had done by offering things to the devil or thought I had offered things to the devil and not put right; I would have to put them right when I thought that way. Rationalising things as just obsessions could be killing my conscience. Where things to me are real, I can't think of them as irrational.

T: And therefore –

P: Then I haven't the confidence to stop putting right, you've got to do the absolution.

T: If you do kill your conscience, then what?

P: Then I'll be living an anti-religious life, I really will be offering things to the devil because I haven't neutralised it.

T: So that leaves us with two possibilities. Either that the thoughts are correct and you could be living the life of an anti-christ; or that you have an obsessional problem. Are these the two possibilities you see, and swing between?

P: Yes, sometimes I can say 'this is my stupidity', then there are things I really feel guilt for and the ritual has to be done because it seems I really have offered things to the devil. I lose my temper or have impure thoughts, then think I'm going to offer that to the devil and still give in. That makes it more real, because by implication I wanted to commit the sin, I chose to do it. Other times the thought comes when I am walking through a door, then that's not a problem in the same way; that seems like it really is an intrusion. Guilt from a real, chosen sin makes it very real so I have to put it right then.

T: So some thoughts you can see are an obsession for sure; then there are thoughts which go with something which is really a sin, then you're not so sure?

P: It means I really have offered things to the devil because I have the wrong attitude of mind; if I continue and say 'Blow it', there is a conscious decision on my part, therefore I must neutralise. I'm responsible for my actions then, no matter what.

T: But the other possibility is that the whole lot is part of your obsession?

P: Yes. But if I accept that, it's easy for me to go throught life saying it's all obsession; but it might be just that I'm learning a trick to kill my conscience. I can't be confident.

T: Right, so we have two possibilities which really come into conflict in obsessions where your action could mean you have chosen to offer things to the devil. Let's write these down [*writes*]: first, 'my problem is obsessions'; second, 'my problem is sin; calling this obsessions is killing my conscience'. Look at these; do you agree these are the possibilities?

P: Totally.

T: Right, now look at the first one; could you rate how likely that is to be true, using 0 to 100, where 0 is no truth at all, 100 is completely true.

P: Well: the first one, about 30 per cent now; when they happen, only 10 per cent. The second one, 70 per cent now, nearly 100 per cent when they happen.

T: OK, so you are not completely sure either way, although this can vary. Could both be true?

P: Definitely not. Only one of these can be correct.

T: That's really useful to know. If the problem is obsessional thoughts, then the idea that the problem is sin will be untrue, *or* if the problem is sin, then it couldn't be an obsession. I think that the main thing we need to work on today is to find a way of resolving this question, which is why I have written it down. How does that seem to you?

P: Yes, I agree that that's what we should do. I don't think I can stop putting things right unless I'm sure the thoughts really are an obsession.

T: OK, so look at the card where I have written the two ways of looking at your problem. Can you think of how we might be able to decide on this, between these possibilities?

P: Well, if I don't commit sin, fine, there is no obsession.

T: How likely is it that you won't commit sin?

P: Very unlikely; I've been brought up to believe that you should always try to be free of sin, but that you always fall.

The therapist has thus pin-pointed one of the main obstacles to treatment, and has made deciding on the nature of the thoughts (and therefore resolving this obstacle) the target for the session. Leaving the card with the patient (and referring to it from time to time), the patient and therapist go on to examine the obsessional thoughts and how they occur. The thoughts can occur any time, and are always associated with urges to put right. The only difference that the patient can identify between obsessions associated with a sinful act or thought and those which are not is the context; when obsessions occur in the context of urges they are associated with increased belief in responsibility, while intrusive thoughts not associated with this type of behaviours are simply seen as an obsession.

P: I need that confidence; priests have often told me that, but the question keeps coming up, have they got it right on this occasion?

T: So it is important to identify whether the thought is an obsession; rather than trying to say on each occasion whether or not the thought is a sin, the alternative is to clarify whether the thoughts are obsessions.

P: Right. If I believed that I wouldn't have to put right.

T: We need tests of the ideas on the card; do you have any evidence already?

P: Well, the very fact that I'm here; everybody apart from me says it's an obsession, and that's evidence. I'm not so sure.

T: Right, but you think there is a small possibility that everybody could be wrong. Is there anything else?

Tests of this view carried out by the patient included attempts to exclude various non-obsessional thoughts from his mind and trying to gain certainty that various harmful events (such as being knocked down by a car) would not happen. These exercises served to illustrate the 'mechanics' of intrusive thoughts, and the impossibility of proving that something would *not* happen. A further component of treatment involved identifying and making explicit the thoughts of harm which were linked to the idea of not 'putting right'.

Having thus elaborated on the evidence for and consequences of the thoughts as an obsessional problem, the therapist next asks the patient for further details of his beliefs about what it would mean if the thoughts really were sinful. Doing this means that the patient is unlikely to perceive the discussion as an attempt to 'trick' him. The therapist works out with the patient what would be bad about not neutralising the obsessional thoughts when he had offered some intentional act (such as lustful thoughts or being angry) to the devil. The technique used was the 'downward arrow', in which the therapist questions the patient about how bad each of a succession of steps would really be.

T: So you say that the worst thing which could happen if you don't do the neutralising is that everything you do would be against God. What would be so bad about that for you?

P: Yes. My life would be a continual offence.

T: How bad would that be?

P: Terrible. Nothing I did would be worthwhile; watching television, anything I do. I couldn't look forward to a holiday, going to the theatre, anything like that, it would all be pointless, an offence against God.

T: Supposing these things were stopped being worthwhile; what would be bad about that?

P: It's all part of life having no meaning, no enjoyment.

T: So if this were happening, you really wouldn't be able to enjoy anything?

P: Definitely not.

T: Would that be the same for anyone else in the same position?

P: No. I have the wrong attitude of mind. That's the problem, that's what will spoil things.

T: How has that happened?

P: It has come up through habit, the obsession.

T: The obsession can destroy your life if you don't neutralise?

P: Yes, I just have this kink.

This brief discussion brings the consequences of not putting right into the more concrete form of not being able to enjoy things; this is added to the idea of deadening his conscience.

T: Would you accept, from what we have discussed before, that the putting right keeps the obsession going?

P: Yes.

T: So, as it stands, there is no escape from the obsession.

P: Unless I actually stop putting right, but to me that would have to mean killing my conscience.

T: So morally, you have to keep on being obsessional, if your life is to be worthwhile, if you are to be able to enjoy even simple things?

P: Yes, if I keep offering things to the devil in my thoughts.

T: And unless you stop putting things right, then offering things to the devil will continue?

P: Yes. Yes.

T: So you can't stop being obsessional in any way?

P: Yes. It sounds like the problem has me trapped; it goes round and round.

T: So if you do what I recommend, you might offend against God and deaden your conscience. You can keep doing the ritual, but you know from years of experience that that makes you worse.

P: It's like a whirlpool. That's not how it should be. I think I must let it go; there really is no choice in that pattern, so I shouldn't ritualise; it can't be intended in that way, with no escape. I can't keep the upsetting thoughts out, and there is nobody who can be a saint all the time.

T: So the major obstacles to stopping the ritual would be the problems of deadening your conscience and not being able to enjoy things?

P: Yes.

T: Supposing you were to try stopping the ritual for three months; if that had deadened your conscience and stopped you enjoying things, would you know?

P: Yes.

T: Supposing you tried it, and your worst worries turned out to be true; could you then go back to how things are now, with the ritualising?

P: Um . . . yes, I think so.

T: Are you absolutely certain?

P: Yes.

T: OK, then how about stopping the rituals for just three months; at the end of three months, we review the situation very carefully and see what has happened. If your fears are confirmed, you can get back to how things are now, and I'll help you do that. If your fears are not confirmed, then you will be in a really strong position. How does that sound?

P: I need to think about that . . . it sounds like a good idea.

T: Well, the idea is just that you find out which of the possibilities you identified earlier is accurate: I wrote these down on the card as 'my problem is obsessions' and 'my problem is sin; calling this obsessions is killing my conscience'. Stopping the putting right for three months will help you solve this?

P: Yes.

T: OK. Well, I've got my diary here; what I'm going to do is book a specific appointment in three months' time to review how this experiment works out. I'll write in large letters: 'Three-month review of Mr Johnstone's experiment'. In all the sessions up to then, we will do our best to get rid of all the putting right. Are you happy about that?

P: I really want to get started now.

This strategy proved effective, and the patient improved rapidly. The following transcript was taken from the session which was specifically arranged to review whether response prevention had deadened his conscience or not.

P: I'm not so obsessed about sin, if it occurs then it occurs, I'm not bothered by it now in the same way. When the thoughts occur, they are far, far less.

T: So have you sinned more: has your conscience been deadened?

P: No, not at all. I now feel that this is the right way to deal with it.

T: Even when you have the thoughts?

P: Yes, even then.

T: So if you compare how much you 'offended' when you were putting right to how much you are offending now?

P: Much less.

T: What do you make of that?

P: Yes, I'm not seeing everything as a sin. The obsession with sin has been removed, now I'm dealing with real sin and not my imaginary scruples and so on.

T: How does that fit in with your concerns of before?

P: I'm better off now, in my religion and in myself.

T: The other prediction you made was that you would not be able to enjoy yourself; how did that work out?

P: I'm enjoying myself much more now, even in the little things.

T: So what happens when you have one of these thoughts now?

P: Thoughts just pass through; for instance, if I have a blasphemous thought, I don't fight it and try and throw it out, I just say to myself, it's coming, so what. It's a more effective way of dealing with them; fighting them seems to bring them on. That's gone now, I don't fight them at all.

T: How is the evidence looking, now you've had a chance to try this out?

P: What you said would happen has happened, I'm less bothered and sinning less.

Further enhancing exposure treatments

The simplest cognitive view of exposure treatment is that exposure and response prevention provides the best conditions for the patient to make a more accurate appraisal of the extent to which his obsessional thoughts truly represent threat. This being so, the response prevention component is particularly crucial, because the patient comes to believe that each occurrence of the obsession represents a disaster only just prevented, thereby providing fuel for the continuation of the belief in the potential for disaster. It therefore follows that anything which increases the extent to which exposure contains information relevant to the patient's fears should enhance the effectiveness of exposure. Information about such fears readily emerges when exposure is proposed; patients often say 'I can't do that because if I do then . . . will happen'. This kind of information has often been regarded as something of a nuisance by behaviour therapists, having to be passed over as quickly as possible; however, for the cognitive therapist, this kind of statement represents invaluable information which is vital when it comes to devising the treatment programme. It follows from the cognitive account of the effectiveness of exposure that removing the perception of threat will also have the effect of reducing or abolishing discomfort.

Once the patient's beliefs about their obsessions are elicited, this information is exploited by focusing on the patient's fears and working on a detailed specification of the conditions which would represent a proper test of the validity of his fears. For instance, a patient thought that he might lose control of his behaviour while walking down the street, resulting in him jumping into the path of an oncoming car and being killed. Exposure alone seemed unlikely to be effective, as this patient was not avoiding walking in the street. Notice in the following transcript that the therapist pays particular attention to covert neutralising.

T: You don't avoid the street?

P: No.

T: OK, so could we run through the last time you walked down the High Street. As you got to the bit where the cars go faster, what happened then?

P: Well, I had the thought that I might jump into the road.

T: When you had the thought that you might jump into the road, did you try to do anything?

P: I tried to keep in control.

T: How did you try to keep in control?

P: Sort of mentally.

T: Right, so that you tried to stop yourself jumping out by keeping mental control of yourself. Is that what you usually do?

P: All the time. Otherwise I think I might do it [jump].

T: Is there anything else you do?

P: I walk further away from the pavement edge.

The therapist at this point formed the hypothesis that the patient's fears were being maintained by the avoidant behaviour described. From here, the therapist went on to discuss this possibility with the patient. To illustrate how this might work, he used the example of the apprentice builder who is asked by his workmates to hold a wall up while they have a break; the wall is actually perfectly secure, but the apprentice does not know this. Whilst they are gone, he worries about his responsibility, and pushes against the wall harder and harder, becoming more and more concerned about the consequences of letting the wall go. When his workmates come back, he discovers the wall to be quite secure when he lets it go; only by letting it go is he able to determine the true risk of the wall falling (or not). The patient was asked whether the apprentice was helping his worries when holding the wall up; this discussion was directed towards allowing the patient to arrive at the conclusion that unnecessary avoidance behaviour serves to focus the mind on the feared disaster and leads to an unrealistic (if understandable) perception of the risks involved, rather than giving any peace of mind. The patient agreed with the point, but thought it was possible that his situation was different, because in his instance the risk seemed more likely. He also agreed that the apprentice would say something similar. This led on to consideration of whether it was possible to check it out for his particular situation. The therapist and patient did this by conducting an experimental exposure session where both went to a main road, stood on the edge, and 'tried to lose control' for half an hour! Discussion of this last exercise showed that the patient did not feel 'loss of control' increasing during this behavioural experiment, however hard he tried to make himself lose control. One possible explanation for this is that there are no 'mental muscles' which can be employed in this situation. Having made this discovery, the patient was then able repeatedly to go down the street he feared *without exerting 'control'*. He quickly lost his fear of this situation without any more exposure than had previously been occurring in the normal course of events. Thus, exposure had been adapted in a way which specifically changed the patient's belief that it is possible to come to harm because of spontaneously losing control of one's behaviour. This generalised to a wide range of situations, including social situations where the patient had believed that he constantly ran the risk of losing control.

Dealing with negative automatic thoughts

The way in which negative automatic thoughts of obsessional patients are challenged and tested does not substantially differ from the style adopted in other problems. Factors identified on p. 62 need to be borne in mind, particularly the way in which negative automatic thoughts concern responsibility for harm arising as a result of inaction following an intrusive thought, image, or impulse. In general, care should be taken to ensure that the thought being challenged is an evaluation of the intrusive thought rather than the intrusive thought itself. Arguing with obsessionals about the rationality of the intrusion is a time-honoured and highly *unsuccessful* approach, however attractive it may seem when the patient describes doubts about some improbable disaster.

For example, a 27-year-old woman worked part time in a clothes shop. Her principal complaint was of checking, particularly late at night before going to bed. Checking was always carried out with her husband or daughter looking on. Some degree of checking had always been present, but she dated the worsening of her problem to a specific incident. She awoke to the smell of smoke, and managed to escape with her young son just before the entire house was engulfed by flames. She was subsequently troubled each night by images of her family being horribly burnt; these images led her to the extensive checking of her house and all electrical appliances in it. During exposure she was able to identify this occurrence of the image and her appraisal which went: 'This image shows what might happen. I can't risk it in any way.' In the course of exposure she was taught to identify negative automatic thoughts which represented appraisals of responsibility, and to answer these. The patient devised a striking example for herself when she was unable to resist checking her cooker. On the third night that resisting this was her target (she had failed the previous two nights), she asked herself, 'What is *really* the worst thing that could happen?' and concluded, 'I will have a bigger electric bill.' She went straight back to sleep, and stopped checking the cooker from then on, with no subsequent discomfort.

The cognitive model of obsessions gives *the perception of responsibility for harm to self or others* a key role in obsessional problems. Treatment should aim to change the patient's views about responsibility by demonstrating that the taking of previously avoided responsibility does not have dire consequences. There are three principal ways in which exposure to responsibility can be implemented: (1) by getting the patient to undertake previously avoided activities involving elements of responsibility

(Salkovskis and Kirk 1989); (2) by demonstrating the effects of, and then preventing, reassurance seeking (Salkovskis and Westbrook 1987; Salkovskis and Warwick 1988); (3) by getting the patient to seek out responsibility actively without revealing any details to others (including the therapist) so that the patient alone is responsible (Salkovskis and Westbrook 1987).

Dealing with concurrent depression

The association between obsessions and depression is an important component of the cognitive model. Depressed or anxious mood can affect the likelihood of intrusive thoughts, of negative evaluation of those thoughts, and the likelihood that that evaluation will contain an element of personal responsibility for harm and therefore have implications for neutralising behaviour. Clinically, these phenomena have been identified as the cause of treatment failure (Foa 1979) and of worsening of obsessions (Gittleson 1966). Such associations have led to the suggestion that tricyclic antidepressant medication is indicated where severe concurrent depression complicates an obsessional problem. This view is supported by outcome trials such as the MRC study (Marks *et al.* 1980). There has been some argument as to the relative merits of clomipramine in the treatment of obsessional problems, with the MRC study suggesting that the drug effects are purely antidepressant, whilst others suggest a more specific anti-obsessive effect (Christensen *et al.* 1987). This issue could be clarified by a trial of cognitive therapy focused on depression in obsessional patients with severe concurrent depression, given the evidence that cognitive treatment of severe primary depression is as effective as tricyclic antidepressant medication in the short term (Blackburn *et al.* 1987) and more effective at follow-up. Treatment of depression in obsessional patients should follow similar lines to that employed with patients with primary depression; an additional focus would be on episodes where depressed affect contributed to obsessional problems and vice versa. (See Salkovskis and Warwick 1988.)

Dealing with obsessions not accompanied by compulsive behaviour

Early behavioural treatments were considered particularly suitable for obsessive–compulsive disorder because of the prominence of overt avoidance and distressing compulsive behaviours. Consistent with learning theories current at that time, it was assumed that if obsessions *with* compulsions could be dealt with effectively, then the knowledge so gained would be easily generalised to obsessions *without* compulsions, which have the appearance of a less complicated variant of the same problem. This quite reasonable expectation has not been fulfilled. Rachman (1983) stated that 'the main obstacle to the successful treatment of obsessions is the absence of effective techniques'. We have argued elsewhere (Salkovskis and Westbrook 1987; Salkovskis and Warwick 1988) that this pessimism is based more on methodological grounds than actual difficulty. That is, the emphasis on *overt* behaviour served to mask the extent to which *covert* ritualising and avoidance behaviours are involved. Obsessions without overt compulsions are characterised by mental rituals. When ritualising becomes covert, this can have the effect of making the obsessional problem more severe and particularly resistant to treatment. This is because mental rituals are more difficult to identify (by both patient and therapist), more 'portable' in the sense that mental ritualising can be carried out almost anywhere, usually without fear of social embarrassment, and are often briefer and therefore potentially more frequent. Where response prevention is initiated, the scope for 'sneaky ritualising' is greater. Finally, making the occurrence of obsessional stimuli (thoughts) predictable can be particularly difficult when exposure is to thoughts alone. Unpredictability tends to retard habituation.

Despite these complicating factors, the solution to the problem of treatment of obsessional thoughts is principally to be found in the careful application of both cognitive and behavioural treatment techniques used in obsessive–compulsive disorder, following the principles outlined earlier in this chapter. Obsessions without overt compulsions present problems of predictability of stimuli and difficulties in implementing response prevention. Salkovskis and Kirk (1989) and Salkovskis and Westbrook (1989) provide detailed solutions for the more specific problems. Avoidance of particular situations or stimuli is discovered and reversed. Predictability of exposure to obsessional thoughts can be increased by getting patients to record their obsessional thoughts on loop audiocassette tapes, then play them back in situations which increasingly approximate to those in which the obsessional thoughts usually occur. Response prevention requires careful instruction in the rationale for stopping covert neutralising; the audiotape procedure can then be used as a way of pin-pointing and overcoming difficulties in the detection of neutralising responses and the implementation of response prevention (Salkovskis 1983). The audiotape also helps to detect covert avoidance and neutralising, because it provides an opportunity to present obsessional thoughts under controlled conditions.

In the case of Mr Johnstone, described above, covert neutralising persisted for some considerable time after overt ritualising and avoidance had been eliminated. The patient still experienced occasions in which he would be troubled by having the thought that he was going to offer his behaviour (such as being angry) to the devil, not being able to suppress either the thought or the behaviour, then neutralising by 'making a firm purpose of amendment', usually with mental ritualising including prayers. Quite often he would experience this as prolonged sequences of intrusive thought, neutralising, further intrusive thought, neutralising, and so on. The patient was instructed in the use of thought-stopping techniques *for the neutralising thought*. Whenever the intrusive thoughts occurred, he would first try to deal with them 'as if they hadn't occurred', by just letting the thought drift through. If he felt the urge to respond to the thought by neutralising build up, then he would mentally shout 'stop' and, if necessary, switch into a pre-arranged thought sequence (e.g. he would imagine eating his favourite meal). If, despite this cognitive thought stopping he still began to neutralise, he would then undo the neutralising as thoroughly as he could, e.g. by offering the same thing to the devil again *then* using the same procedures. Note that the complicated sequence described here was to cover contingencies; although the thought-stopping based cognitive response prevention was sometimes used, the other procedures were very seldom required. The procedures were first taught in the context of the patient describing a particularly troublesome blasphemous sexual image onto an audiotape loop, then exploring the use of the response prevention techniques with the help of the therapist. Daily homework practice with the audiotape played on a personal stereo was used; this structured practice was successfully generalised from home to work and leisure activities within a period of 6 weeks. The patient reported that the audiotaped practice in the range of settings helped considerably with the application of cognitive response prevention when the obsessional thoughts occurred unprompted.

Relapse prevention

Relapse prevention is best accomplished by ensuring that *all rituals* (overt and covert) have been fully response prevented, and the patient has a clear idea of how they might react if the obsessions were to recur. Discussing hypothetical situations in which this might happen can be helpful. The therapist points out that one of the things which has been helpful in therapy has been identifying problems, and that a great deal has been learned from problems which have arisen; any setbacks in the future will provide similarly useful information. This goes with the idea that having a setback is not the same as having a relapse, but is an ideal opportunity to practise the skills the patient has learned during therapy. The patient writes down as part of a homework exercise towards the end of treatment a list of (1) what they have learned from treatment; (2) how to recognise an obsessional thought and how to recognise neutralising behaviours; (3) how they would advise a friend to set about tackling upsetting thoughts which had just started to occur, and were causing some upset to them. Having reviewed these with the therapist and discussed the range of potentially problematic situations with the therapist, the patient then makes up a 'setback package', which includes the material they have written and the audiotape of the session in which how to deal with future stress and setbacks was discussed. Sometimes, the patient will identify some residual problems which require more specific attention.

For example, towards the end of treatment, Mr Johnstone reported that his obsessional problem had ceased to trouble him in most respects. However, there were occasions when he would still experience the obsessional thoughts and go on to ritualise. These were not associated with extreme discomfort, but were occasions when he was enjoying himself; for instance, when he was sitting in his garden relaxing with a beer. At that time, he would feel a sense of loss or emptiness, and *deliberately* offer something to the devil *so that he could then have the opportunity to ritualise.* Rather than giving him a sense of relief from anxiety, he said that the feeling was one of comfort, and that he wanted to be able to retain this sense of comfort and closeness to his religion. He did not regard this behaviour as a problem. The therapist agreed that it was not necessary to stop this behaviour in its own right, so that one possibility would simply be to allow this to continue. However, given that this was the last trace of his obsessional problem, another possibility would be that this could form something of a focus for relapse if he became stressed (depressed or anxious) for some other reason. The therapist and patient discussed alternative strategies Mr Johnstone could use when he had that feeling, and settled on the occasional saying of prayers as a way of obtaining 'indulgence', so that the whole sequence was a positive one and did not have to involve a revival of his obsession.

Finally, it is often helpful to discuss with the patient the factors which might be helpful in predicting setbacks. These usually include factors which previously served to exacerbate the obsessional problem, including stress and anxiety arising from external sources, depressed mood, extra responsibilities, and being tired. Being able to predict setbacks in this way is consistent with the model which has been presented to the patient, and helps him to strengthen his belief that the problem is upsetting thoughts and not the threatened disasters. That is, when a setback occurs, rather than focusing on the content of the upsetting thoughts themselves, the patient is able to attribute correctly the distress they are experiencing to their thoughts.

Conclusions

This chapter has outlined the ways in which cognitive strategies can be used in conjunction with exposure and response prevention. There would be little point in applying cognitive therapy separately from exposure, given the good outcome obtained in behavioural treatment. The need for the addition of cognitive strategies to behaviour therapy for obsessional problems lies principally in the limitations which are apparent in the poor treatment acceptance and compliance rates. It is nevertheless encouraging to note that Emmelkamp and his colleagues have been able to demonstrate that cognitive procedures are as effective as exposure treatment in two controlled trials (see Emmelkamp 1987). Work on the relationship between normal intrusive thoughts, obsessional behaviour, and mood has opened up an exciting area of development, suggesting that an understanding of the basis of obsessional problems may improve understanding of a range of other psychological problems (e.g. Warwick and Salkovskis, this volume), and perhaps of much wider aspects of cognitive functioning in non-clinical populations (Edwards and Dickerson 1987; Salkovskis 1988).

Acknowledgements

The author is grateful to the Medical Research Council of the United Kingdom for their support, to Joan Kirk for help with some of the material in this chapter, and to Hilary Warwick for help with the material and for comments on an earlier version.

References

Beck, A.T. (1976) *Cognitive Therapy and the Emotional Disorders*, New York: International Universities Press.

Beech, H.R. and Liddell, A. (1974) 'Decision making, mood states and ritualistic behaviour among obsessional patients', in H.R. Beech (ed.) *Obsessional States*, London: Methuen.

Blackburn, I.M., Eunson, K.M., and Bishop, S. (1987) 'A two-year naturalistic follow-up of depressed patients treated with cognitive therapy, pharmacotherapy and a combination of both', *Journal of Affective Disorders* 10: 67–75.

Christensen, H., Hadzi-Pavlovic, D., Andrews, G., and Mattick, R. (1987) 'Behaviour therapy and tricyclic medication in the treatment of obsessive–compulsive disorder: a quantitative review', *Journal of Consulting and Clinical Psychology* 55: 701–11.

Edwards, S. and Dickerson, M. (1987) 'On the similarity of positive and negative intrusions', *Behaviour Research and Therapy* 25: 207–11.

Emmelkamp, P.M.G. (1987) Chapter in W. Huber (ed.) *Progress in Psychotherapy Research*, Louvain: University of Louvain Press.

Espie, C.A. (1986) 'The group treatment of obsessive–compulsive ritualisers: behaviour management of identified patterns of relapse', *Behavioural Psychotherapy* 14: 21–34.

Foa, E.B. (1979) 'Failures in treating obsessive–compulsives', *Behaviour Research and Therapy* 17: 169–76.

Foa, E.B. and Goldstein, A. (1978) 'Continuous exposure and strict response prevention in the treatment of obsessive–compulsive neurosis', *Behaviour Therapy* 9: 821–9.

Foa, E.B., Steketee, G., Grayson, J.B., and Doppelt, H.G. (1983) 'Treatment of obsessive–compulsives: when do we fail?' in E.B. Foa and P.M.G. Emmelkamp (eds) *Failures in Behaviour Therapy*, New York: Wiley.

Gittleson, N. (1966) 'The fate of obsessions in depressive psychosis', *British Journal of Psychiatry* 112: 705–8.

Marks, I.M. (1987) *Fears, Phobias and Rituals*, New York: Oxford University Press.

Marks, I.M., Stern, R.S., Mawson, D., Cobb, J., and McDonald, R. (1980) 'Clomipramine and exposure for obsessive–compulsive rituals: I', *British Journal of Psychiatry* 136: 1–25.

Rachman, S.J. (1971) 'Obsessional ruminations', *Behaviour Research and Therapy* 9: 229–35.

Rachman, S.J. (1981) 'Unwanted intrusive cognitions', *Advances in Behaviour Research and Therapy* 3: 89–99.

Rachman, S.J. (1983) 'Obstacles to the successful treatment of obsessions', in E.B. Foa and P.M.G. Emmelkamp (eds) *Failures in Behaviour Therapy*, New York: Wiley.

Rachman, S.J. and de Silva, P. (1978) 'Abnormal and normal obsessions', *Behaviour Research and Therapy* 16: 233–8.

Rachman, S.J., de Silva, P., and Roper, G. (1976) 'The spontaneous decay of compulsive urges', *Behaviour Research and Therapy* 14: 445–53.

Rachman, S.J. and Hodgson, R. (1980) *Obsessions and Compulsions*, Englewood Cliffs, NJ: Prentice-Hall.

Roper, G. and Rachman, S.J. (1975) 'Obsessional–compulsive checking: replication and development', *Behaviour Research and Therapy* 13: 25–32.

Roper, G., Rachman, S.J., and Hodgson, R. (1973) 'An experiment on obsessional checking', *Behaviour Research and Therapy* 11: 271–7.

Salkovskis, P.M. (1983) 'Treatment of an obsessional patient using habituation to audiotaped ruminations', *British Journal of Clinical Psychology* 22: 311–13.

Salkovskis, P.M. (1985) 'Obsessional–compulsive problems: a cognitive-behavioural analysis', *Behaviour Research and Therapy* 25: 571–83.

Salkovskis, P.M. (1988) 'Intrusive thoughts and obsessional disorders', in D. Glasgow and N. Eisenberg (eds) *Current Issues in Clinical Psychology 4*, London: Gower.

Salkovskis, P.M. and Dent, H.R. (1988) *Intrusive Thoughts, Impulses and Imagery: Cognitive and Behavioural Aspects*, manuscript in preparation.

Salkovskis, P.M. and Harrison, J. (1984) 'Abnormal and normal obsessions: a replication', *Behaviour Research and Therapy* 22: 549–52.

Salkovskis, P.M. and Kirk, J.W. (1989) 'Obsessional problems', in K. Hawton, P.M. Salkovskis, J.W. Kirk, and D.M. Clark, (eds) *Cognitive–behaviour Therapy for Psychiatric Problems: A Practical Guide*, Oxford: Oxford University Press.

Salkovskis, P.M. and Warwick, H.M.C. (1985) 'Cognitive therapy of obsessive–compulsive disorder–treating treatment failures', *Behavioural Psychotherapy* 13: 243–55.

Salkovskis, P.M. and Warwick, H.M.C. (1988) 'Cognitive therapy of obsessive–compulsive disorder', in C. Perris, I.M. Blackburn, and H. Perris (eds) *The Theory and Practice of Cognitive Therapy*, Heidelberg: Springer.

Salkovskis, P.M. and Westbrook, D. (1987) 'Obsessive–compulsive disorder: clinical strategies for improving behavioural treatments', in H.R. Dent (ed.) *Clinical Psychology: Research and Development*, London: Croom Helm.

Salkovskis, P.M. and Westbrook, D. (1989) 'Behaviour therapy and obsessional ruminations: can failure be turned into success?' *Behaviour Research and Therapy* 27: 149–60.

Warwick, H.M.C. and Salkovskis, P.M. (1985) 'Reassurance', *British Medical Journal* 290: 1028.

Chapter four

Hypochondriasis

Hilary M.C. Warwick[1] and Paul M. Salkovskis[2]

Introduction

Hypochondriasis is defined in *DSM III-R* as an unrealistic interpretation
of bodily sensations, leading to preoccupation with the fear of, or belief
that one has, a serious disease, despite medical reassurance (American
Psychiatric Association 1987). There are no reliable estimates of the
prevalence of hypochondriasis, but it has been estimated that 30–80 per
cent of patients who consult physicians, present with symptoms for which
there is no physical basis (see Barsky and Klerman 1983). Despite the
implications for resources at all levels of medical practice, current
treatment of hypochondriasis is unsatisfactory and its prognosis is generally
regarded as poor (Nemiah 1985), indicating the need for new approaches
to understanding and treatment of this problem.

We have recently suggested a cognitive–behavioural approach to the
condition and reported the successful treatment of two cases using
cognitive–behavioural strategies (Salkovskis and Warwick 1986; Warwick
and Salkovskis 1985, 1987). This chapter briefly summarises the model and
gives a detailed account of assessment and treatment based on it,
illustrated by case examples. The hypothesised maintaining factors and the
efficacy of the treatment approach have yet to be fully experimentally
validated, although preliminary results are encouraging.

As the *DSM III-R* definition suggests, hypochondriasis can be a fear of
or belief in a serious illness. It is not clear whether two distinct subgroups
are described within the category. Pilowsky (1967) utilised a factor analytic
approach to investigate this question, and found that three dimensions of
hypochondriasis could be identified – bodily preoccupation, disease
phobia, and disease conviction. His study provides support for the view
that separate conditions may exist, consistent with the clinical impression
of the validity of such a distinction (e.g. Bianchi 1971; Leonhard 1968;
Marks 1987; Ryle 1947). However, no studies have attempted to
differentiate hypochondriasis and illness phobia in terms of symptoms
experienced and extent of avoidant behaviours exhibited (such as

reassurance seeking and avoidance of illness-related situations). It is likely that these behaviours occur to some extent in most patients and it may also be the case that patients fluctuate between disease conviction and fear that they may contract a disease, depending on their levels of anxiety. Table 4.1 summarises the core clinical and psychological features of hypochondriasis from a cognitive–behavioural perspective, derived from a review of the literature (Warwick and Salkovskis 1987).

Table 4.1 Core features of clinical conditions characterised by anxiety about health

1. Preoccupation with health
2. Insufficient organic pathology to account for the concerns expressed
3. Selective attention to bodily changes or features
4. Negative interpretation of bodily signs and symptoms
5. Selective attention to and disbelief of medical and non-medical communications
6. Persistent seeking of reassurance/checking bodily status/information.

Cognitive–behavioural hypothesis

The cognitive hypothesis addresses factors involved both in aetiology and in the maintenance of hypochondriasis. Treatment mostly emphasises the modification of maintaining factors, although for specific patients a formulation in which both are considered is sometimes helpful, as will be described below.

The cognitive view of the development of hypochondriasis set out in Figure 4.1 proposes that attitudes and dysfunctional assumptions related to health are formed, usually, as part of early experience. Note, however, that these assumptions should not be regarded as static and may be modified by later experience and information. Such assumptions can also lead the patient selectively to attend to information consistent with having an illness, and selectively to ignore or discount evidence indicating good health. Thus, particular assumptions tend to produce a *confirmatory bias* in the patient's thinking once a critical incident has resulted in the misinterpretation of bodily symptoms and signs as being indications of serious illness. Critical incidents are events which specifically mesh with and serve to activate dysfunctional assumptions. These range from the death of a close relative from a previously undiagnosed illness to hearing information about a particular illness on the radio or television. Sometimes the critical incident is the occurrence of a particular symptom or noticing a bodily change. This leads to the increased likelihood that distressing thoughts (or images) of illness may occur, or that previously unnoticed sensations are focused on and misinterpreted. The physiological, cognitive, affective, and behavioural correlates of these negative thoughts and their interaction with the beliefs held by the patient then play a vital role in the degree to which the anxiety about health persists or simply fades.

Previous Experience

Experience and perception of:
(i) Illness in self, family; medical mismanagement
(ii) Interpretations of symptoms and appropriate reactions
'My father died from a brain tumour.'
'Whenever I had any symptoms I was taken to the doctor in case it was serious'

Formation of dysfunctional assumptions

*'Bodily symptoms are always an indication of something wrong; I
I should always be able to find an explanation for my symptoms'*

Critical incident

Incident or symptom which suggests illness

*'One of my friends died of cancer a few months ago;
I have had more headaches recently.'*

Activation of assumptions

Negative automatic thoughts /imagery

*'I could have a brain tumour;
I didn't tell the doctor that I have lost some weight.
It may be too late.
This is going to get worse.
I will need brain surgery'*

HEALTH ANXIETY, HYPOCHONDRIASIS

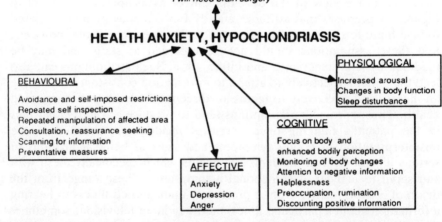

BEHAVIOURAL

Avoidance and self-imposed restrictions
Repeated self inspection
Repeated manipulation of affected area
Consultation, reassurance seeking
Scanning for information
Preventative measures

PHYSIOLOGICAL

Increased arousal
Changes in body function
Sleep disturbance

COGNITIVE

Focus on body and
enhanced bodily perception
Monitoring of body changes
Attention to negative information
Helplessness
Preoccupation, rumination
Discounting positive information

AFFECTIVE

Anxiety
Depression
Anger

Figure 4.1 Cognitive–behavioural model of the development of hypochondriacal problems

The perception of bodily changes or symptoms is followed by negative automatic thoughts concerning danger or threat. Such thoughts are most commonly misinterpretations of normal bodily variations (variations in normal bodily appearance, sensations, or functions). The belief that these sensations are indications of a dangerous physical condition is usually based on what the patient regards as convincing evidence. Such evidence most commonly stems from particular idiosyncratic beliefs about health along with persist symptoms in the absence of any satisfactory and believable alternative interpretation. Information (simple reassurance) will only be helpful at this stage if it is relevant to patients' evidence that they are ill, and if it is both relevant and new, rather than bland reiteration. Trying to convince such patients that they do not have a particular illness is seldom effective unless accompanied by a satisfactory alternative account of their problem.

We hypothesise that three main mechanisms operate to further increase anxiety, preoccupation with illness, and the misinterpretation of bodily variations and hence result in the persistence and maintenance of anxiety, symptoms, and preoccupation with health. As described above, the assumptions which characterise many of these patients can result in the addition of a confirmatory bias which interacts with all three of the factors described here, further fuelling the misinterpretation of bodily symptoms and bodily state.

Increased physiological arousal

Increased physiological arousal (which stems from the perception of threat) leads to increased occurrence of autonomically mediated sensations; these sensations are often interpreted by the patient as further evidence that they are ill. For example, if a patient notices an increase in sweating and has the thought that this is a sign of a serious hormonal imbalance, sweating will increase when this thought occurs, appearing to provide further evidence of 'disturbance'.

Focus of attention

Normal variations in bodily function (including those which give rise to bodily sensations) or previously unnoticed aspects of appearance or bodily function may be noticed more readily than had previously been the case. The patient is then likely to conclude that these perceived changes represent pathological changes from 'normal function' when this is not actually so. For example, a patient noticed that the roots of his fingernails looked pale and he had white spots on his nails, and interpreted this as a sign of a 'hormone problem'. He found this observation extremely upsetting, and could not believe that he could have missed something so distressing in the past, strongly supporting his view that this must represent a new phenomenon. Focus of attention may also lead to actual change in physiological systems where both reflex and voluntary control are involved (breathing, swallowing, muscular activity, and so on). For example, patients may notice difficulty in swallowing dry foods which they interpret as a possible sign of throat cancer. Focusing on swallowing can lead to undue effort and increased discomfort and difficulty.

Avoidant behaviours

Disease conviction and illness phobia can both be conceptualised from a behavioural perspective. In both instances, anxiety has become conditioned to stimuli associated with illness; for the illness phobic, these stimuli are most often external (hospitals, doctors, medical information, other people being ill, and so on). For hypochondriacal patients the stimuli are predominantly internal (bodily sensations such as stomach discomfort, bodily signs such as lumps under the skin), although the hypochondriacal patient's attention is often brought to the bodily variation by external factors such as reading about a particular disease. The illness phobic copes with the anxiety by avoidance of the stimuli concerned. However, because of the nature of the stimuli involved, the hypochondriacal patient seldom has this option, so resorts instead to behaviours designed to neutralise the anxiety, like the behaviour more typical of obsessional patients. In both instances, avoidant behaviours are prominent and serve to terminate exposure to the feared stimuli, thereby preventing habituation from taking place and perpetuating the condition.

The cognitive–behavioural hypothesis we have formulated gives avoidant behaviours even broader functional properties than a purely behavioural view. Avoidant behaviours are crucial in three respects. First, they prevent the patient from learning that the things which they fear do not actually happen. That is, the things which the patient fears are accompanied by negative thoughts; in normal circumstances, the reality of these thoughts about negative outcomes would become clear in the course of time. However, avoidance prevents this reappraisal of threat. Second, avoidance functions to keep the patient's attention focused on the negative thoughts, resulting in a characteristic preoccupation. Third, in some patients the checking behaviours have a direct impact on the bodily variations which elicited the thoughts in the first instance. For example, a patient noticed a mild pain in one of his testicles. He had the thought that this may have been caused by cancer. Over the next few days he repeatedly probed his testicle, which became more painful and inflamed, which he believed confirmed his self-diagnosis. When he stopped checking, the symptoms (including pain) resolved within three days.

The importance of reassurance

The significance of reassurance seeking as a type of avoidant behaviour is often neglected in hypochondriacal patients, despite it being so prominent that it is part of the definition of the disorder. Reassurance seeking and provision may be of fundamental importance in the maintenance of the condition. According to the *DSM III-R* criteria, a patient cannot be diagnosed as hypochondriacal until they have had some unsuccessful medical reassurance. Hypochondriasis can be seen to be unusual in that the diagnosis depends not only on the characteristics of the patient but also on the actions of doctors. The nature, quality, and extent of such reassurance will differ greatly between practitioners and future diagnostic criteria must include a definition of appropriate reassurance.

We have previously pointed out (Warwick and Salkovskis 1985) that inappropriate reassurance, such as repetition of information of which the patient is already aware and clinically unnecessary physical investigations, can serve to exacerbate the patient's problems. It seems that this occurs because such reassurance serves the same function as rituals in obsessive–compulsive disorder – that is, a short-term reduction in anxiety and a longer-term return of and increase in fear and the urge to seek further reassurance. Indeed, although present diagnostic criteria require that the problem 'persists *despite* medical reassurance' (emphasis added), in some cases it might be that the condition persists *because* of medical reassurance. This is not to say that the provision of appropriate new information will cause these difficulties, but that repeated and irrelevant information can have this effect. A recent study (Salkovskis and Warwick 1986) illustrates these points in the successful management of two cases.

Hypochondriacal patients often seek reassurance from a variety of sources, sometimes in a very subtle manner. Several doctors may be being consulted simultaneously and friends and families questioned repeatedly, often in a way which does not immediately seem to be connected to their health concerns. Reassurance may also be obtained from literature and bodily checking. The role of reassurance seeking in maintaining their problems must be explained to the patients in a way which they clearly understand (see Salkovskis and Westbrook 1987). Sometimes it is necessary to demonstrate this as described above and in Salkovskis and Warwick (1986). When treatment provides a clear rationale for controlling this behaviour and thereby helps them to tolerate the initial anxiety caused, compliance will be enhanced and treatment is much more likely to be successful. Families and others involved with the patient must be included in such discussions and shown how to deal with requests for reassurance, preferably using role-play. The case examples given below highlight the importance of reassurance seeking and the implications of its prevention in successful management of hypochondriasis.

Many hypochondriacal patients have exaggerated dysfunctional beliefs about health and illness which will specifically prevent them responding to attempts to rule out physical illness. For example, a patient reported that he had always been 'the type of person who had to know the cause of a problem; for example, I would *completely* take my car apart to find why there was a rattle'. Being told that 'We have ruled out, beyond reasonable doubt, the possibility that your symptoms indicate a serious condition' is unlikely to be helpful as long as the symptoms persist. A similar problem occurs in patients who perceive health professionals as likely to make errors of diagnosis with potentially serious consequences. Such beliefs may occur as a result of personal experience or because of examples publicised in the media.

Note that each of the mechanisms described as involved in the maintenance of hypochondriasis has a dual effect; it increases the extent to which the patient is preoccupied with health and acts to increase the weight of evidence that they are suffering from a physical illness. For treatment to be effective, it should be directed at changing both.

Principles of cognitive treatment of hypochondriasis

As already described, hypochondriacal patients specifically do not respond to repeated reassurance; most patients have been repeatedly told that they are *not* suffering from a physical condition, often backed up by a range of physical examinations and investigation. The explicit aim of psychological treatment is for the patient and therapist to identify what the problem *is*, not simply to rule out every possible physical cause. To be most effective, this information needs to be accompanied by a clear demonstration of the way in which anxiety and symptoms are maintained, backed up by specific assignments designed to provide further evidence for a more accurate interpretation.

Treatment starts with the explicit engagement of the patient in active treatment of their anxiety about health. This is often the most difficult part of the entire therapy process. Most patients are willing to come along to therapy, but have a quite different implicit set of goals from the therapist; they regard the therapist as a potential ally in their attempts to have their medical problems taken seriously, and as a potential source of expert reassurance. If the patient and therapist continue to have quite different but parallel agendas, therapy is unlikely to be effective. It would be unreasonable for the therapist to expect the patient to 'admit' that their problem is 'just anxiety', especially as they are seeking treatment precisely because they truly believe that their problem is that they have an undiagnosed physical illness.

This apparently impossible situation is resolved by careful discussion which neither rejects the patient's beliefs nor adds weight to them. The therapist must accept that the patient does indeed experience the symptoms complained of, and firmly believes that these symptoms mean that they have a serious physical illness. It is explained that, in the experience of the therapist, patients base such beliefs on particular evidence which they find convincing, and that this evidence is unlikely to be imaginary. However, it is also possible that there are alternative explanations of the evidence. Assessment and treatment will involve the examination of the evidence and possible alternative explanations of it. Treatment in this way does not simply involve the patient taking the therapist's word for things, but will involve specific tasks designed to test out alternative explanations. However, physical tests and checks would not be a part of treatment, nor would lengthy discussions of symptoms and reassurance. Because this would be a completely different way of dealing with the problem, it is important to consider the overall usefulness of each of the alternative ways of tackling the problem. How long had the patient been trying to rule out physical causes of their problem? How effective had this been? Had they ever properly tested the alternative psychological approach that the therapist is suggesting to them? It is then proposed that they work totally with the therapist in this new way for four months. If they had been able to do all the things worked out with their therapist and the problem had not been helped at the end of that time, then it would be reasonable to come back to their original way of tackling the problem, and the therapist would then be happy to reconsider the problem from a more physical perspective. In this way, the patient is not asked to give up their view of their problems, but to consider and test an alternative for a limited period. In patients who believe that they may have a physical illness which is being neglected this is an attractive proposition (Salkovskis 1989).

Once the patient has been engaged in treatment, therapy is directed at gathering and testing evidence for a more accurate interpretation of the evidence the patient believes supports the idea that they are ill. This process emphasises testing hypotheses about the true cause of the problem rather than reassuring. However, sometimes it is profitable to discuss and evaluate evidence against the patient's interpretation of the evidence. The crucial distinction here is between giving relevant information as opposed to irrelevant or repetitive information. Rather than discounting a belief, discover the evidence and consider it with the patient. At no point should treatment become combative; questioning is the preferred style, as in cognitive therapy in general. If therapy becomes confrontational, then the therapist should 'fall back' and consider the thoughts which the patient is experiencing at that time. For example, if the patient is arguing that the pains in their chest cannot be the result of anxiety, the therapist, rather than saying 'But anxiety often causes chest pains, and yours sounds like that', says, 'Right. You are having chest pains, then the thought that these are not caused by anxiety. Do you have any thoughts about what they might be caused by? . . . Is there anything about the chest pains which particularly makes you think they are caused by a heart condition? . . . What is it about the chest pains which makes you think they can't be anxiety?' Case 1 is an illustration of the difficulties involved in assessment and engagement of such a patient, and the type of questioning which can be used to deal with these problems. The interview also serves to illustrate the combined operation of confirmatory bias (particularly with respect to well-intentioned medical communications), misinterpretation of normal sensations (stiffness and muscular tension), a behaviour intended to check bodily function ('clicking'), avoidance behaviour preventing exposure and reappraisal of risk (her interview style and attempts to focus on the detail of symptoms to the exclusion of their feared consequences), and focus of attention.

Case 1

A 57-year-old former teacher was referred who had extensive involvement with first aid work. She had a 37-year history of worrying about her health. She was referred to psychiatric services complaining of depression and feeling unable to cope, related to her being ill. She was admitted to the psychiatric ward when it became clear that her family were currently unable to manage her demanding behaviour. Her immediate family included her mother, who spent much of her time looking after the patient, and the patient's husband who had recently cancelled a surgical operation in order to look after his wife. On admission, the patient continued the pattern of behaviour she had established at home, repeatedly seeking reassurance from anyone who would listen to her, particularly from medical staff. When interviewed, a striking characteristic of her behaviour was that she talked incessantly and rapidly about physical symptoms to the exclusion of all else, and with an almost complete absence of emotional expression. On the few occasions it was possible to get her to discuss her general situation and mood, she denied any anxiety and psychological problems, appeared to begin to show some signs of being upset, and immediately returned to talking about her symptoms very rapidly and in great detail. A videotaped assessment was arranged; we will use sections of this to illustrate the characteristics of this kind of patient, and some of the elements of cognitive assessment with this not uncommon presentation.

T: I wonder if you could tell me about the sorts of problems you have been having recently.

P: [Sighs] I actually came here because I became very agitated about my throat.

T: So you became agitated about your throat. What was the problem with your throat?

P: [*Sighs*] I don't know. It is a long story, and it's absolutely true, but I
     don't think people really believe it, but it's absolutely true, and my
     family believe it.
T: All right, well I don't know the story.
P: Do you want to know?
T: I'd be very grateful if you would tell me.

Here the therapist is establishing his interest in the patient's problems as
she herself sees them.

P: Well – I was blackmailed into having an experiment done when I had
     my tonsils out in September 1952. The nurse who was there wouldn't
     have it done, she had more sense. I had a gold clip put here to clip
     something back here, so I like a fool said yes. So I had it done, and
     it was so uncomfortable that I had to swallow down the left side for
     the rest of the day, and I had to go and have it X-rayed right across
     to see what effect the gold clip had. So I swallowed one side, all day,
     and I had it taken out under the anaesthetic. After the operation the
     muscles and tendons seized up down that side, and I couldn't open
     my mouth for about five days, it was just like this [*demonstrates*].
T: U-huh.
P: The nurse who didn't have it done could open hers wide. It was ever
     so painful. For over a year I had trouble with it, I kept swallowing
     and swallowing, because it was so awful, it felt so awful on this side,
     they kept saying there was nothing wrong with it. It looks as though
     the tonsils are out as clean as a whistle, but I always have trouble
     with it.
T: At that time, what went through your mind about what was wrong
     with it?
P: Well, it had seized up. The doctor said I had been unlucky. That I
     was one in 2,000, that the muscles had pulled up. I clicked it over the
     years, and had trouble with it. Now it's here, and right down here . . .
     [*Points, opens mouth*].
T: That was quite a long time ago; has it been the same ever since?
P: Yes, it's always been the same, sometimes it's worse. Now it doesn't
     seem to matter if I click it –
T: Er –
P: – not click it, swallow –
T: Er –
P: – not swallow; it's worse than it's ever been now . . .

The patient then runs through a list of medications, symptoms, increases
in symptoms; the therapist is unable to break in for some time.

P: A month ago come Monday I got excruciating pain, how it started, I ate a cream doughnut, had a sudden pain there [*points*], the cream had a nasty taste.

T: So you started to get pain about a month ago?

P: Yes, and I started to click my throat, because it was so bad and I was so fed up with it.

T: I'm not clear what you mean by clicking your throat.

P: Well, the arch [*points*], there, is uncomfortable when I draw my tongue back in my mouth, it's the arch which hurts, that's what I click.

T: Can you show me?

P: [*Click . . . click*] Like that.

T: Right. So does that hurt?

P: No, it doesn't hurt, I'm just in the most terrible, terrible discomfort with it, Dr X said to stop clicking it, and I tried, but this is the one time when it's not responded to not clicking, because it doesn't make any difference. . . . I have to . . . it's compulsive; I think I've altered the structure of my throat. . . .

The patient continues to give an over-detailed account of her symptoms, doing so rapidly and with some agitation. She gives details of clicking, investigations and symptoms, and their timing. Questioning reveals that she believes that many of the symptoms are due to medical mismanagement. After some time, the therapist attempts to summarise, with the patient frequently adding extra points.

T: Let's see if I understand what's happening. At the moment, you've got a lot of discomfort –

P: Enormous amounts . . . it comes [*starts talking over*] –

T: Hold on. . . . I want to see if I have this right. You are uncomfortable at the back of the throat, and you feel you have to click in order to swallow. You do that compulsively, every second or so. If you don't, what will happen?

P: If I hold on for a few seconds . . . if I don't . . . [*pauses, becomes upset*] I have to click after a few seconds, it's uncomfortable, here, I have to swallow, it's like swallowing a piece of wire, just like after the operation. . . . [*Calms down, talks over the therapist for a few minutes.*]

The therapist next attempted to get details of the patient's interpretation of her symptoms by asking what will happen if the avoidance behaviour (clicking) is not carried out. This normally successful strategy fails, apparently because another avoidance behaviour (discussing symptoms in detail) intervenes to 'switch off' the upsetting thoughts. The therapist is formulating a tentative hypothesis about what the obstacle to assessing the upsetting thoughts might be (judging by the patient's reaction to questioning such thoughts are probably present). The task now is to try to break through this barrier, and to get at the thoughts themselves. Note that any therapist with this type of patient has the difficult task of conducting the assessment on the basis of working hypotheses about both the problem itself and the difficulties in assessing it. A useful strategy which helps to circumvent the kind of avoidance exhibited here involves finding some area of agreement with the patient, preferably connected to the distress the patient is experiencing.

T: So it is uncomfortable if you delay clicking.
P: Yes, terrible.
T: The other thing obvious to me now is you are a bit frightened about what is happening. What is it about the throat that makes it so frightening?
P: Well, because it's so uncomfortable, and I think, where the hell is it all going to end?

This is what the therapist has been looking for; it is important to try to capitalise on this.

T: Where do *you* think it's going to end? What is the worst thing that could happen?
P: [*Close to tears.*] Well, I've been thinking, I've got a good imagination, I've been pushing my food down [*cries for a few seconds, then speaks very rapidly*], it's very uncomfortable to eat, the food scrapes down, over that arch, and I can drink. . . . I think because of the clicking, it's given me terrible tension, it's like I've been kicked in the ribs –
T: Hold on a minute; I'm still not clear what you think is going to happen; what's the worst thing that could happen because of this?
P: [*Quickly.*] Well . . . yesterday, the doctor said that nothing would happen.
T: Before the doctor said that, what sort of things went through your mind when the throat was bad?
P: [*Long pause, then rapidly.*] It's getting worse and worse every day. . . . [*Goes into lengthy detail of symptoms.*]

There seems to be increasing support for the hypothesis that talking in great detail about aspects of symptoms is functioning as avoidance of thoughts involving the catastrophic misinterpretation of those symptoms. The therapist explains to the patient that upset and anxiety often come, not from the symptoms themselves, but from the kind of thoughts which accompany symptoms. The patient accepts this general idea; however, when the therapist tries to get details of the specific thoughts about the patient's throat, he gets the same response as before. None the less, some new information emerges.

T: What do you think might be the cause of it?

P: The operation and clicking have changed the structure of my throat; I had it X-rayed by the chiropractor, and he said that it was a bit cock-eyed; that was all the clicking; Dr X also said I had an asymmetrical soft palate.

T: Do you think this is going to cause you further harm, then?

P: Yes. . . . [*Starts to be upset.*] In the end I expect I shall. . . . [*Quickly.*] The tension has got so bad, I'm wobbling about, I can scarcely walk, the tension has got worse, the tension was easing off, I could sleep before, now I have to have sleeping tablets, the swallowing is getting worse . . . [*and so on*].

By this stage, the therapist knows roughly the type of misinterpretations which are having the greatest impact on the patient's anxiety; the concerns surrounding the patient's fears about 'where it will end' seem crucial. However, the avoidance strategy used by the patient is so effective that the therapist cannot break through it without losing the rapport he has established. He therefore spends a further twenty minutes gathering background information for the cognitive–behavioural analysis, whilst at the same time looking for another way of gaining access to thoughts associated with the patient's intense anxiety about her throat symptoms. The information gained during this period includes details of a number of other symptoms: depersonalisation, tension, sleeping problems, visual disturbance, and many others.

T: What happens when the doctors tell you that your throat is all right?

P: Well, if they tell me that it's all in my mind, I know that it jolly well isn't.

T: You believe that it is all physical?

P: I admit it gets on my nerves, but I put it all down to the experiment.

T: Right. Sounds like you've been through a lot.

P: I have. It's been hell.

T: What is it about the throat that makes it so bad?

P: I don't feel it's going to get better this time.

T: Mm. What's going to happen?

P: There's nothing I can do about it. See, I'm clicking it all the time.

T: OK, let's make a list of all the problems. [*Takes out paper.*]

At this point, the therapist wants to try to bring all the problems together as a brief summary, and to emphasise how upsetting each of them is to the patient. This confronts the patient with the full force of the symptoms which she is afraid of, whilst at the same time cutting out the obsessive detail which is serving to avoid the core thoughts of ultimate unpleasant outcome. At the end of the period spent compiling this list, as the therapist begins talking about the patient's husband going into hospital, she becomes tearful again.

P: I won't be able to cope, I'm not well, I can't do anything like this, I'm frightened all the time. [*Starts to cry.*]

T: What went through your mind right then, when you started to cry?

P: Nothing, except that I'm upset.

T: You keep saying that you are frightened. . . .

P: [*Still crying.*] Yes, because where's it all going to end, it's been getting worse every day.

T: Where do you think it's going to end? Is it going to kill you?

P: [*Crying, rocking to and fro.*] Yes, because in the end I shan't be able to walk, shan't be able to breathe, eat properly, and then I'm afraid [*almost screaming*] I shall be taken away from my family [*cries*], nobody will look after me, I can see it.

T: Do you get pictures of this?

P: Yes. . . . I will be taken away, made to be still, taken away, people say I'm making it up.

As is often the case, the patient at this point is acutely distressed, crying; this is distressing for the therapist as well. However, it is crucial to pursue the upsetting thoughts which have taken so long to elicit; this is an ideal opportunity to identify them fully so that they can be properly and fully dealt with. The therapist has to resist the temptation to allow the patient to change to a different, less threatening topic in order to reduce the distress she is expressing.

T: Who will take you away?

P: Doctors.

T: What will happen then?

P: [*Crying more.*] I don't want to be taken away. I won't be able to see to myself any more.

T: So you get terrified you will be taken away, put in a home or die, because you just stop functioning.

P: Yes, but it'll take a long time, and it'll be very painful.

T: Like being senile?

P: No. My brain will be fine, I will be physically unable to cope.

Further questioning, taking care to keep the patient focused on her fears, reveals that, when she has the symptoms, she believes this 100 per cent. The evidence for this is that, when she complained of specific tension in the throat, a consultant physician told her that tension could 'go all over you, but you would go on breathing' (another example of reassurance backfiring). The patient was experiencing frequent visual images accompanied by intense and frightening sensations of tension in her throat and other areas.

T: Have you ever heard of this happening to anyone?

P: No, but I'm stiff now; this arm is numb right up to here; my legs are; I can feel the tension spreading.

T: OK. Let me see if I'm getting this right. Can I summarise the thoughts? What you are saying is that you get very frightened about the throat and you can see a number of possible things happening in the long run. One of those is that you get taken away, you will lose your faculties, that your brain will be OK but you will be completely unable to look after yourself; related to that is the thought that you will become so stiff that you will not be able to move.

P: Yes, because I can feel it coming on.

The patient goes on to mention being able to picture these things; it transpires that she has a number of frightening images, which she does her best to avoid, and which are usually followed by an increase in symptoms; for instance, she said: 'I can see myself being made to be still, restrained, but still being kept alive. I can see that clearly.' (Note that where the discussion in this chapter has referred to negative thoughts and misinterpretations, these may often take the form of visual images rather than words.)

Having completed the assessment, the therapist used the video tape as a means of engaging the patient fully in treatment. The technique used is a slightly different way of generating the competing psychological and medical hypotheses, then gathering evidence to test the two alternatives. In this case, this was done in an unusual but, in this instance, highly effective way. On the session after the assessment interview outlined above, the therapist said to the patient, 'I have thought a great deal about your problem, and believe I have some idea about what is happening. However, I would like you to help me out a little. What I would like you to do is to watch the video film we made two days ago and go over what is happening. I want you to look at it as if it were someone else you were watching. In particular, I want you to tell me now and then whether the person on the video has a problem because she is physically ill, or whether she has worries about the future and dreadful things which might happen.' This strategy allowed patient and therapist to proceed rapidly to and agree a psychological formulation emphasising catastrophic misinterpretation of bodily sensations and avoidance behaviours. After seven further sessions of treatment focused on the exploration of her catastrophic misinterpretations, this patient was free from health anxiety.

Treatment strategies and reattribution

The principal treatment strategy involves the construction and testing of alternative explanations of symptoms which the patient currently misinterprets as signs of physical illness; this is done through the use of 'behavioural experiments'. The patient is asked to rate their negative (illness-related) belief. The belief is stated as clearly as possible (e.g. 'so your belief is "I am suffering from multiple sclerosis"') then rated on a 0–100 scale ('where 0 is don't believe this at all and 100 is being absolutely convinced it is true'). Then all evidence the patient considers supports their belief is carefully identified and noted down; any inconsistent evidence is also elicited and noted. Alternative explanations are generated, preferably through careful questioning, then any observations consistent with this alternative. If there are any tests of the alternative which can be carried out in the session (see below), these are tried at this point, and the results examined. The evidence for all alternatives is summarised (often on paper) making sure therapist and patient agree on the summary; often the summary helps generate yet further information. The patient is then asked to re-rate their negative belief and rate their belief in the alternative explanation. Finally, therapist and patient agree on follow-up behavioural assignments as homework specifically designed to provide further evidence discriminating between the alternative hypotheses.

Alternative hypotheses

A variety of alternative explanations can be used to account for the symptoms experienced by hypochondriacal patients. They encompass the range of mechanisms involved in the maintenance of anxiety disorders. All such mechanisms converge on the role of preoccupation with ill-health and the anxiety resulting from this; however, the diversity of presentations reflects the variety of ways in which anxiety may manifest. The maintaining factors (and therefore the behavioural experiments which can be used to bring about the reattribution away from serious illnesses) can, for convenience of discussion, be divided into three systems.

1. *Behavioural* A variety of behaviours can serve to maintain preoccupation, keeping the patient's mind on illness-related matters. These include reassurance seeking, checking bodily state, avoidance of activity, early coping, and the effects of rubbing or otherwise irritating affected areas (often explained to patients as equivalent to 'spot picking', with similar impact on irritation experienced).
2. *Cognitive* Cognitive factors which can lead to the misinterpretation of bodily sensations and signs include the deliberate focusing of attention on bodily responses, the effects of frightening illness-related imagery, and the way particular attitudes can lead to the misinterpretation of symptoms and confirmatory bias.
3. *Physiological* The most common physiological factors which can lead to the perception of bodily functions as being 'out of order' include autonomic arousal (as a result of externally threatening situations or

of particular thoughts about health), changes in breathing (hyper-ventilation and/or alteration in pattern of breathing, such as breathing normally but with the lungs kept relatively full), unaccustomed exercise, loss of fitness due to changes in exercise pattern. Some external factors can contribute, including caffeine, alcohol, and other drugs.

Education in the effects of these factors is a helpful preliminary intervention; in most instances a direct demonstration of their effects is most persuasive. This most commonly involves manipulating the provoking factor or agent by reducing it or increasing it. Increases are often more convincing as demonstrations.

As already discussed, confirmatory bias in which patients selectively attend to information which is consistent with the negative interpretation of their condition can be a key factor in hypochondriacal problems. This often affects the way in which patients understand conversations with others, particularly health professionals. This is as likely in cognitive therapy as in a medical clinic, making the usually desirable practice of checking the extent to which the patient has accurately received sense of any communications absolutely imperative. This is best done by asking the patient to summarise any important points which arise during the discussion, and to summarise what they have learned at the end of the session. Finally, the patient should be asked whether they were worried by anything that was discussed during the session. Not only does this prevent the therapist inadvertently increasing the patient's anxiety, but can be used as an illustration of the way in which communications can be readily misinterpreted and may subsequently form the basis of a discussion of the extent to which this type of process may be a more enduring characteristic serving to maintain anxiety about health. This is a further useful alternative hypothesis to employ with these patients.

Cases 2 and 3 describe the application of specific cognitive–behavioural treatment techniques. In Case 2, the behavioural component is particularly prominent, and the presentation similar to obsessional disorders, requiring similar interventions.

Case 2

A 48-year-old housewife was referred with a 20-year history of fear that she had cancer. This fear was constantly present but was exacerbated when she was aware of bodily symptoms, especially those involving her throat. The most common symptoms which provoked the fear were feelings of dryness or pain in her throat (particularly if these were unilateral), difficulty swallowing, changes in her voice (especially when singing), and lumps or blotches on her skin. The fear had led to a variety of abnormal behaviours which could be divided into three main categories – repetitive checking directly related to the symptoms, repetitive checking of routine daily activities, and avoidance. Checking directly related to symptoms included constant scanning for changes in her body. If a symptom was noticed she would check the afflicted area, e.g. perceived changes in her throat would lead to inspection with a dental mirror, repeated swallowing and 'clearing the throat', palpation of buccal mucosa with her tongue, and ingestion of proprietary cough lozenges and medicines. She repeatedly asked her husband for reassurance and visited her GP at least weekly. Repetitive checking and ritualising affected virtually every activity – an example was complicated counting during household tasks such as peeling vegetables, actually being able to use the knife only whilst thinking certain numbers which were 'safe'. Other examples were repeating prayers for two hours each night, cleaning furniture always from the right-hand side, and positioning household objects so that they faced the hospital – if an object had two handles, one would have to face the hospital and the other the doctor's surgery. The extent of these activities caused her great handicap and distress. Examples of avoidance were refusing to switch off the radio or television if the programme concerned health and refusing to say 'I'm fine' if asked about her health.

Further information was obtained in the course of the cognitive–behavioural analysis. She was brought up by her mother and maternal grandmother, following the sudden death of her father during the war. Her only sibling died aged 7 years from whooping cough, and from that time her mother kept her at home frequently. If she developed symptoms, she was taken to the doctor immediately. In her early twenties she married and had her first son. Her labour was protracted and the child anoxic, being subsequently diagnosed as severely mentally impaired. He is now 27 and lives at home; his mother feels responsible for his condition because she did not insist on being taken to hospital during the labour. He demands constant attention from her, refuses to be left with anyone else, and she will not allow him to attend social service facilities. She subsequently divorced his father and remarried, and is very concerned about the fate of her son after her death. Her own health worries commenced some twenty years ago after a famous actor underwent surgery for throat cancer. Four years ago, she noticed that her mother had a lump; she was currently undergoing treatment for lymphoma. Her husband has recently suffered two myocardial infarctions, from which he has made only a limited recovery.

She read and watched programmes about illness extensively, e.g. she videotaped and repeatedly watched every programme about AIDS, and developed a series of assumptions about her health. Typical examples were as follows: 'If I get an illness it will be untreatable'; 'Both sides of the body must be absolutely identical or there is something wrong'; 'Symptoms inside the body are more serious than ones on the outside'; 'Symptoms always mean something or they wouldn't be there'.

Such assumptions were activated regularly, by the type of symptoms described above and by publicity about illness, e.g. a singer's recent throat surgery. This led to a familiar set of negative automatic thoughts, e.g. 'This must be cancer'; 'I'm going to die and there will be no one to care for my son'; and to images, such as seeing herself emaciated and her family pitying her.

Her extensive illness-related behaviours were easier to understand in this context. Behaviours directly related to symptoms were to monitor their progress, and hence to prevent serious harm by early consultation. The other rituals and avoidance behaviours are perceived as a means of keeping her and her family safe from illness and not 'tempting fate'.

The cognitive–behavioural analysis of this case is summarised in Table 4.2.

Table 4.2 Cognitive–behavioural analysis of Case 2

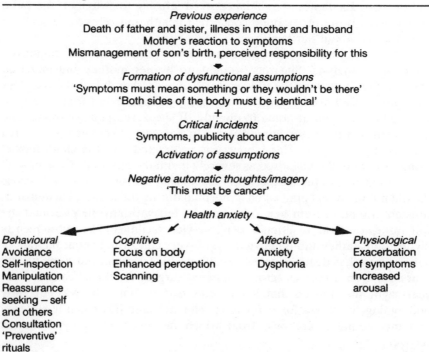

Previous experience
Death of father and sister, illness in mother and husband
Mother's reaction to symptoms
Mismanagement of son's birth, perceived responsibility for this

Formation of dysfunctional assumptions
'Symptoms must mean something or they wouldn't be there'
'Both sides of the body must be identical'
+
Critical incidents
Symptoms, publicity about cancer

Activation of assumptions

Negative automatic thoughts/imagery
'This must be cancer'

Health anxiety

Behavioural	*Cognitive*	*Affective*	*Physiological*
Avoidance	Focus on body	Anxiety	Exacerbation
Self-inspection	Enhanced perception	Dysphoria	of symptoms
Manipulation	Scanning		Increased
Reassurance			arousal
seeking – self			
and others			
Consultation			
'Preventive'			
rituals			

Cognitive–behavioural intervention

As with any cognitive treatment, the first stage of treatment was to inform the patient of the link between thoughts and feelings. However, particular attention had to be paid to the basis of bodily symptoms in general. Like many cases of hypochondriasis, this lady initially gave little credence to the suggestion that symptoms can be caused by anything other than organic pathology. Common examples of how worry can lead to tangible physical symptoms such as palpitations and diarrhoea were understandable and relevant, and enabled the patient to question her initial general assumption. Information about the role of illness-related behaviours in the maintenance and even exacerbation of physical symptoms was given, again using general examples, such as the effect of repeatedly palpating healing wounds. At all times it was stressed that the veracity of her symptoms was not in question; but that alternative explanations for them were being explored.

The next stage was to give an example of a case of typical 'cardiac phobia', explaining how the unexpected death of a relative had caused a man constantly to monitor chest symptoms, and repeatedly to check pulse-rate and for tingling in his left arm by applying pressure to the muscles. She was told how he avoided exertion and repeatedly asked his wife for reassurance, despite his doctor's assurance that his cardiac status was entirely normal. She was asked for her view of this case and identified the importance of the death of the relative immediately. Further questioning led her to volunteer that his behaviour would 'keep his mind on the problem all the time', and 'would make him notice symptoms which could well have occurred anyway'. By squeezing her left forearm firmly for a few seconds, she quickly noticed parasthesiae. Finally, she considered the cause of the man's symptoms and suggested that they were due to his worry about his heart. It was very important that enough time was given to the use of this example, so that the patient could generate the information herself.

We then decided to test out whether it was possible that a similar mechanism could be operating in her case. A version of Table 4.2 was drawn up during the session, in terms understandable to the patient – again the patient was questioned in such a way that she generated most of the information. It was particularly important to identify all sources of checking and reassurance seeking and to include them in the analysis.

Homework set in the first session was to take home the figure, which was seen as a possible explanation for her problems, and to test out if specific symptoms did indeed lead to negative automatic thoughts about health. When she next noted anxiety about health she was asked to record the circumstances and the thoughts experienced. As a result of this exercise, she accepted that these episodes fitted in with the hypothesis, and the next stage was to test out the effects of repetitive checking behaviours directly related to the symptoms. An example arose in the next few days when she became concerned about her swallowing; she reported: 'I couldn't stop thinking about it; every time I wanted to swallow it got harder, so I made myself swallow ten times more often than I should. I got to the stage where I couldn't swallow at all.' It is important to fit such information directly to the hypothesis wherever possible. In this case, asking the patient what it was that had made her unable to swallow reinforced the idea that the cause of her difficulty was the repeated behaviour and preoccupation with the symptom rather than an organic cause. The patient had, in this way, constructed and tested an alternative explanation for her symptoms, and been able to bring about the required reattribution.

After two sessions of monitoring thoughts and testing the effects of her behaviours (continued between the sessions), she was asked to stop the abnormal behaviours related to the symptoms. Despite the success of these interventions, the therapist was not content to continue treatment on this basis alone. Attempting to find an alternative explanation for every feared symptom has a limited usefulness when the patient has fears about a wider range of symptoms than normal because of more general beliefs and assumptions. In the next session, dysfunctional assumptions were considered, focusing on those which were leading to the misinterpretation of normal bodily sensations and variations. We had previously identified the assumption that 'Both sides of the body must be identical or there is something wrong' and her initial belief was 100 per cent. She was then asked to look at her hands to see if they were identical, and to check if they felt identical and was able to identify several differences in both appearance and sensations. She was asked to inspect the therapist's hands to see if they were identical and again found differences. Other evidence, such as taking different sized left and right shoes, was generated. Internal structure was considered, as she regarded internal changes as more dangerous, and the asymmetrical distribution of major organs was explained and accepted. At the end of this session she rated her belief in the original assumption as 30 per cent. Homework was to cease 'preventive' ritualising during her daily activities and avoidance.

After three sessions she was much improved but was concerned that her symptoms had not disappeared altogether. Discomfort was associated with the automatic thought 'It's come back' and the urge to check. Further explanation of the frequency of symptoms in *normal* individuals dealt with this concern.

At the time of writing, the patient does no checking in direct response to symptoms and has stopped 75 per cent of her 'preventive measures'. The latter had been performed very frequently for a long period and had themselves almost become automatic. As she prevented some behaviours, she became more aware of other behaviours which she had not recalled during initial assessment. She is continuing, with vigilance, to decrease these activities. She rates a 50 per cent improvement in her preoccupation with symptoms and is 100 per cent convinced that the hypothesis generated in the first session adequately explains her problems.

Case 3

This case is an example of disease conviction which was associated with acute distress, depressed mood and fleeting suicidal thoughts, which required rapid treatment. A 29-year-old married ambulance driver had a 15-year history of anxiety associated with intrusive thoughts about his health. In the past he had been afraid that he had contracted hepatitis, cancer, and multiple sclerosis, and exhibited a variety of avoidant behaviours in response to thoughts about illness.

Over the month prior to this consultation, he had become increasingly alarmed that he might contract AIDS. He had no history of homosexual contact, but thought that he might be at risk through contact with infected blood, when dealing with trauma cases. He had worked in Sydney three years previously and dealt with AIDS cases; since that time he had wondered about the risks occasionally and kept a mental note of about half a dozen drug addicts he had dealt with. Publicity about AIDS increased during the weeks prior to consultation and the media gave inconsistent reports of the ways in which the condition could be contracted. A colleague was in hospital with an undiagnosed viral illness and his wife had lost a considerable amount of weight. He began to avoid dealing with high-risk cases whilst at work and refused to touch any patient unless he was wearing two pairs of gloves – in case they had unknowingly had a transfusion of infected blood. On his return from a call he would fill the gloves with water to ensure that they had not been punctured; an action which caused much comment amongst his colleagues. He checked his appearance for evidence of weight loss every thirty minutes, asked his wife for reassurance frequently and palpated his neck for swollen lymph glands. Sexual contact with his wife was avoided and he was reluctant to touch his daughter.

Following an incident at work when he injured his hand whilst dealing with a homosexual patient, he developed a coincidental viral infection with symptoms of malaise and enlarged lymph glands – both described in the media as typical symptoms of early AIDS infection. He was convinced that he had AIDS and became acutely distressed with fleeting suicidal thoughts.

A cognitive–behavioural analysis of the problem resulted in the following formulation. His previous fears of illness had led to the following dysfunctional assumptions: 'If I don't worry about my health, I am more likely to fall ill', 'I have a high risk of falling ill', and 'Health workers have a very high risk of contracting illness'. These assumptions had been activated intermittently during the preceding weeks by publicity about the condition and he had been experiencing automatic thoughts, e.g. 'I may have AIDS'. He continued to carry out preventive measures to minimise the perceived risks and to ensure that he did not infect his family. However, the two final critical incidents described above were associated with automatic thoughts, 'I have got AIDS', 'I will have caused my family to become ill and die'. This analysis is summarised in Table 4.3.

Table 4.3 Cognitive–behavioural analysis of Case 3

Previous experience
Previous history of worries about health,
colleague with viral illness

Formation of dysfunctional assumptions
'If I don't worry about my health, I am more likely to fall ill'
'I have a high risk of falling ill'
'Health workers have a great risk of catching AIDS'

+

Critical incidents
Conflicting publicity about AIDS
Injury whilst dealing with homosexual patient
Physical symptoms

Negative automatic thoughts/imagery
'I have got AIDS'
'My family may die'
Images of lying emaciated in a coffin

Behavioural	*Cognitive*	*Affective*	*Physiological*
Checking self	Focusing on	Depression	Exacerbation
Checking family	'AIDS' symptoms	Anxiety	of perceived
Reassurance seeking	Preoccupation		physical changes
Avoidance at work	Increased perception		Increased
'Protective'	of symptoms		arousal
measures at work			

At the beginning of the first consultation, depression was rated at 65 on a 0–100 scale; belief that he had AIDS was 100 per cent. Initially, the critical incidents were discussed in an effort to generate rational responses to the automatic thoughts. Evaluating the risk of contact with blood which may have been infected during the critical incident led to discussion of how long the HTLV-III virus could survive in the atmosphere and how big an injury would be necessary to contract AIDS. There was no change in belief or depression – the therapist had fallen into the trap of discussing the probability of intrusive thoughts being true and attempting to provide reassurance that there was no risk of contracting AIDS in this way. Such an intervention is not likely to be effective, as we have already seen (Salkovskis and Warwick 1986; Warwick and Salkovskis 1985). It was then decided to challenge the assumption that health workers are at risk of contracting AIDS. This intervention is summarised in Table 4.4, and was successful; final belief that he had AIDS was 30, and depression rated at 50. He felt able to stop the checking, reassurance seeking and preventive behaviours and resumed normal contact with his family. He stopped wearing gloves for routine cases at work, and dealt with a case of AIDS with no anxiety. Currently, his belief that he has AIDS is rated at 0 and he has no other hypochondriacal concerns.

Table 4.4 Cognitive intervention in Case 3

Evidence for the assumption

1. ? one health worker has contracted the AIDS virus by accidental injection of infected blood.

Evidence against the assumption

1. There is no increased incidence of AIDS in colleagues in Sydney or San Francisco, where they have more cases of AIDS than we do.

2. Paramedics and ambulance men have not changed their practice in Sydney or San Francisco.

3. Paramedics in Sydney and San Francisco do more direct work and have more contact with their cases than British ambulance men.

4. I know that all of my colleagues have cut themselves on duty, so it is reasonable to assume that foreign colleagues have also. Some of my colleagues have been jabbed accidentally with needles, as will have foreign colleagues.

5. Evidence 1–4 applies to doctors and nurses working in Sydney and San Francisco.

6. No increase in AIDS antibodies in health workers in Sydney or San Francisco. They have had the condition for much longer than us and the antibodies are detectable after 3 months, so it would have shown up by now.

7. They are not barrier nursing at new AIDS wards, as they do for hepatitis.

8. No instructions from ambulance service chiefs to change practice.

9. Wife's family and friends in the Australian health service would have contacted us if there had been any increase.

Conclusions

This chapter has emphasised the need for a new treatment approach in hypochondriasis. A cognitive–behavioural formulation, emphasising the way in which psychological processes interact to produce the core features of the condition, has been described. We have tried to illustrate some of the strategies which, in combination with other more standard techniques, are specifically required for the treatment of hypochondriasis. More than in any other condition these patients are likely to have been dissatisfied with previous treatment; this is neither the fault of the patient nor of previous therapists, but rather is a consequence of the nature of the factors involved in the condition itself. Most hypochondriacal patients appear to have an involuntary style of attending to and interpreting well-intended information and reassurance in a way which acts to provide confirmation of their worst fears. Furthermore, given the beliefs which characterise this disorder, it is not surprising that they are frequently reluctant to accept psychological treatment. Treatment efforts with hypochondriacal patients all hinge on how effectively the patient has been engaged in treatment; we have described several ways in which this can be done. Finally, we emphasise the importance of using collaborative treatment strategies in order to help the patient reach and accept a positive *psychological* explanation of their symptoms rather than asking that the patient trust in our (uncertain) ability to rule out all possible physical causes. There is little point in depending on interventions which attempt to prove to the patient that the problem which has been troubling them so badly, and which is accompanied by so much distress, has no basis in fact. Even if this were to be possible in the majority of cases (and, by definition, it is not), patients continue to experience distress and perceive continuing physical disturbance, so that sooner or later they are likely to question the disproof they have been offered. We suggest that the use of cognitive–behavioural strategies such as those outlined here may lead to a more encouraging outlook for hypochondriacal patients.

Notes

1. Authorship is equal.
2. Paul Salkovskis is grateful for the support of the Medical Research Council of the United Kingdom.

References

American Psychiatric Association (1987) *Diagnostic and Statistical Manual of Mental Disorders*, 3rd revised edn, Washington DC: American Psychiatric Press.

Barsky, A.J. and Klerman, G.L. (1983) 'Overview: hypochondriasis, bodily complaints and somatic styles', *American Journal of Psychiatry* 140: 273–81.

Bianchi, G.N. (1971) 'The origins of disease phobia', *Australia and New Zealand Journal of Psychiatry* 5: 241–57.

Leonhard, K. (1968) 'On the treatment of ideohypochondriac and sensohypochondriac neuroses', *International Journal of Social Psychiatry* 2: 123–33.

Marks, I.M. (1987) *Fears, Phobias and Rituals*, New York: Oxford University Press.

Nemiah, J.C. (1985) 'Hypochondriasis', in H.I. Caplan and B.J. Saddock (eds) *Comprehensive Textbook of Psychiatry. Vol. 4*, Baltimore: Williams & Wilkins, pp. 1538–43.

Pilowsky, I. (1967) 'Dimensions of hypochondriasis', *British Journal of Psychiatry* 113: 89–93.

Ryle, J.A. (1947) 'Nosophobia', *Journal of Mental Science* 94: 1–17.

Salkovskis, P.M. (1989) 'Somatic problems', in K. Hawton, P.M. Salkovskis, J. Kirk, and D.M. Clark (eds) *Cognitive Behaviour Therapy for Psychiatric Problems: a practical guide*, Oxford: Oxford University Press.

Salkovskis, P.M. and Warwick, H.M.C. (1986) 'Morbid preoccupations, health anxiety and reassurance: a cognitive behavioural approach to hypochondriasis', *Behaviour Research and Therapy* 24: 597–602.

Salkovskis, P.M. and Westbrook, D. (1987) 'Obsessive–compulsive disorder: clinical strategies for improving behavioural treatments', in H.R. Dent (ed.) *Clinical Psychology: Research and Development*, London: Croom Helm.

Warwick, H.M.C. and Salkovskis, P.M. (1985) 'Reassurance', *British Medical Journal* 290: 1028.

Warwick, H.M.C. and Salkovskis, P.M. (1987) *Clinical and Research Aspects of Hypochondriasis: A Review of Current Problems and A Cognitive–Behavioural Perspective*, manuscript submitted for publication.

Chapter five

Cancer patients

Jan Scott

Introduction

The use and efficacy of cognitive behaviour therapy (CBT) in the treatment of primary major depressive disorders is now well established on both sides of the Atlantic (e.g. Rush *et al*. 1977; Blackburn *et al*. 1981). More recently, its use in anxiety disorders has been similarly well described (Beck *et al*. 1985). The use of CBT in the treatment of depression or anxiety that arises as a secondary consequence of physical illness has been less extensively researched. A small number of studies have been published in the literature pointing to the possible use of CBT in patients with multiple sclerosis (Larcombe and Wilson 1984), epilepsy (Tan and Bruni 1986), and irritable bowel syndrome (Schwarz and Blanchard 1986), as well as with those suffering from painful conditions such as rheumatoid arthritis (Bradley 1985), or coping with the consequences of coronary surgery (Valliant and Leith 1986) or myocardial infarction (Stern *et al*. 1984). The sample sizes were small; the applications of CBT varied between group, individual, and telephone sessions; the outcomes were variable, with evidence of both success and failure. These modest results may dampen some therapists' enthusiasm for trying CBT with physically ill patients, but the studies quoted so far can only be regarded as a preliminary attempt to 'test the water'. Few of the reports gave details of the problems of applying CBT to these patients and relatively little information is available on if, or how, the CBT approach was modified to tackle the specific needs of this group.

One of the most interesting potential applications of CBT to the physically ill is its use with cancer patients. Again there is a small, but growing, literature. Maguire and colleagues (1985) in the UK, and Worden (1987) and colleagues in the USA, have provided some preliminary studies in this area. The early results suggest that CBT can be an effective therapy for cancer patients, used either alone or in combination with antidepressant drugs. These groups of researchers also made preliminary attempts to identify factors that made some cancer sufferers more vulnerable to emotional disorders.

In this chapter I will briefly review the prevalance of psychological morbidity in cancer patients and outline why CBT may have a role to play in such disorders. In addition, I will describe some of the specific issues that need to be addressed in applying CBT to this patient population and try to identify potential problem areas. A case study of the use of CBT in a female patient with breast cancer will be described to highlight some of the strategies that may be used.

Prevalence of psychological problems in cancer patients

The diagnosis of cancer represents a major and catastrophic life event to most individuals (McIntosh 1974). As Massie and Holland (1984) point out, an individual's ability to adapt depends on the threat it poses to their 'age-appropriate' goals (e.g. family, career); their prior level of emotional adjustment; the presence of a social support network; and disease-related factors such as the site of the tumour, the presence of disabling symptoms, treatment variables, and prognosis. The commonest emotional response of any individual to the diagnosis of cancer follows the classical sequence of a crisis reaction: initial shock and disbelief are followed by anxiety, anger, guilt, and depression. The period of adjustment is variable, but the acute reaction usually begins to resolve over 7–14 days. In some cases, this adaptation may be considerably delayed or may never occur, whilst in others the illness is denied.

In a significant number of individuals the emotional response takes the form of a depressive or anxiety disorder. At least 25 per cent of post-mastectomy patients develop these disorders in the twelve to eighteen months following surgery (Morris 1979). A similar figure is reported for patients with a colostomy following treatment for bowel cancer (Devlin et al. 1971). Exacerbations of these symptoms may occur with evidence of recurrence of the cancer (Silberfarb et al. 1980), or at the end of the course of radiotherapy (Holland et al. 1979). Psychiatric morbidity may also be a direct consequence of specific chemotherapy regimes (Hughson et al. 1980).

Estimating the prevalence of psychiatric disorders in the physically ill is often problematic, but there is well-documented evidence that the actual level of morbidity in an oncology unit greatly exceeds that recognised by the staff caring for the patients (e.g. Levine et al. 1978). This lack of detection may be a function of the patients' reluctance to reveal their fears or the staff's failure to respond to verbal and non-verbal cues. Unfortunately, even when anxiety or depressive disorders are recognised they frequently remain untreated. Greer (1985) suggests that the staff tend to regard these conditions as an understandable response and so fail to consider that psychiatric help is either feasible or indicated.

The lack of adequate recognition and treatment of the emotional consequences of cancer is disappointing for two reasons. First, over the last decade there has been a rapid expansion in the physical therapies available to treat a wide variety of cancers. The survival times for many patients have been significantly lengthened, although some of the treatments are themselves difficult to tolerate. These factors have led to an increasing awareness of the need to maintain the quality of life experienced by the patient. It is no longer merely a question of being 'grateful to be alive'. Second, there is evidence that the psychological response to the cancer may affect the length of survival. Several studies (e.g. Greer *et al.* 1979) indicate that the outcome at 5 years is better in those patients who either deny the existence of the illness or show a 'fighting spirit', shorter survival rates being associated with stoic acceptance or a helpless–hopeless response.

There are some data available on which individuals are most vulnerable to psychological problems. First, with regard to physical status, patients most at risk of psychological problems are those who undergo mutilating surgery (Dean *et al.* 1983), those with inadequately controlled pain, those in poorer physical health generally, and those with advanced stage illness (Holland *et al.* 1983). Patients who fail to cope with radiotherapy show 'extremes of behaviour' (e.g. withdrawal), engage poorly with health professionals, and have unrealistic expectations about their prognosis (Schmale *et al.* 1982). Poor psychosocial adjustment after mastectomy is associated with premorbid neurotic traits (Schonfield 1972), lack of close personal relationships (Weisman and Worden 1977), lack of employment (Bloom 1982), and a history of previous psychiatric disorder (Morris 1979). Weisman and Worden (1977) have also identified a group of poorly coping patients with a wide variety of different tumours. They found that 'poor copers' showed a long history of inadequate problem solving in a variety of situations.

Why use cognitive behaviour therapy?

Maguire and co-workers (1985) have often advocated the use of anti-depressant or anxiolytic drugs in patients with cancer. They feel that there has been a reluctance to prescribe psychotrophic drugs because of the obvious 'reactive' nature of the psychological problems. In many instances the severity of the symptoms and the type of illness do warrant drug therapy. In other instances, pharmacotherapy is required in order to enable the patient to engage in counselling and support. However, the use of drugs in cancer patients presents a number of difficulties that may realistically make people wish to avoid prescribing them:

1. The patient's psychological symptoms may not fit neatly into the pattern of a particular syndrome and may not show features that would

be resolved by drug therapy. Often the presentation is a mixture of anxiety and depressive symptoms, frequently coming under the rubric of *DSM III-R* 'adjustment disorder' (American Psychiatric Association 1987). CBT may tackle the combination of problems presented in a more comprehensive way than pharmacological treatment.

2. Even when drugs seem to be indicated, patients with cancer are frequently more sensitive to their side-effects. This is particularly true of tricyclic antidepressants; cancer patients are less tolerant of the anticholinergic side-effects, possibly due to changes in hepatic enzyme activity (Massie and Holland 1984).

3. Antidepressant drugs may be contra-indicated because of interactions with other physical treatments. Monoamine oxidase inhibitors should not be combined with opiate analgesics. Tricyclic antidepressants are contra-indicated with the chemotherapeutic agent procarbazine (Massie and Holland 1984).

4. The risk of a suicide attempt may be high in a depressant and hopeless patient. Psychotropics may merely provide the patient with the means to carry this out.

5. It is important to consider the 'message' being given to patients and their families. With CBT, the statement being put forward focuses on helping the individual to participate actively in the development of coping strategies. Drug therapies make the patient the passive recipient of a 'cure'. The patients' preferences also become important here. Do they have more faith in pharmacology or do they prefer a psychological approach?

If pharmacotherapy is used, it should be seen as an adjunct to rather than a replacement for psychological treatment. However, as Worden (1987) points out, whilst there is a vast array of psychosocial interventions available for cancer patients, most are aimed at helping them and their families cope with dying. CBT differs from many of these therapies because it attempts to enable the patient to adjust to the problems of living. The focus is on controlling the quality of life in a situation where the 'quantity' may be an unpredictable variable. This is not to suggest that CBT should replace other psychological interventions. The use of counselling and supportive psychotherapies is generally known to be beneficial (e.g. Bloom *et al.* 1978). However, it is interesting to note that some of the most effective programmes tend to incorporate many techniques that would come within the classic CBT framework. Sobel and Worden (1980) focused on problem-solving skills, whilst Gordon *et al.* (1980) utilised a programme of supportive therapy with education and information giving and environmental manipulation. This aimed to give patients a more realistic outlook, increase their daily activities, and improve their adjustment to the disorder.

Specific issues in applying cognitive behaviour therapy to cancer patients

The following section refers to specific issues that may need to be tackled in a course of CBT with a cancer patient who is suffering from psychological problems. It is obvious that some of these difficulties may also be experienced by patients with other physical illnesses.

Grieving for the 'lost self'

One of the major problems confronting the patient will be the effect of the illness on their self-esteem and self-image. The role of the individual in the family and work situation may change significantly. Self-esteem will be affected by loss or changes in role. Cancer sufferers often feel stigmatised by colleagues and friends. Those close to them often feel uncomfortable in the patient's company, not knowing if they are or are not allowed to discuss the illness.

The disfigurement brought about by surgery can have a tremendous effect on the individual's self-image. Many women report sexual difficulties following mastectomy related to their anxieties about their body image (Morris 1979). These difficulties are often compounded by a sense of personal failure and self-blame that the individual has developed cancer in the first instance.

In many ways the patient's view of themselves is tackled in the same way as it would be in CBT in general (e.g. see Beck *et al.* 1979; Williams 1984). In addition the following points should be remembered:

1. With the physically ill, subjective perceptions of personal worth and degree of handicap may be distorted, but in tackling these issues there is also a need for a realistic appraisal of the patient's role and help is needed in adjusting to actual changes that may be required.
2. It is often important to involve the spouse in discussions about self-image in patients who have undergone disfiguring surgery.
3. Role-plays can be used to enable the patient to take the lead in interactions with friends and colleagues. This allows the patient to take control of discussions about the illness and its treatment.

Locus of control

Patients frequently feel hopeless because of the overwhelming sense of lack of personal control over their illness and prognosis. This sense of powerlessness is very demoralising. At some point a sensitive exploration of the patient's fears about coping with death is necessary. The patient can be helped in several ways:

1. An acknowledgement that the future is uncertain, accompanied by the

provision of clear information about what is and is not known about their particular illness.

2. According to Gomez (1987), most patients' fantasies about their death include images of 'disastrous dyscontrol' and an agonising, often painful and lonely end. It is important to take on these anxieties and to talk in detail about all aspects of concern. Additional meetings can be organised with the clinicians to discuss pain control, etc.

3. Avoiding overgeneralisation of feelings of lack of control by getting the patient to define those aspects of life that they are in control of and those which no one can control.

4. Helping the patient overcome any guilt or anger they feel about their lack of control.

Physical status

There may be realistic limitations placed on the patient because of physical disability or side-effects of treatment. This needs to be taken into account when planning activity schedules by:

1. planning activities that require less exertion or mobility;
2. using activities that enhance residual abilities rather than expose deficits;
3. putting limitations on what the patient is allowed to tackle at a given time, e.g. in the initial time after radiotherapy (which can be particularly tiring) only allowing the individual to choose from a specific number of activities that have been preselected as feasible for someone in that physical state.

Pain

For some patients the control of pain is a major problem. There is a fairly extensive literature available on the application of CBT techniques to control pain (e.g. Pearce and Richardson 1987). As well as ensuring that adequate physical treatment is being employed, additional strategies include the following.

1. The use of a pain diary to monitor fluctuations in intensity and duration and allow any factors that reduce the pain to be identified.
2. Examination of pain-related cognitions.
3. Distraction techniques.
4. As with physical disability the pain may limit the patient's ability to engage in particular activities. The intensity of the pain may be 'coded' by the patient, e.g. using a 'colour coding': pain of medium severity equals orange, more severe pain equals green, etc. Activities are similarly coded depending on difficulty in accomplishing them with a

particular level of pain. The patient then chooses activities from the list according to the colour coding. This often avoids disappointment and anger at not being able to achieve or enjoy a specific activity at any time and engenders some feelings of control, e.g. a male cancer patient enjoyed golf, but had a metastatic lesion in his spine. He coded severe pain as green and moderate pain as orange. Nine holes of golf were coded as orange and eighteen holes as green. He overcame some of his frustration by avoiding attempting too much and got positive reinforcement from successful outings.

Treatment issues

The patient may wish to discuss their radiotherapy or chemotherapy treatment, as the side-effects of these can be very distressing. Some may wish to stop treatment entirely. In addition, issues of long-term hospitalisation or moving into a hospice may need to be tackled. The following strategies may be helpful:

1. Examining the pros and cons of continuing treatment; this includes issues such as the quality of life, prognosis without treatment, and effects on significant others. Collaboration with treating physicians and family is vital.
2. Generating alternative solutions with regard to whether to accept hospice or other care and discussing the timing of any moves that may be desired or become necessary.

Longstanding deficits in coping strategies

Many patients who fail to cope with cancer show longstanding deficits in coping strategies (Worden 1987). It was found by Weisman and Worden (1977) that 'poor copers' showed two main deficits in their coping repertoire. First, they tended to over-use strategies that were least effective in resolving problems e.g. drinking as a means of avoidance of issues. Second, they were unable to generate alternative coping strategies. These deficiencies were accompanied by high levels of emotional distress.

'Good copers' not only generated more alternatives, but were more effective at evaluating and rank ordering the potential solutions to a variety of problem situations. Hopefully, it is obvious from this description that standard CBT interventions could be used to deal with 'poor copers'.

Specific problems in applying cognitive behaviour therapy in cancer patients

There are many potential pitfalls in trying to apply CBT to cancer patients. Perhaps one of the most important is simply that for many patients their negative view of reality is not a distortion but an accurate reflection of the problems they are facing. This does not preclude the use of CBT, but it must be acknowledged. The therapist must not attempt to make the patient into an unrealistic optimist, nor should they identify with the patient's hopelessness to the extent that they cannot function effectively. Other problems that may need addressing are the following:

1. The prevalence of organic brain syndromes in cancer patients is estimated to be about 40 per cent (Levine *et al.* 1978). It should be borne in mind that the patient may have or may develop subtle cognitive deficits that impair their ability to engage in CBT. In some instances these problems can be overcome by modelling task assignments within the sessions and 'overlearning', as described by Hibbard *et al.* (1987) in their work with brain-damaged patients.
2. Co-operation with other health care professionals. A vital feature of CBT in physically ill patients is its role in giving information about the disorder and discussing the patient's views about the treatment options available. Close collaboration is required with other members of staff to ensure consistency in these communications.
3. The patient's family or significant others may want or need to be involved. This has many potential benefits in reinforcing the therapist's work. It can also afford an opportunity to examine the family's cognitions and emotional responses to the illness.
4. If the patient is a medical or psychiatric in-patient, CBT may need to be adapted to take this into account. These problems have been discussed by Blackburn (this volume) and Scott (1988).

Finally, it is important to remember that in a significant subgroup of cancer sufferers, denial is an adaptive coping strategy that may be associated with longer survival times (Greer *et al.* 1979). In some patients, denial may reduce the individual's sense of hopelessness and so it should not automatically be challenged.

Case study

Margaret was a 37-year-old female who was referred by a hospital social worker to a specialist centre for CBT. Margaret was a widow who worked as a shop assistant and lived with her 15-year-old daughter. She had recently had a partial mastectomy with breast reconstruction, followed by a course of radiotherapy. When that treatment came to an end she was seen by the social worker who felt she was suffering from 'stress and depression'. A psychiatric assessment revealed that the patient was suffering from major depression without melancholia, accompanied by symptoms of generalised anxiety disorder. Her past history revealed three previous episodes of major depression over the past 12 years that had all been precipitated by stressful life events. Margaret's mother (who lived several hundred miles away), appeared to have a longstanding untreated paranoid psychosis.

At the 'intake' interview, an assessment was made to determine if CBT might be a suitable approach to Margaret's problems. This interview was carried out by an experienced cognitive therapist (who then allocated the patient to the most appropriate therapist at the clinic). Margaret expressed the view that she did not wish to receive medication and that she wanted to 'learn to help herself'. The assessment recorded that her mood was depressed and anxious. She was more irritable than normal and felt hopeless. Behaviourally, she was withdrawn and restless. Physiological complaints included insomnia, anorexia, weight loss and fatigue, loss of libido, loss of interest, and poor concentration. She also complained of the physiological concomitants of anxiety. Cognitively, Margaret was pre-occupied by her health, her sense of powerlessness and her perceived lack of support from family and friends. Although feeling hopeless, she denied any suicidal intent, declaring that her fate was 'in God's hands'. Objective data collected at the initial interview are shown in Table 5.1.

Table 5.1 Ratings over the course of treatment

Measure	Intake	Session 6	Session 10
Beck Depression Inventory (BDI)	27	7	1
Anxiety Checklist (ACL)	18	4	0
Hamilton Rating Scale: for Depression (HRSD)	28	9	3
for Anxiety (HRSA)	19	6	2
Hopelessness Scale (HS)	15	2	0
Scale of Suicidal Ideation (SSI)	4	0	0
Dysfunctional Attitudes Scale (DAS)*	284	–	212

*Initial high scores on perfectionism and issues of control. Scores on these dropped significantly by the end of therapy, although the overall change on the DAS was not significant.

Margaret was allocated to me after the assessment interview. It had been decided that she might well benefit from CBT. With her permission, all the sessions were audiotaped. This can be beneficial to therapists as a self-teaching exercise and also for use in supervision sessions. As will be seen in this case, it can also be useful for the patients.

Sessions 1 and 2

The first two sessions focused on three issues:

111

Establishing a rapport between patient and therapist It was important to emphasise the collaborative nature of the approach and the active role the patient would take in the therapy. This was particularly important for Margaret as she had engaged in a different style of therapeutic relationship when previously treated for depression. It was also important to acknowledge that, in this particular clinic, Margaret had been seen by one therapist for the initial assessment and was now having to transfer to another therapist and establish a new relationship.

Socialising the patient into the cognitive model of emotional disorders As Margaret was already assessed as a suitable candidate for CBT, every opportunity in the sessions was used to reinforce the cognitive model. Examples of 'event–thought–affect' links were demonstrated whenever possible. If the patient showed a particular cognitive distortion, e.g. selective abstraction, not only was the dysfunctional thought pointed out, but the type of error was given an appropriate 'label'.

Generating a problem list Over the two sessions Margaret and I talked in detail about all her current difficulties. We established links between some of the issues she brought up and gradually clarified the specific problem areas. We were then able to come up with the following list of goals of the therapy:

1. Reducing anxiety related to health.
2. Learning to recognise stress-provoking situations and thoughts.
3. Learning to cope with 'stress and depression' and altering previous maladaptive coping strategies.
4. Examining and improving her social and family relationships.

Within these goals, it would be important to incorporate work on hopelessness, locus of control, and perfectionism. These had been highlighted as problem areas in the assessment interview and had again been recognised as major issues during the initial sessions. The first two sessions were held within a week. Margaret was then going to visit her mother, so there was a one-week gap before Session 3. It was agreed that the next session would focus on Margaret's anxieties about her physical health and how to deal with them.

Session 3

At the beginning of the session the Beck Depression Inventory (BDI) and Anxiety Checklist (ACL) were repeated; the BDI score had risen and Margaret said she felt much worse. Although the preliminary agenda had previously been set for the session, it was important in the first instance to 'check out' what had happened to make Margaret feel more distressed.

T: You seem to be feeling worse today and I see from the Beck that your score has gone up. Is that a true reflection of things? How are you feeling?

Even though there are obvious clues, it's still important to check out the facts with the patient.

P: Yeh, I feel really down. I've had an awful week, it was quite traumatic visiting my mother. Then to top it all, even the damn rent-a-car got stolen. These things *always* happen to me.

Although the last statement is an obvious overgeneralisation, it is not appropriate to tackle that comment at present, but rather to note it and to continue to gather more information.

T: It sounds like things really didn't go the way you planned, visiting your mother and getting the car stolen. Were there any other problems that made the week particularly difficult?

Again the therapist is clarifying with the patient if she understands the situation and also checking out if there were other problems.

P: No, but that was quite enough. I feel really miserable. [*Pause.*] It's all so hopeless. [*She begins to cry.*]
T: [*Pause.*] What's going through your mind right now?

The therapist is trying to identify the automatic thought or image that accompanies the emotion.

P: I'm no help to my mother and she's not well. I'm useless as a daughter.
T: That thought seems to be very powerful for you. I know that we had planned the agenda for today. But it seems to me that maybe our priority should be to deal with the situation in hand and tackle how you're feeling and thinking right now. Is that what you want to do?

In crisis situations it is totally acceptable to leave the planned agenda.

P: Yeh, I think it would help to talk about my visit to my mother.
T: Tell me about the time you spent there. . . .

We established that Margaret was particularly upset during the first few days of her visit. Her mother expressed the idea that the CIA were watching her and at the beginning of the week this topic dominated the conversation. Margaret allowed her mother to talk about these beliefs, but stated that she felt helpless and didn't know how to deal with the situation. Her mother's delusions were encapsulated, she did not act out on them, and overall functioned at a high level. However, she was not easily dissuaded from these ideas and Margaret did occasionally have the fleeting thought that there might be some truth in what her mother told her because her mother had previously been a government employee.

The therapist noted two important factors from the discussion. First, Margaret had used a coping strategy, i.e. allowing her mother to ventilate. From the details given, this actually seemed to be an effective technique; however, more evidence was required to establish if that was the best approach. If it was, it was also important that Margaret *discovered that for herself*, rather than the therapist trying to convince her of it. Second, the difficulties had not continued for the entire week, but only for the first two days; at the present time Margaret perceived the whole week as dreadful.

T: From what you've told me the way you coped with your mother's difficulties was to allow her to talk it through for a few days until she felt less upset. Is that right?

P: Yeh.

T: But it also comes across that you don't feel that that's the solution to the situation?

P: Well, if I was a better daughter, I'd help her more.

T: Perhaps we can look in detail at this problem of how you deal with your mother when she's upset like this. The technique we're going to use is called generating alternatives. What I'd like us to do in the first instance is just try and list all the possible ways we think someone could handle this situation. In the first instance, I want us just to list *all* the possibilities. I don't want you to filter any out because you don't think they're right, let's just identify all the alternatives. OK? [*The patient nods.*] One way is to allow her to ventilate her worries for a couple of days, which is what you already do. What other things might someone in that situation do? [*Patient and therapist make a list of the alternatives.*]

P: I could refuse to talk about it. That's often how I feel.

T: Right, that's a possibility; anything else?

P: Well, I guess I could get the doctor.

T: OK, anything else?

P: I could get the police, in case she's right.

T: OK, anything else?

P: Well, I could stop visiting her altogether.

T: Anything else?

P: I could challenge what she's saying, although she gets upset if I do. Maybe I should just leave.

T: OK. Let's now go through each one of the alternatives in some detail and decide what the advantages and disadvantages are to each approach and try and check out how feasible they are. If you've tried any of these things in the past we can also look at the evidence for whether or not they work. Let's start with not visiting at all. . . .

The patient and therapist carried out the above exercise in some detail, and wrote down all the relevant data for each option that had been put forward, e.g. getting the doctor in the past had led to considerable family disharmony. Margaret's mother had been very guarded when talking with the doctor and very angry that he had been called. She had refused to comply with the medication prescribed (she did not want hospitalisation and was not sectionable).

T: OK, having checked this all out, which approach do you feel seems to be the most effective?

P: Well, I guess, allowing her to talk for a couple of days suits us both best. [*Smiles.*]

T: You're smiling, what's going through your mind?

P: Maybe I'm not such an incompetent daughter after all. It's silly really, for the past few years I've really been down on myself about not coping with her problems better. I thought I should be doing more, but now I sort of feel like I'd been doing the best thing all the time, I just assumed I could do more.

T: On the evidence we have that does seem to be true. I think we should reword the statement as well, it ought to read 'I am a competent daughter'.

P: [*Smiles again.*] I guess that's true. My mother does say that so long as she can talk it through it's OK.

T: Did she say that to you when you were there this time?

P: Yeh, by Tuesday she seemed more relaxed and it was easier to distract her onto other topics. . . .

The patient then went on to make a more realistic appraisal of the week's holiday. She acknowledged that, after the first few days, she had enjoyed herself and she and her mother had been on quite a few outings that they had both taken pleasure in.

P: When I came in today I really felt life wasn't worth living any more. My mother has been such an important support to me and I felt like I wasn't able to repay any of that.

T: You seemed really hopeless?

P: Yeh, I was, I feel much better now. . . .

The session had been a particularly important one for Margaret. It had helped her overcome her hopelessness, and she felt more secure about her ability to help her mother. It was decided that one of the homework assignments would be for Margaret to take the tape of the session home to listen in detail to what had happened and what techniques were used to tackle the problems she had presented. The therapist recorded that Margaret had not discussed her own problems with her mother. Whilst this might be appropriate in view of her mother's mental state, the therapist noted this fact. It also came to light that she had never discussed her mother's difficulties with any of her friends and so had never received any support in coping. This information would be used in later sessions.

Session 4

During the preliminary stages of the session, Margaret reported that, although a little better overall, she had felt very down for the last three days. After going to the radiotherapy department for a post-treatment check-up she had been very distressed and had spent the last few days crying for long periods. This seemed an ideal opportunity to tap into any automatic thoughts associated with Margaret's anxieties about her illness, so the therapist used the opportunity to pursue these.

T: We had said at the last session that today we would start to look at ways to deal with your anxiety about your physical health. In fact from what you say about the last few days, perhaps it would be helpful to start with your visit to the clinic and then to move onto your anxieties. Is that OK?

Agenda setting is always a joint exercise and therefore the patient and therapist must collaborate closely at this stage of the session. The therapist must seek feedback from the patient about the ordering of the agenda and the priorities.

P: Yes, that would be helpful. I still feel bad about it. [*Starts to cry.*]
T: OK. [*Pause.*] Let's just take things steadily. Can you tell me some more about what happened when you visited the clinic?
P: Well, I was anxious when I got there, but it wasn't too bad until I actually went in for my check-up. The doctor seemed very pleased and said I was doing real well. He said they were going to throw the body mould [used for radiotherapy treatment] away and gave me the 'all clear'. I started to cry. He was very nice and reassuring, but then I felt angry. . . .
T: So first of all you felt upset and then you felt angry. Let's just try to go back in your mind to the clinic and try and find out what thoughts went with those feelings. What went through your mind at that moment in time?

The last question is actually a better phrase to use than just asking for thoughts. Occasionally, patients have automatic images and saying 'what went through your mind' avoids missing out on these.

P: Well, first of all, when he said they were going to throw the mould away I felt very panicky. He was saying I wouldn't need any more treatment and I thought 'if it [the cancer] comes back, I won't be able to handle it'. Then I felt annoyed. . . .
T: What do you think went through your mind then?

The therapist chose the option of gathering the other automatic thoughts, rather than focusing in too quickly on the first one.

P: I suppose I was angry . . . with him and myself. I didn't want his pity. . . . [*Pause.*] 'I should be stronger and cope better on my own.'

At this point the patient and therapist wrote these two automatic thoughts onto a dysfunctional thought record; Margaret was then asked to rate the percentage belief in each thought and the intensity of the emotional response.

These automatic thoughts were tackled in the standard way. First, with regard to 'handling' any recurrences, Margaret believed 90 per cent in the statement 'If the cancer recurs I won't be able to handle it'. She rated her emotional response as Anxiety (80 per cent) and Depression (70 per cent). Examining this statement, we established that Margaret had a good track record in coping with difficult practical situations in general. However, we did not have so much evidence about how she 'handled' illness. We therefore listed all the different aspects of handling any recurrence of the cancer as:

1. coping with her own emotional response, e.g. anxiety;
2. accepting and tolerating any treatment prescribed;
3. coping with pain, e.g. from secondaries;
4. dealing with the reactions of others;
5. being able to discuss her treatment and prognosis with the staff.

Being specific in this way and breaking the issue down allows patient and therapist to determine which aspects of the problem are already being dealt with appropriately, and which require further interventions.

We established that she was prepared to accept the treatment prescribed despite the side-effects she had experienced before. Discussion of the problems of coping with pain revealed that she had a strong image of seeing herself in a hospital bed dying alone without pain relief. As we analysed this, Margaret remarked that, in fact, people did visit her in hospital and there was no reason to jump to any conclusions that they would not again. However, she needed more reassurance about methods of controlling any pain. We discussed in detail the use of analgesia. Her anxiety was partially alleviated, but not totally resolved. In addition, there seemed a need for more information about her illness in general. The patient had not felt able to discuss her prognosis at her last clinic visit; she anticipated the worst and did not wish to hear her fears confirmed. After exploring the thought and examining its validity (noting that she had not acknowledged that the doctor had given her positive feedback, i.e. he had said 'all clear'), the next step was to define what further action was required. With coaxing, Margaret agreed that her assignment before the next session was to arrange to revisit the clinic to discuss her illness. She would take responsibility for making the appointment but together we drew up a list of questions she wanted to ask. (The oncology unit frequently arranged additional appointments for 'information giving'.)

The two other aspects that needed to be dealt with – Margaret's ability to cope with her own anxiety and depression, and talking to significant others – partly linked into the general goals of therapy. These were tackled in this and later sessions. Belief in the original automatic thought had dropped to 40 per cent; her Anxiety and Depression ratings also fell to 50 and 35 per cent respectively. Within the session Margaret's mood had also shown a significant shift. She was now brighter and more cheerful.

The second automatic thought – 'I should be stronger and cope better on my own' – was also examined. First, the therapist tackled the 'should' statement, helping the patient discover that this was a personal rule she was trying to live by, not a generally accepted principle. Second, we established what Margaret meant by being a strong and coping individual. She believed that 'normal' people were strong and coping. However, her definition of strong seemed to be analogous with invincible. With inductive questioning we were able to show that this definition was unworkable and also that Margaret applied double standards: she expected herself to be invincible, but did not expect it of others. The therapist also noted that Margaret seemed to be expressing an underlying belief that 'in order to be liked by others I must not show any signs of weakness'. It was not appropriate to tackle this assumption at this stage as it was too early in the therapy. Also, the therapist had to find further supporting evidence for this hypothesis before working on it with the patient.

The remainder of the session focused on Margaret's anxieties about her health. We established that a key automatic thought that made her particularly anxious was 'I don't have any control over anything that happens to me'. Margaret tended to attribute most things to luck or fate. She felt both anxious and hopeless in response to this thought. However, this idea seemed to be applied globally across all aspects of her life so initially we tackled this overgeneralisation.

T: First, can we look at the evidence to support the belief that you have no control over anything that happens to you. I wonder if we can fill out this [activity] schedule for the past three days and then try and see what events or activities were within your control and which were controlled externally.

Margaret and the therapist made out a schedule and determined locus of control.

T: Looking at the schedule and the data, what do you conclude?
P: Well, I guess I control far more things than I gave myself credit for.

In fact, more things are controlled by me than by somebody or something else. I guess I was just focusing on what I couldn't control.

T: That seems to be true on the past few days' evidence. And being so fixed on what you couldn't control was making you feel anxious and hopeless. What's that type of reasoning error called?

Using the opportunity to reinforce patient's knowledge of types of distortions.

P: Selective abstraction. [*Smiles.*] And before you ask, I was over-generalising as well!

T: That's right. [*Patient and therapist laugh.*] Is there anything else that you notice from the data?

P: I'm not sure what you mean.

T: Well, is the control either all internal or all external?

Therapist is now trying to get Margaret to examine her dichotomous thinking on the subject.

P: Oh, you mean that I was doing my black and white bit again?

T: That's it, it came across from looking at the events of the past few days that some things are more in your control than others, but often it's to do with degrees of control.

Margaret had found that particular discussion useful and decided to note the conclusions. She wrote down:

1. I have some degree of control over 75% of the events that happen to me or activities I take part in.
2. Control is not an all or nothing phenomenon. In different situations I have differing degrees of control.

To supplement this, we also looked at how advantageous or disadvantageous it had been for her constantly to put everything that happened to her down to luck or fate. The conclusion was that it was maladaptive. Margaret decided that she would keep a record over the next few weeks of how she could effect change on a day-to-day basis, by simply applying problem-solving techniques to the task in hand. This again was aimed at increasing her sense of control.

The next phase of the discussion about locus of control focused more specifically on her illness. Margaret did not feel she had much control over this in general, e.g. she could not control whether secondaries occurred. However, she stated spontaneously that her compliance with the radiotherapy treatment had been an attempt to reduce this risk as much as possible. We defined Margaret's role in controlling her illness as taking responsibility for being as healthy as possible. The elements of this are listed in Table 5.2.

Table 5.2 Margaret's action list for reducing her anxieties related to her health

Problem	Action
1. Control of anxiety in general	Learn anxiety management techniques Take up yoga again
2. To become as fit as possible	Pay attention to diet Take more exercise (gradually) Stop smoking
3. To understand my illness	To go and seek information actively e.g. at clinic, education material
4. To look for other supports	To make enquiries about support groups in the area

Sessions 5 to 7

These sessions predominantly focused on working on Margaret's list. Her mood was improving and she appeared more relaxed. We reviewed her visit to the hospital to discuss her illness. We examined her automatic thoughts and feelings before and after the visit. Margaret concluded that her depression, anxiety, and hopelessness were all reduced by seeking out information and dealing with the realities of her illness and her prognosis rather than focusing on her fantasies about the situation.

She had started to exercise by walking a mile a day through some fields near her home. Ultimately, she decided she would like to join a health club she had previously been a member of, but she would work towards this in a graded way. In the past, she had managed to give up smoking, but had lapsed and now smoked more than twenty cigarettes a day. To try to aid reducing this, she was shown how to make a 'flash card'. This was a small card that she carried around with her. On it she listed the key reasons for not smoking, e.g. to be healthy, you have to make some effort; think of the money you save; how could you smoke after treatment! This card was available to her to re-read at appropriate moments to maintain her motivation to give up. Margaret managed to stop smoking, and derived considerable pleasure from this success experience. She was worried, however, that she would gain weight. This in fact reinforced her desire to get fit and eat a healthy diet.

During the sessions Margaret learned anxiety management techniques and incorporated these into her assignments. In session 7 we also discussed the possibility of joining a support group. Margaret showed some ambivalence towards this. As a homework assignment she generated a list of the pros and cons of joining.

Session 8

The list of pros and cons seemed to favour making a commitment to a support group. On further exploring her reluctance to take this step it came out that Margaret felt going to such a group might be seen as a sign of personal weakness. (Again, this issue of Margaret's view of a strong person came to the fore.) In addition, Margaret felt she would rather receive support from relatives and friends than from 'strangers'. A theme that came out, however, was that Margaret's behaviour (attempting to be strong and coping) did not allow her friends to offer the response she would like (i.e. caring and supportive). Since her operation, she had become rather withdrawn socially and was feeling lonely. Also she had not spoken in any detail to her daughter or mother about her problems. The agenda for this session was to look at her support network and to examine if she should change her approach.

T: It seems that what you're saying is that you feel you should put on a brave face for your friends?
P: Yeh, I think they expect it from me. People don't want to listen to my moans.
T: Do you listen to theirs?

Instead of taking the stated automatic thought that 'people don't want to listen to my moans' and then going through all the evidence, the therapist decided to check out whether Margaret was applying double standards, a tendency that had been obvious on many occasions previously.

P: Yeh, I'm regarded as a good listener. I never turn people away.
T: Do you mind that you do that for them, but they don't reciprocate?
P: No . . . well, I guess that's not entirely true. [Margaret smiles, an acknowledgement that she knows there is a problem for her here.] Sometimes I feel a bit annoyed. . . .

This line of enquiry proved to be very fruitful and through further questioning we were able to elicit a number of underlying assumptions. Margaret had grown up in an environment (both family and school) where open expression of distress was perceived as weakness. Since then she had been reluctant to confide in people. On one occasion after her husband's death she had talked at length to Rosemary, a close friend. It was later reported back to Margaret that Rosemary had then remarked to someone else that being with Margaret was depressing. This incident confirmed for Margaret her belief that 'weak people are unlovable'. From then on Margaret had avoided expressing any difficulties to others. She acknowledged that she would like more support, but resisted approaching anyone for fear of rejection. (She also demonstrated the belief that 'good people are selfless, bad people are selfish'. According to her definition, however, even talking about her own problems would be selfish.) In addition, Margaret promoted a false self-image of being totally coping and would not accept even tentative offers of support. She constantly failed to assert her own needs in her friendships, she always put others first. The outcome tended to be that failing to assert herself left her feeling frustrated and ultimately angry that people did not support her more, i.e. this rigid pattern of behaviour left Margaret feeling uncomfortable with herself. More importantly, she found her friendships unfulfilling as she concluded that she cared about her friends more than they cared about her.

As a homework assignment Margaret agreed to try to be more open about her difficulties. She agreed to re-establish contact with two of her closest friends and, if the opportunity arose, to tell them about some of her anxieties. With encouragement she also agreed to talk to one of them about her mother's mental health problems. Margaret had never disclosed this to anyone, but was getting worried about her mother's impending return visit to her. These conversations would be used as experiments to:

1. see the effect on Margaret's self-image of allowing people to know about her true anxieties and feelings; and
2. to look for evidence that expressing these anxieties would lead to rejection.

A further assumption came to light in these discussions, namely that Margaret also held the belief that 'I cannot be happy if I am independent of others', i.e. she desired a close network of supportive friends. Again, she was encouraged to make contact with her friends. This statement was also explored by asking her several key questions. Could she identify people without close personal relationships who were happy? Were there people who were in a close relationship who were unhappy? Were there activities that she did or could enjoy alone? Could she only feel happy in other people's company? Lastly, could we distinguish between what she wanted (i.e. was desirable) and what was needed (i.e. fundamental to survival). We established that, whilst she desired close relationships and gained many positive benefits from them, they were not absolutely essential to her.

We also looked at Margaret's relationship with her daughter and mother. Her daughter had apparently withdrawn from her. The discussion suggested that Margaret's daughter was probably scared about her mother's illness and was uncertain about what the future held. Margaret (in an attempt to be strong and coping and to try to protect her daughter) had not shared her anxieties with her, nor had she shared any of the information she had about her illness and prognosis. She decided to tell her daughter the information she had gained from her visit to the clinic and from the educational booklets she had been reading. Margaret also agreed to ring her mother and try to talk through her recent difficulties.

Sessions 9 and 10

The very positive feedback and support that Margaret received from relatives and friends surprised her and helped her adapt her coping strategies. She no longer felt she had to be invincible to keep her friends. Margaret and her daughter started exercising at home to 'workout' tapes. This gave them a joint activity that they both enjoyed that allowed them to spend some time together and work on their relationship. Over the next few weeks we repeatedly tested out her rigid schemata and tried to develop more flexible, adaptive assumptions.

The last few sessions focused on helping Margaret identify stress-provoking situations and thoughts. We included her perfectionism, her difficulty in asserting herself and her difficulty in asking for help or confiding in friends as stressors, again reinforcing the advantages of relinquishing these ideas and patterns of behaviour. Many of these issues overlapped with other aspects of Margaret's problems and had been dealt with in previous sessions. However, she also read some self-help material on perfectionism, e.g. *Feeling Good* (Burns 1980), and on assertiveness training, e.g. *Your Perfect Right* (Alberti and Emmons 1975).

Finally, we spent time dealing with Margaret's anxieties about leaving therapy and being her own cognitive therapist. She was still debating whether to join a support group but on balance was now in favour as she felt that anxieties about her health and how to cope would never fully disappear. What seemed important, however, was that she no longer suffered from incapacitating anxiety and depression.

Outcome

Objective data from the final CBT session are given in Table 5.1, Margaret was still alive and free of cancer at 4-year follow-up. She had not required any referrals for psychiatric help.

Conclusions

CBT is widely used to treat a variety of emotional disorders. It successfully exposes people's misinterpretations of reality. But in this case, on first analysis, the reality is bad. The patient is confronted with a diagnosis of cancer and an uncertain future. Her past history of depression in response to stressful life events made her vulnerable to the current illness. However, further examination reveals that this vulnerability was compounded by rigid, unrealistic expectations of herself. A prominent and organising schema seemed to be a belief that in order to be liked she should not manifest any weakness in the face of stress. The Dysfunctional Attitudes Scale (DAS) demonstrated further vulnerability with respect to high scores on issues of control and perfectionism. Having cancer made this woman feel powerless. This rapidly generalised to all aspects of her life. Her most frequent cognitive distortions were selective abstraction, dichotomous thinking, and overgeneralisation.

Through CBT she regained control over those aspects of her life that she *could* control and took on as much responsibility as possible for her health status. However, though she had initially arrived at the clinic in crisis because she had cancer, the CBT sessions also afforded an opportunity for the patient to re-examine her coping strategies as applied to other situations and to correct her distorted interpretations of her subjective reality. One of the most significant sessions in reducing her hopelessness and alleviating her distress revolved around how she coped with her relationship with her mother. This session had engaged the patient in therapy; she went away from that session knowing that the techniques could be effective and seeing the benefit that changing her perceptions had on her emotional state.

This is a single case study and many aspects of the application of CBT to cancer patients described earlier in the chapter (e.g. lowered self-esteem in the face of mutilating surgery) were not included. However, it does offer some validation of the view that CBT can be a powerful tool in treating the physically ill in general and cancer patients in particular.

References

Alberti, R.E. and Emmons, M.L. (1975) *Your Perfect Right: A Guide to Assertive Behaviour*, San Luis Obispo, CA: Impact.

American Psychiatric Association (1987) *Diagnostic and Statistical Manual of Mental Disorders 3rd (R) edition*, Washington, DC: American Psychiatric Press.

Beck, A.T., Emery, G., and Greenberg, R.L. (1985) *Anxiety Disorders and Phobias: A Cognitive Perspective*, New York: Basic.

Beck, A.T., Rush, A.J., Shaw, B.F., and Emery, G. (1979) *Cognitive Therapy of Depression*, Chichester: Wiley.

Blackburn, I.M., Bishop, S., Glen, I.M., Whalley, L.J., and Christie, J.E. (1981) 'The efficacy of cognitive therapy in depression: a treatment trial using cognitive therapy and pharmacotherapy, each alone and in combination', *British Journal of Psychiatry* 39: 181–9.

Bloom, J.R. (1982) 'Social support, accommodation to stress and adjustment to breast cancer', *Social Science and Medicine* 16: 1329–38.

Bloom, J.R., Ross, R.D., and Burnell, G.M. (1978) 'The effect of social support on patient adjustment after breast surgery', *Patient Counselling and Health Education* 1: 50–9.

Bradley, L.A. (1985) 'Effects of cognitive behavioural therapy on pain behaviour of rheumatoid arthritis patients: preliminary outcomes', *Scandinavian Journal of Behaviour Therapy* 14: 51–64.

Burns, D. (1980) *Feeling Good: The New Mood Therapy*, New York: William Morrow.

Dean, C., Chetty, U., and Forrest, A. (1983) 'Effects of immediate breast reconstruction on psychological morbidity after mastectomy', *Lancet* 1: 459–62.

Devlin, H.B., Plant, J.A., and Griffin, M. (1971) 'Aftermath of surgery for anorectal cancer', *British Medical Journal* 3: 413–18.

Gomez, J. (1987) *Liaison Psychiatry: Mental Health Problems in the General Hospital*, London: Croom Helm.

Gordon, W.A., Freidenbergs, I., Diller, L., *et al.* (1980) 'Efficacy of psychological intervention with cancer patients', *Journal of Consulting and Clinical Psychology* 48: 743–59.

Greer, S. (1985) 'Cancer: psychiatric aspects', in K. Granville-Grossman (ed.) *Recent Advances in Clinical Psychiatry: Number 5*, London: Churchill Livingstone.

Greer, S., Marcus, T., and Pettingale, K.W. (1979) 'Psychological response to breast cancer: effect on outcome', *Lancet 2*: 785–7.

Hibbard, M.R., Gordon, Egelko, and Langer, K. (1987) 'Issues in the diagnosis and cognitive therapy of depression in brain-damaged individuals', in A. Freeman and V. Greenwood (eds) *Cognitive Therapy: Applications in Psychiatric and Medical Settings*, New York: Human Sciences Press Inc.

Holland, J.C., Hughes, A., Silberfarb, P., *et al.* (1983) 'Patients with depression in pancreatic and gastric cancer' (abstract), *Proceedings of the American Society of Clinical Oncology* 2: 127.

Holland, J.C., Rowland, J., Lebovits, A., and Rusalem, R. (1979) 'Reactions to cancer treatment: assessment of emotional response to adjuvant radiotherapy as a guide to planned intervention', *Psychiatric Clinics of North America* 2: 347–57.

Hughson, A., Cooper, A.F., McCardle, C.F., Russell, A.R., and Smith, D.C. (1980) 'Psychiatric morbidity in disease-free survivors following radiotherapy and adjuvant chemotherapy for breast cancer: a two year follow-up study', *British Journal of Surgery* 67: 370.

Larcombe, N.A. and Wilson, P.H. (1984) 'An evaluation of cognitive therapy for depression in patients with multiple sclerosis', *British Journal of Psychiatry* 45: 366–71.

Levine, P.M., Silberfarb, P.M., and Lipowski, Z.J. (1978) 'Mental disorders in cancer patients', *Cancer* 42: 1385–91.

McIntosh, J. (1974) 'Processes of communication, information seeking and control associated with cancer', *Social Science and Medicine* 8: 167–87.

Maguire, P., Hopwood, P., Tarrier, N., and Howell, T. (1985) 'Treatment of depression in cancer patients', *Acta Psychiatrica Scandanavica* (Suppl) 320: 81–4.

Massie, M.J. and Holland, J.C. (1984) 'Psychiatry and oncology', in L. Grinspoon (ed.) *Psychiatry Update: Volume III*, Washington, DC: American Psychiatric Press.

Morris, T. (1979) 'Psychological adjustment to mastectomy', *Cancer Treatments Review* 6: 41–61.

Pearce. S. and Richardson, P.H. (1987) 'Chronic pain: treatment', in S. Lindsay and G. Powell (eds) *A Handbook of Clinical Adult Psychology*, Aldershot: Gower.

Rush, A.J., Beck, A.T., Kovacs, M., and Hollon, S.D. (1977) 'Comparative efficacy of cognitive therapy and imipramine in the treatment of depressed outpatients', *Cognitive Therapy and Research* 1: 17–37.

Schmale, A.H., Morrow, G.R., Davis, A., *et al.* (1982) 'Pre-treatment behavioural profiles associated with subsequent psychological adjustment in radiation therapy patients: a prospective study', *International Journal of Psychiatry in Medicine* 12: 187–95.

Schonfield, J. (1972) 'Psychological factors related to delayed return to an earlier life-style in successfully treated cancer patients', *Psychosomatic Medicine* 45: 163–9.

Schwarz, S.P. and Blanchard, E.B. (1986) 'Behavioural treatment of irritable bowel syndrome; a 1 year follow-up study', *Biofeedback Self Regulation* 11: 189–98.

Scott, J. (1988) 'Cognitive therapy with depressed inpatients', in P. Trower and W. Dryden (eds) *Developments in Cognitive Psychotherapy*, London: Sage Publications. In press.

Silberfarb, P., Maurer, L.H., and Crouthamel, C.S. (1980) 'Psychological aspects of neoplastic disease: I: Functional status of breast cancer patients during different treatment regimes', *American Journal of Psychiatry* 137: 450–5.

Sobel, H.J. and Worden, J.W. (1980) *Helping Cancer Patients Cope: A Problem Solving Intervention Programme for Health Care Professionals*, New York: Guilford Press.

Stern, M.J., Plionis, E., and Kaslow, L. (1984) 'Group process expectations and outcome with post-myocardial infarction patients', *General Hospital Psychiatry* 6: 101–8.

Tan, S.Y. and Bruni, J. (1986) 'Cognitive behaviour therapy with adults with epilepsy: a controlled outcome study', *Epilepsia* 27: 225–33.

Valliant, P.M. and Leith, B. (1986) 'Impact of relaxation training and cognitive therapy on coronary patients post-surgery', *Psychological Reports* 59: 1271–8.

Weisman, A.D. and Worden, J.W. (1977) *Coping and Vulnerability in Cancer Patients: A Research Report*, Boston, MA: Massachusetts General Hospital.

Williams, J.M.G. (1984) *The Psychological Treatment of Depression: A Guide to the Theory and Practice of Cognitive Therapy*, Beckenham: Croom Helm, and New York: Free Press.

Worden, J.W. (1987) 'Cognitive therapy with cancer patients', in A. Freeman and V. Greenwood (eds) *Cognitive Therapy: Applications in Psychiatric and Medical Settings*,

Chapter six

Eating disorders

Shelley Channon and Jane Wardle

Introduction

Anorexia nervosa and bulimia nervosa are closely related disorders characterised by intense concern about body shape and the use of strategies to avoid weight gain. Anorexia nervosa is specifically marked by severe emaciation, and bulimia nervosa is marked by frequent episodes of binge eating (American Psychiatric Association 1980; Russell 1979, 1981). Although current diagnostic systems differentiate the two disorders, the distinction between them is clouded by several features, including (1) the similarities between them, (2) the frequency of binge eating in anorexic patients, (3) the fact that many patients move between the two diagnoses and (4) the difficulty in defining normal weight for an individual (Fairburn and Garner 1986).

The diagnostic difficulties suggest that anorexia nervosa and bulimia nervosa might best be understood as manifestations of the same core disorder of body image, with the symptom profile modified by the level of weight loss and the predominant methods of weight control (Fairburn and Garner 1986). This assumption underlies much of the recent therapeutic work on eating disorders, in that procedures for modifying concerns about body shape, fear of weight gain, restrictive eating patterns, and fear of loss of control over eating are common to both disorders, with techniques for managing binge eating or weight restoration being included where necessary.

The incidence of eating disorders, particularly normal-weight bulimia nervosa, is said to be rising (Crisp *et al.* 1976; Willi and Grossman 1986), no doubt in part because of the prevailing western cultural preference for a thin appearance in women (Garner *et al.* 1980). Once established, eating disorders run a serious and chronic course. Toner *et al.* (1986) followed up fifty-five anorexic patients treated previously at the Clarke Institute in Toronto. They found that about one-third were asymptomatic and just under one-third were unchanged, with no difference between restrictive and bulimic subgroups. Five patients (two bulimic and three restrictive) had died. Psychometric assessment revealed continuing disturbances in attitudes to eating and weight, and in addition there was a high incidence of anxiety and depression. These results confirm other findings that eating disorders are resistant to change (Hsu 1980; Schwartz and Thompson 1981; Abraham *et al*. 1983; Swift *et al*. 1987).

Treatment for anorexia nervosa has undergone several changes over the past few decades. Initially bed-rest, naso-gastric feeding, and a variety of different pharmacotherapies were the main prescriptions, directed principally at weight restoration. With the advent of behavioural treatment programmes (e.g. Bachrach *et al*. 1965), a regime based on reinforcing weight gain became popular, and more or less formal versions of this remain in use for very underweight patients (Agras 1987). Most weight-gain regimes are fairly successful in the short term but the relapse rate is high, and even if weight is stabilised, many patients continue to show disturbances in their attitudes to eating and weight (Morgan and Russell 1975). This has prompted the development of treatments directed at the specific cognitive and behavioural disturbances which characterise these patients (Garner and Bemis 1982; Cooper and Fairburn 1984).

Bulimia nervosa has been identified much more recently (Russell 1979) and treatments have been predominantly in the cognitive–behavioural domain (Fairburn 1981; Garner 1986; Wardle 1987a).

There are still relatively few controlled studies evaluating the outcome of cognitive–behavioural treatment, especially for anorexia nervosa. Uncontrolled case series and cross-over designs comparing two treatments constitute the major evidence for the efficacy of these techniques (Fairburn 1981; Smith and Medlik 1983; Cooper and Fairburn 1984; Johnson *et al*. 1986; Wolchik *et al*. 1986; Wilson *et al*. 1986). The few controlled studies that have been reported find that cognitive behaviour therapy is a promising treatment for bulimia nervosa (Lacey 1983; Kirkley *et al*. 1985; Fairburn *et al*. 1986).

The outcome for anorexia nervosa is less clear, and undoubtedly more work is needed to identify the critical ingredients of cognitive–behavioural treatment programmes, to improve the therapeutic impact, and to identify the patient characteristics which are associated with a successful outcome (Channon *et al*. 1989). However, despite their relatively short history, treatment procedures which are broadly cognitive–behaviourally based have proven popular and acceptable to patients and have opened new avenues for these difficult disorders.

Cognitive behaviour therapy for eating disorders has developed from a systematic analysis of the characteristic emotional, cognitive, and behavioural disturbances. The treatment programmes draw widely upon basic techniques for anxiety reduction, self-management of behaviour, and modification of maladaptive cognitions. Compared to cognitive therapy for some disorders, depression for example, the behavioural components of eating disorders are given greater emphasis in treatment. This is because behavioural disturbances (e.g. starving or vomiting) are central features of the disorder which have to be controlled.

The aim of the present chapter is to describe the application of the main elements of a cognitive–behavioural treatment programme. Clinical examples are given to illustrate the practice and the problems of the procedures.

Case history

Carol's history is very similar to that of many anorexics. She was referred through her general practitioner to a unit specialising in eating disorders. At the time of referral she was a 19-year-old hotel receptionist who had left home a year before to take up her present job. She had done a secretarial course after leaving school at 16 with five 'O' levels, and had worked for a market research firm for eighteen months. Until taking up hotel work she had lived at home in a small town sixty miles away with her mother, sister, and stepfather. Her decision to leave home had been partially prompted by her mother's remarriage, which she had initially found difficult to accept. Since leaving she had maintained regular contact and now felt that she got on well with them all.

She now lived in a staff flat which she shared with three other hotel employees. They all worked shift hours, and days off were often during the week rather than at weekends. Carol liked her fellow workers, but had not got to know them very well as yet. She tended to work overtime hours when extra work was available, in order to save for driving lessons and buying a car. Otherwise she would read or knit, go shopping, visit her family or occasionally go to the pub with the others from the flat.

Her presenting problem was progressive weight loss over the previous fifteen months, with amenorrhoea for the past nine months. Her mother had become worried about her daughter's deteriorating health, and had finally persuaded her to seek treatment. She had a history of treatment for anorexia nervosa which had resulted in one in-patient admission nearly three years previously. At this time she had presented with low weight and depressed mood, but no bulimic symptoms. She had apparently responded well to treatment, regained her weight, and maintained it until around the time of leaving home. There was no other psychiatric history in the family, although her younger sister did show a tendency to diet.

Carol finally agreed to seek help because she herself had become concerned that she was losing control over her eating. In the previous few months she had started to go on binges where she would eat large amounts of left-over food from the hotel kitchen. This now occurred several times a week, usually in the evenings if she was not working. At other times she restricted her food in an attempt to eat a 'healthy' diet, but felt continuously preoccupied with thoughts of food. In the first six months of dieting she had lost a stone (14 pounds) slowly from a premorbid level of nearly 9 stone (126 pounds). Since this time weight loss appeared to have escalated until she reached 6 stone 2 pounds (86 pounds), at which weight she looked emaciated. She also described low mood and physical exhaustion in carrying out her job.

The general issues raised by a case such as Carol's will be discussed next, before returning to their specific application to Carol.

Medical assessment

In any out-patient treatment for disorders of eating and weight, the issue of medical involvement should be considered since there are a number of physiological correlates of severe weight loss, obesity, or binge eating and vomiting or purging which may need to be closely monitored (see Table 6.1). The severity of the particular features of the illness will determine the need to collaborate with a sympathetic physician who will assess physical well-being at regular intervals. For a discussion of the physical complications of eating disorders, see Garfinkel and Garner (1982). Carol's physical condition was assessed by a psychiatrist attached to the Eating Disorders Unit. Despite severe emaciation, she did not appear to have any serious complications which would require immediate hospitalisation. It was therefore decided that she would receive a trial of cognitive–behavioural treatment, and would be examined physically every four weeks.

Historically, attempts to treat anorexia nervosa were initially almost entirely hospital-based and aimed at rapid weight gain through a variety of operant and drug methods. However, follow-up studies found that weight restoration in hospital was not necessarily maintained after discharge (e.g. Morgan and Russell 1975), and Channon and de Silva (1985) showed that improvements in attitudes to eating and weight were only partially maintained at follow-up. The emphasis has therefore shifted towards finding more effective out-patient treatments. From a long-term perspective, out-patient treatment has a number of advantages over hospitalisation. First, patients are often very resistant to the idea of going into hospital, and may be more willing to accept out-patient treatment. Second, out-patient treatment provides the opportunity to learn to deal with factors in the environment which may maintain the presenting difficulties. Hospital can provide a temporary respite, but upon return to the community the same issues are likely to arise again. Finally, in out-patient treatment the responsibility remains firmly in the hands of the patient, whereas hospitalisation can be perceived as a handing over of responsibility to the caring team.

Despite these drawbacks, there are several situations where hospital care offers advantages over out-patient treatment. The first consideration must be the preservation of life in cases of extreme weight loss or medical complications. It may be required for the care of a patient who is felt to be a serious suicide risk. There is a case to be made for considering admission for patients who are not in acute physical danger, but who remain chronically underweight over an extended period of time and do not respond to out-patient treatment. Hospitalisation can also provide an opportunity for interrupting the vicious circle of binge eating and vomiting for severe bulimic patients who do not achieve control in an out-patient setting.

It is often necessary to set individual thresholds beyond which admission to hospital will be required, such as continued weight loss below a certain weight, or low potassium levels over a specified period of time. It is difficult to specify an exact weight criterion, since the degree of emaciation which will cause concern will vary individually, but once weight drops below about 70 per cent of average then close monitoring should be instigated. In any such negotiation, it is important that hospitalisation be presented not as a punishment, but rather as a means of regaining control over behaviour which the patient is currently unable to regulate. Discussion of the possible need for hospitalisation should be held at an early stage in the treatment if it seems likely that this may be necessary, with careful explanation of why admission will be considered. The therapist may then develop an alliance with the patient focused on avoiding the need for hospitalisation, and with clear goals for producing improvement in an out-patient setting. In Carol's case it was agreed that if weight loss progressed, or if any new signs of ill-health developed, she would be seen more urgently by the physician and the need for hospitalisation would be reviewed.

Psychological assessment

The assessment of eating disturbance and body size concerns must address several different areas. A clinical history is useful in giving clues to broad problem areas and possible causal and maintaining factors. Standardised questionnaires, self-monitoring methods, and experimental techniques may then be used to supplement information obtained from clinical interviews. Table 6.1 provides a guide to some important aspects of assessment which could be taken into consideration. A detailed knowledge of eating habits, weight fluctuation, and dysfunctional thoughts and attitudes to eating and body size should form the basis of the assessment. Selection amongst the different problem areas and assessment tools would depend upon the particular difficulties of each individual patient. For a more detailed discussion of the investigation of eating and weight disorders, see Wardle (1987b).

The first session with Carol included discussion of her dieting and binge

Table 6.1 The assessment of eating disorders

Problem area	Type of information	Method of collection
Body fat	Weight	Scales
	1. ideal weight tables (e.g. Metropolitan Life Insurance 1983)	
	2. Ponderal index – weight ÷ height squared (Florey 1970)	
	Skinfold thickness – amount of subcutaneous fat	Callipers
Physical complications	Weight loss	Medical examination/laboratory tests
	1. severe muscle weakness	
	2. susceptibility to infection	
	3. hypertension	
	4. amenorrhoea	
	5. infertility	
	6. osteoporosis	
	Bulimia or rapid refeeding	
	1. gastric dilatation and perforation	
	2. sodium overload with oedema and cardiac failure	
	Self-induced vomiting	
	1. dental erosion	
	2. parotid swelling	
	3. hypokalaemic alkalosis	
	4. renal disease	
	5. cardiac arrhythmias	
	6. tetany	
	7. muscle weakness	
	Laxative abuse	
	1. hypokalaemic alkalosis	
	2. colonic denervation and atony	
Eating behaviour	Type of food eaten	Food diary/dietary interview/ behavioural test
	1. protein, fat, carbohydrate, vitamins, minerals, etc.	
	2. sweet versus savoury food intake	

		Assessment method
	Pattern of eating	Food diary
	1. meals versus snacks	
	2. regular versus erratic eating	
	3. avoidance of specific foods or situations	
	4. speed of eating and amount of chewing	
	Responses to food	
	1. amount eaten	
	2. speed of eating	
	Fluids and alcohol intake	
	Binge eating	
	1. types of food eaten	
	2. frequency of binges	
	3. precipitating factors	
	4. urge to binge	
Compensatory behaviours	Vomiting, laxative abuse	
	1. frequency	
	2. precipitating factors	
	3. type of laxatives and quantity taken	
	Exercise	
	1. frequency and duration	
	2. type of exercise taken	
Affective responses	Anxiety	Subjective ratings
	1. before, during, and after eating	
	2. about weight gain and getting on scales	
	Obsessionality	
	Depression	Questionnaires, e.g. Rosenberg (1965)
	1. low self-esteem	Questionnaires, e.g. Beck Depression Inventory (Beck et al. 1961)
	2. severity of depressed mood	Clinical interview
	3. suicidal ideation	

Table 6.1 (continued)

Problem area	Type of information	Method of collection
Cognitive and perceptual factors	Overvalued ideas about dieting, thinness and body size	Recording of dysfunctional thoughts
	Fear of eating and weight gain	Self-report questionnaires, e.g. EDI (Garner et al. 1983)
	Fears of loss of control over eating and body size	Recording dysfunctional thoughts DEBQ (Van Strien et al. 1986)
	Preoccupation with food	Stroop test (Channon et al. 1987b)
	Attractiveness of specific body parts	
	1. ratings of a list of body parts	Rating scale, e.g. Pearlson et al. (1981)
	Body size estimation	
	1. techiques measuring specific body parts	E.g. moving lights (Slade and Russell 1973)
	2. techniques assessing entire body image	E.g. distorting photos (Garner et al. 1976)

Figure 6.1 Recording form

DAILY DIARY   Date ....   Name: ....

Time	Place/company/ feelings	Hunger (0–100)	Craving (0–100)	Food eaten	Anxiety (0–100)	Difficulty stopping (0–100)	Binge/not binge

Please complete this as soon as possible after eating   Also mark down any episodes of vomiting (V) or laxatives (L) eating, and she was asked to keep a diary which included the type and amount of food eaten, the cognitive, emotional, and situational preceding events, and ratings of anxiety, hunger, and craving. During discussion it emerged that she also vomited after every binge, and she was asked to keep a note of this on the diary sheets. An example of the type of recording form used may be seen in Figure 6.1. She was initially asked to keep these records daily for two weeks, to form a baseline. Records for the first week revealed that most of the time she restricted her eating to about 800 calories daily, and avoided sweet foods, fats, and most carbohydrates. She would eat cereal and skimmed milk for breakfast, cottage cheese and green salad for lunch, and have an extremely small portion of the hotel evening meal for supper, followed by a natural yoghurt. During restrained eating times she was very anxious about the prospect of eating what she saw as 'bad' or 'forbidden' food. She had eating binges two or three times a week, and these took place in the evenings after she had finished working. Then she would eat numerous sweets, cakes, and desserts until she felt intolerably full, when she would make herself vomit, and occasionally take two Senokot laxative tablets. She binged mainly when she was alone and was feeling bored and lonely, but also when very tempting food was readily available.

Carol was weighed, and her weight was calculated with reference to both ideal weight tables (Metropolitan Life Insurance 1983) and body mass index (Florey 1970). It emerged that she was currently 68 per cent of the ideal population weight-for-height, with a body mass index of 14.6. This represented a serious degree of emaciation, indicating that regular medical assessment would be important in ensuring that she could safely be treated as an out-patient. She reported that she would prefer to be about half a stone heavier, but was terrified of losing control over her weight and becoming fat.

She also filled in self-report questionnaires. The Eating Disorders Inventory (Garner et al. 1983) was used to measure attitudes to food and eating. This showed her to have high scores on the Drive for Thinness and Body Dissatisfaction scales, and a fairly high Bulimia score. The Dutch Eating Behaviour Questionnaire (DEBQ) (Van Strien et al. 1986) was used to measure the degree of control exercised over eating ('restraint') and responsiveness to external or emotional eating cues. She scored highly on restraint and emotional eating. She was also asked to complete the Beck Depression Inventory (Beck et al. 1961) and a self-esteem scale (Rosenberg 1965). These suggested that she was fairly depressed (BDI score = 22), and her pattern of responding on the Rosenberg scale indicated her self-esteem to be low. Body image satisfaction was assessed by asking her to rate how satisfied she felt with a range of body parts, showing her to be particularly dissatisfied with her stomach and thighs.

Treatment plan

On the basis of this assessment, it was clear that the most urgent aims of treatment were to help Carol gain control over both her progressive weight loss and her bingeing and vomiting, since these behaviours presented a significant risk to her health. This would necessitate addressing the relationship between the cognitions and behaviours which were maintaining her current problems. A second aim of treatment would be to examine the factors relating to her low mood and self-esteem, to see how closely these were linked to her eating problems. Finally, treatment would aim to address wider aspects of functioning such as career, family, and social issues.

The results of the assessment so far were discussed with Carol at the second session. A formulation of her problems was presented to her using the cognitive–behavioural model put forward by Garner and Bemis (1982), and the outline of a treatment based on these principles was negotiated with her. The treatment plan can be seen in Table 6.2. It was agreed that sessions would take place on a weekly basis for the first 2 or 3 months, and that this would gradually be reduced depending upon her rate of progress.

Table 6.2 Treatment plan

1. Present cognitive–behavioural model of anorexia nervosa and rationale for treatment.
2. Provide information and education about:
    (i) the dangers of weight loss, binge eating, and vomiting
    (ii) cultural pressures on eating and body size
    (iii) dietary restraint and binge eating
    (iv) nutrition and normal eating patterns
    (v) normal weight regulation and fluctuation
3. Increase amount and range of foods eaten to reduce dietary restraint and restore weight to a normal healthy level.
4. Identify dysfunctional cognitions associated with eating, weight, and body size.
5. Challenge dysfunctional thoughts through a collaborative, didactic approach.
6. Address other areas such as self-esteem, depression, career, family, and social issues.

Developing motivation for treatment

In the case of anorexia nervosa, the initial contact with a treatment centre is commonly made by people other than the patient herself (we will refer to the individual patient as 'her'; the majority of anorexia nervosa and bulimia nervosa patients are female). Referrals by family and friends who are concerned about progressive weight loss are often valuable in identifying the existence of a problem, but reluctance or active hostility on the part of the patient who arrives for treatment in this manner is not unusual. Bulimic patients who do not lose a substantial amount of weight may find it easier to conceal their difficulties from relatives, and are more likely to pursue treatment in order to control their binge eating. The other central issue in accepting treatment may be focused on the concept of desirable weight, since a central feature in both anorexic and bulimic disorders may be the pursuit of thinness and a refusal to accept the necessity for a body weight within or even above the normal range. The first task in developing a therapeutic alliance is to anticipate ambivalence about reaching or maintaining a normal body weight. Typically patients are keen to get rid of preoccupation with eating and size, and to gain control of symptoms such as craving and binge eating, but not at the expense of weight gain.

It is important to understand the degree of fear which may be aroused by the prospect of change through accepting treatment, particularly when there is a long history to the problem. Rituals around eating or resisting food, calorie counting, getting on the scales to monitor weight, and so on, may occupy a substantial part of daily life and even be perceived as valuable in that they may serve to maintain food restriction and emphasise the value of thinness. The therapist's ability to empathise with the conflicting emotions which are likely to be experienced is likely to be important in gaining the patient's trust. It is also helpful to show tolerance and lack of surprise at symptoms which may be presented by the patient as shocking confessions, such as the amount of food consumed in a binge. The patient's beliefs, such as perceiving herself to be extremely fat, should be accepted as currently genuine for her, even if she is severely emaciated. As with the example below, taken from the case study of Carol, the beliefs can be reinterpreted as a part of the overall problem.

T: Do you see body size and weight as a problem for you at the moment?

P: I'm worried about getting fat.

T: Do you think you are fat right now?

P: I feel very fat at the moment, it's all on my stomach and thighs.

T: How can you tell that you are fat?

P: When I get on the scales I'm terrified in case my weight goes up a pound, and I can tell from my clothes if they get tighter at all.

T: How do you think you look to me – would I see you as very fat?

P: You'll probably say that I'm too thin. I know I've lost a lot of weight, but I feel so fat.

T: So you realise that you are thinner than most people at the moment, but you feel so worried about your weight that it doesn't seem that way to you. Is that right?

P: Yes – I know other people think I'm too thin but I want to lose some more weight.

T: I think that's part of the illness you have – it doesn't seem to matter how much weight people lose, they always feel that they're too fat and want to lose more. I expect that when you started dieting, you thought that everything would be fine after you'd lost some weight, but after you got there it didn't seem enough?

P: I suppose so – I don't know if I'll be satisfied even when I've lost some more weight.

T: So it's important that we distinguish between your actual weight loss, which is very worrying because you are so underweight at the moment, and your worries about feeling fat, which you probably have even at a very low weight, and which are part of the illness you have.

There may be difficulties in persuading the patient to acknowledge that there are any real problems for her which need to be addressed in treatment. It can at times be useful to use strategies such as stressing the specific dangers of the conditions, and spelling out the consequences of continuing to lose weight or vomit/abuse laxatives in order to increase motivation for treatment.

P: I wouldn't mind if I could just put on a little bit of weight gradually – but I know I wouldn't be able to stay there, I'd just get fat like I used to be, and I couldn't stand it.

T: That's something we can work on together. You're bound to be frightened of putting on weight, but you know that you can't go on at this level – it's too much of a strain on your body. Do you notice that you don't feel as well as you used to?

P: I know I get very tired lately, more than I used to.

T: I expect you do – you probably notice it's more effort to climb stairs, and harder to keep warm, and things like that. Do you know why that is?

P: Not really.

T: Well, as you get thinner you use up more energy than you take in, don't you. Do you know where that energy comes from?

P: I suppose it comes from fat on my body.

T: That's right, it does come from body fat – but there's not much fat left on your body now, is there? You can tell that if you just pinch the skin together on your arm, for instance, and you'll see that there's hardly any fat under the skin. So that means that when your body has used up most of the fatty tissue, it has to take energy from the muscles – and that includes your heart muscle and diaphragm muscle, not just your arms and legs and so on.

P: Is that why I get so tired?

T: I think it's one of the reasons. And you can see why it makes it important for you to put on weight, to take the strain off your heart and the rest of your body. Vomiting puts a big strain on your body as well, you lose the essential minerals that you need like potassium, and that makes it harder for your kidneys to work properly.

P: It sounds a bit frightening – do you think I've already done much damage?

This can be particularly difficult in cases where people have been ill for a long time, and none of the supposed consequences of practising food restriction or compensatory techniques has actually happened to them. It may then be useful to point out not only the acute dangers of cardiac or respiratory failure, but the longer-term risks of kidney damage and osteoporosis, and growth retardation for younger patients.

Rationale for treatment

In persuading patients to accept treatment, a clear rationale should be provided which gives an account of the development of the disorder, and a logical basis for intervention which naturally follows on from this. A detailed descriptive model of the development of anorexia nervosa may be obtained from Garner and Bemis (1982) or Slade (1982).

These describe how an external stressor such as examinations or an internal stressor such as puberty interact with a vulnerable personality type. Dieting is perceived as a solution to these difficulties, and weight loss is initially reinforced both externally by other people and the cultural value system, and internally by a sense of achievement. Social withdrawal becomes increasingly prominent in order to avoid situations involving eating, and this increases the opportunity for preoccupation with eating and body size to develop. An experimental study of the effects of starvation on normal volunteers conducted during the Second World War by Keys et al. (1950) provides evidence of numerous effects of food deprivation such as preoccupation and concern with eating which closely resemble many of the characteristics of anorexic patients. Garner and Bemis (1982) describe how dieting continues to be reinforced by both successful weight loss and fear of weight gain. They emphasise that losing weight rather than being thin becomes the critical factor, maintained by the development of a value system which views thinness as of fundamental importance.

Developmental models of bulimia again place great emphasis on the cultural value system which holds thinness to be a desirable goal. Several authors have suggested that binge eating is caused by food restriction (e.g. Polivy and Herman 1984; Wardle and Beinart 1981; Wardle 1987a). This link is based on parallels between the counter-regulation displayed by dieters who receive a preload of food, and eating binges in patients who attempt to restrict their food severely at other times. Symptoms such as cravings, eating binges, and fears of losing control may then be viewed as a response to the breakdown of strict cognitive control. The eating binges experienced by many of the volunteers in the Keys et al. (1950) semi-starvation study provide further evidence for this viewpoint.

In the following excerpt, the relationship between dieting and binge eating has been described to Carol, and the therapist is helping her to understand its relevance in her particular case.

T: How do you feel after a day where you haven't eaten anything except yoghurt and cottage cheese?

P: I feel really good.

T: I expect it seems that you have achieved something – is that right?

P: Yes, definitely.

T: What happens if you are near to some of your favourite fattening foods?

P: I don't feel tempted, unless something's gone wrong or I'm bored or something.

T: And then?

P: Then I just seem to lose control – I can't stop myself from eating it, and once I start, I think I might as well carry on . . .

T: So once you've broken the rules, you think it's too late and you might as well give up?

P: I suppose that's what happens.

T: Can you see how that might be connected with what we were saying about dieting leading to cravings for food?

P: You mean I get cravings because I'm trying not to eat any of the things I really like?

T: That's right – the more you tell yourself they're not allowed, the more you start to think about them and want to eat them.

P: But that makes it impossible – I can't just stop worrying and thinking about it.

T: That's why it's important for us to work together on the dieting, not just the binge eating.

Providing information and education

A crucial component of cognitive–behavioural approaches is the emphasis on providing information and education about a number of areas related to current concerns. Topics might usefully include nutrition, weight regulation, and the input–output factors affecting energy balance; cues for hunger and satiety; the type and amount of food eaten by normal eaters, and reasons for eating including social and emotional ones; set-point theory of weight, and experimental studies of starvation and counter-regulation; the link between dieting and bingeing; and cultural values and pressures to achieve a lower-than-average weight, combined with data suggesting a steady increase in actual population weights.

An excellent summary of this type of information is provided in a chapter by Garner *et al.* (1985), and it provides ideal material for handing out to patients to read outside the sessions. Provision of reading material may range from academic literature on issues such as the effects of starvation and restrained eating (e.g. Wardle 1987a) through to the personal accounts of illness which have begun to appear in the literature (e.g. MacLeod 1981; Roche 1984), and which may serve to help people realise that they are not alone in their misery. The choice of reading material will depend partly on the patient's level of education and intellectual ability. Setting homework tasks to find out about other people's behaviour may also be useful in getting patients to question their assumptions, such as 'normal people only eat when they're hungry', or 'normal people only maintain a normal weight by eating "healthy" foods'.

In order to explore the postulated link between food restriction and binge eating further in Carol's case, it was agreed during the session that she would do several things. First, she would pay particular attention to the craving ratings in her food diary, to see whether these were related to hunger and to the types of food she was eating. Second, she decided to ask one of her flatmates about whether she attempted to restrict her intake of fattening foods, and how she felt in terms of anxiety, craving, and urge to binge if she did eat anything fattening. Third, she took a copy of the Garner et al. (1985) chapter home to read.

Weight restoration

If patients are severely emaciated, the most urgent aim of treatment is to restore weight to a safer level. The focus of weight restoration should be on the need to return to a normal, healthy weight, and setting a target range within which weight will be maintained is more realistic than aiming for an exact poundage. One criterion for determining a healthy weight is that it is sufficient to permit the return of menses; for a further discussion of this issue, see Treasure (1987). Ovarian ultrasound monitoring has been employed recently to investigate endocrine functioning in anorexic patients, and this is likely to prove a useful index (Treasure et al. 1987). This can usually be identified from the menstrual history. However, in patients who developed an eating disorder whilst they were still growing, there is likely to be a certain amount of trial and error involved in finding the optimal weight for return of menses.

The immediate task of weight restoration is to set short-term, achievable goals of weight gain, and to specify how these might be achieved. A weight increase of one to two pounds a week is probably an acceptable out-patient target. If patients are reluctant to make exact plans as to how they will achieve weight gain, it may be helpful to use a graduated approach whereby they initially attempt to put on weight in an unstructured way, and are given feedback from regular monitoring at treatment sessions. If no gain occurs in the initial weeks of this approach, the therapist may then take increasing control by agreeing a specific eating plan with the patient, and stressing once more the dangers of continued starvation and the rationale for weight gain.

T: I know that you're going to find it frightening to put on any weight. But as we discussed, what we're aiming to do is to put it on gradually and to set an upper limit as well as a lower one for when you get to a normal weight.

P: I don't think I could bear to be more than eight stone.

T: I think that's something we can worry about when we get to it – you're a long way off eight stone now, aren't you.

P: I know – but I couldn't stand going back to being fat again.

T: I can understand that. But right now I'm much more worried about you losing any more weight, because you're not feeling very strong or healthy now, are you?

P: I'm worried about that too. But I don't want to come into hospital.

T: I'm going to try and help you to avoid coming into hospital – but you're the one who's going to have to do the hard work.

P: I'll try. I suppose I've got to put on some weight.

T: Do you think we should agree on how much you're going to try to put on?

P: Yes, OK.

T: What do you think would be a reasonable aim?

P: I don't really know.

T: Well, how about if we aimed for one to two pounds a week?

P: It sounds a lot. But I suppose I'd better try.

T: I think we'd better agree about what to do if you should lose any more weight, as well.

P: Will I have to come into hospital then?

T: First of all you'd have to see the doctor, to see how it affected you, and she might decide you had to come into hospital. I think you should probably see her straight away if you lost even another pound.

With bulimic patients it may also be necessary to encourage some weight gain if past history suggests that the patient's natural weight was on the heavy side. This is a controversial issue, but Garner (1985) found that bulimic patients tend to have high premorbid weights, and suggested that a weight which is 'normal' by average standards could be too low for an individual patient.

Discussion of social and cultural attitudes to weight may enable the patient to adopt a more positive acceptance of her own body shape, and this kind of 'consciousness raising' can be an important background to treatment. Numerous popular books can be recommended which discuss this issue (e.g. Hutchinson 1985).

Eating behaviour

The first step in planning to help a patient to gain weight is to examine in detail the current eating pattern, on the basis of all the information collected from the interviews, food diaries, and so on. The aim now is to see what problems are likely to arise in modifying these eating patterns to reduce restraint and develop a normal meal pattern.

The basic principle of inducing weight gain is simply to start with the current food intake, and increase it sufficiently to produce an energy imbalance. An energy surplus of approximately 3,500 calories is needed to gain 1 pound. Thus a plan might be worked out with the patient as to how she might include an extra 500 to 1,000 calories a day on top of whatever she is already eating to produce a gain of 1 to 2 pounds per week. Weight restoration should focus on a gradual increase in both the amounts of food eaten and the types of food, to include a full range, particularly of fats and carbohydrates which are likely to be avoided.

It is helpful to examine particular difficulties with foods and eating situations by identifying these for the individual patient and working through them. During restricting times, patients usually have great difficulty in including reasonable amounts of sweet, high fat, or carbohydrate foods in their planned eating. It is usually these same avoided foods which trigger binges during times of breaking away from cognitive constraints. The factors implicated in triggering binge eating are likely to be composed of behavioural, emotional, and cognitive components. On the basis of the records obtained during the first two weeks, graded hierarchies of difficult foods and situations were constructed with Carol during the third session. She was asked to generate a list of foods which ranged from mildly to extremely difficult, and these were rated out of 100 per cent. 'Difficult foods' was defined as foods which she tried to avoid eating, but could relate to the tendency to binge once she started to eat them. The range of situations included both social pressures and emotional

Table 6.3 Examples of graded hierarchies

Food item	Degree of difficulty %	Situation	Degree of difficulty %
1. Pasta	30	Shopping for food	35
2. Salad cream	35	In the presence of fattening food	45
3. Creamy cheeses	40	With a friend who eats something fattening	50
4. Potatoes	60	Upset with a friend	55
5. Fish and chips	65	Sight/smell of appetising food	60
6. Crisps	75	Waiting for a meal at home	65
7. Cakes and biscuits	80	Boredom	75
8. Pastries and pies	85	Plans involving eating fall through	80
9. Honey	90	Leaving food on a plate	90
10. Chocolate cakes and biscuits	95	Unspoken rejection by boyfriend	95

states where eating became a particular problem for her. Ten representative items were chosen from each list, and these can be seen in Table 6.3.

These items were used as part of a graded exposure programme; Carol practised eating the items during the sessions, either in her imagination or *in vivo*, until she felt comfortable with each and ready to move to a higher item. Modelling of comfortable eating was provided by the therapist where appropriate. There was a broad aim of progressing at the rate of one item from each list each week of treatment.

Techniques such as relaxation and distraction may be used in conjunction with exposure to aid patients where appropriate. Techniques for dealing with cognitions about restriction and binge eating will be dealt with in a later section.

Binge eating

There are two important principles involved in dealing with binge eating. The first is to decrease the pattern of dietary restraint, as described above, and the cognitions which mediate this (to be described below). The second employs the technique of exposure and response prevention, namely exposure to the factors which serve as cues to binge, and prevention of binge eating in response to these.

Practice sessions of exposure and response prevention should take place both in and out of the treatment sessions, to maximise effectiveness. A typical practice session might involve asking the patient to bring a reasonable quantity of feared food along with her. She would be asked to rate her degree of anxiety, craving, and urge to binge before, during, and after eating some of this food, and to list her thoughts during this procedure. After a portion of the food had been consumed, she would be asked to stop eating for a short period, perhaps ten minutes, whilst the food remained within sight and easy reach. She would then be asked to taste the food again, to see whether she still wanted to eat some more of it. She would be instructed to carry on and eat another portion if she did still want more, but still to leave some uneaten. This procedure would be repeated until any desire to binge or eat more was minimal. This seldom requires more than two or three tasting sessions. The interval between stopping eating and tasting again can be gradually extended to increase control.

This experimentation should be generalised to the home situation as soon as patients feel able to carry this out. Practice should be at least daily, building up to the more difficult items. Patients are also encouraged to keep a supply of feared foods around the home, to maximise their understanding that they can learn to control eating binges. Later in this process, attention can be directed towards sensations of hunger and satiety, to help patients develop appropriate perceptions of these.

Vomiting and laxative abuse

In patients who vomit to compensate for overeating, the desire to do so is likely to decrease once binge eating becomes less of a problem. If this does not prove to be the case, or if vomiting occurs independently of bingeing, then direct steps need to be taken. The most useful strategy involves delaying the interval between eating and vomiting, perhaps by only ten minutes in the first instance, and employing relaxation or distraction strategies. The length of the delay can then be increased until the time of vomiting is so far removed from food intake that the food is mostly digested, and vomiting becomes ineffective.

It is important to focus also on the natural satiety process which will be destroyed if artificial stomach emptying takes place by means of vomiting. It should be explained to the patient that if she induces vomiting, she is likely to feel hungry again in the near future, and this will feed into her fears of loss of control and desires to eat voraciously (Wardle 1987b). She can thus be helped to experience the more gradual reduction in sensations of stomach fullness which come about through the digestion process, since sensations of fullness appear to be a specific trigger for anxiety.

Laxative abuse is dealt with in a similar fashion to vomiting, by encouraging gradual decreases in the amount taken and increasing the delay between eating and ingesting it, and by emphasising the pointlessness of tampering with natural satiety mechanisms. The relative inefficacy of laxatives as a means of reducing energy intake can be mentioned (Bo-Linn *et al.* 1983). Finally, the hazards to physical health which might ensue as a result of each of these methods should also be stressed.

Identifying dysfunctional thoughts

At an early stage in the treatment, work may begin on eliciting cognitions which may represent central themes or schemata underlying the patient's

Table 6.4 Examples of dysfunctional thoughts in anorexic and bulimic patients

Area of concern	Dysfunctional thought
Food and eating	If I eat a sweet, it'll turn into fat straightaway.
	Once I start eating I'll go on and on and I won't be able to stop.
Body size and weight	If I put on weight it'll all go to my stomach.
	I'm special by being thin, and better than other people.
	If I put on 1 pound, it'll get worse and worse and I'll put on more and more weight.
Control over life	The thing in my life I've got control over is my eating. Once I eat, I've given in and lost control over my life.
	I used to weigh more, and I wasn't happy. So I know that if I go back to a normal weight I can't be happy.

belief system. The first stage of identifying such cognitions involves heightening people's awareness of the thoughts which pass through their minds relating to sensitive areas of concern. These can then be further examined to see whether they appear to play a crucial role in maintaining the disorder (Beck 1976).

Garner and Bemis (1982) drew up a list of systematic distortions typifying patients with eating disorders, based on Beck's (1976) classification of types of thinking errors. These included errors of 'overgeneralisation', or extracting a rule on the basis of one example and applying it to all situations; 'magnification', or overestimating the significance of undesirable events; and 'dichotomous' reasoning, or thinking in extreme or absolute terms. Examples of the types of dysfunctional thoughts commonly encountered with anorexic or bulimic patients are given in Table 6.4.

Cognitive–behavioural approaches typically ask patients to keep records of their dysfunctional thoughts, and these are used as a basis for monitoring and challenging the thoughts. Examination of these thoughts is an integral part of treatment, both as an intervention strategy in its own right and as a major aspect of any behavioural task. Patients should be given a clear explanation of the need to identify habitual dysfunctional thoughts and the triggers associated with them, which might be situational, such as mealtimes or trying on clothes, or emotional, such as mood changes. They may then be asked to keep records of every time they start thinking about food and body size. Concurrent recording at the time of getting the thought is obviously preferable, but is not always practicable. If this presents difficulties, sampling procedure can be used, where recordings are made at key points during the day or week to encompass critical times such as mealtimes or getting on the scales.

Patients sometimes have difficulty in recognising these thought processes. They might report that they were unaware of any thoughts in their minds at all, but only of emotional distress. Alternatively they might be able to report a long stream of distressing thoughts, but find these so familiar that they have difficulty in appreciating their potential significance. In these circumstances, *in vivo* techniques or techniques using imagination can be employed during treatment sessions to elicit thoughts. Thus the patients may be asked to eat a small amount of fattening food such as chocolate in the presence of the therapist, and to list their thoughts at four stages:

1. before the food is presented;
2. in the presence of food, before eating;
3. during eating;
4. after eating.

Thought listing, in imagination or *in vivo*, may be used to supplement home-based records as a basis for identifying the presence of dysfunctional thoughts. The skill of making use of this material then lies in selective prompting to enable the patient to make explicit the details and consequences of what might at first appear to be a fleeting or trivial statement.

Carol's list of thoughts elicited by tasting a small bar of chocolate included statements such as 'chocolate is unhealthy'; 'if I have one bit I'll go on and on eating'. Prompts were used to explore these issues further:

T: What do you mean when you say that chocolate is unhealthy?
P: It's just bad for you.
T: Do you think you can try to explain why that is?
P: It doesn't have any nutritional value, and it gives you spots.
T: What else is it about chocolate which is unhealthy?
P: It makes you fat.
T: Can you tell me how it does that?
P: Everyone knows that chocolate is fattening. It's got lots of calories in it.
T: Can you get fat by eating just that small piece you had just now?
P: Yes – I can feel it just sitting in my stomach.
T: And then what will happen?
P: It'll just stay there and I'll have a great big stomach and get fat.
T: Is that a very frightening idea for you?
P: Yes – I'd hate myself and look ugly.

Thus it is important not to accept merely a conventional, socially acceptable answer elicited by questioning, such as 'chocolate is fattening'. As a yardstick, prompting and questioning should continue until the point is reached where the therapist can appreciate that the thought would be distressing to the patient personally.

After spending a session on identifying thoughts in this manner, Carol agreed to record them at home whenever a difficult situation related to weight and eating arose. She was also asked to try eating during the week and recording her thoughts. Inspection of these records revealed that she predominantly worried about losing control over her eating by giving in to sweet things, and that any high-calorie foods she ate would go directly to her stomach and thighs.

Dealing with dysfunctional thoughts

The first difficulty in dealing with dysfunctional thoughts arises in deciding which to choose as targets for intervention. This should be agreed together with the patient. It is useful to gather information on dimensions of both intensity and frequency, since these may operate independently. There may be cognitions which do not occur very often, but are highly distressing when they do arise; and others which are extremely frequent, without being perceived as particularly distressing.

Carol was keen to work first on her fears of losing control over her eating, since it was concern over her eating binges which worried her most and motivated her to seek help. Her records showed that she got this thought every time she was offered high-calorie foods, which happened most evenings in the hotel. She felt particularly distressed by this if she was feeling emotionally upset or lonely. With some discussion, the explicit thought was put into words by Carol: 'Once I start eating something fattening, that's it. I'll lose control and go on and on eating and get fat.'

Initially it may be useful to obtain a rating of the patient's degree of belief in the thought, which can later be compared with her rating after it has been systematically reviewed with her. Such ratings may also be used to monitor fluctuations over time in the degree of belief the thought elicits. Carol believed her statement to be about 85 per cent true at this point in the session.

Another step is to explore with the patient the links between the specific cognition and any associated emotions or behavioural patterns.

T: How does it make you feel when you get that thought?
P: I feel anxious; just the sight of food makes me feel nervous sometimes.
T: Do you feel any other emotions?
P: I'm not sure really, just nervy I think.
T: What about if you taste any of the food?
P: Then I'd feel really guilty, it lasts for ages sometimes.
T: And what about the effects on your behaviour – does that thought affect that in any way?
P: I don't know really.
T: What happens when you do eat? Do you relax and enjoy it?
P: No, I'd just try and eat it as slowly as possible, try and make it last longer than everyone else's.
T: Does it stop you eating at all?
P: Yes, mostly I wouldn't touch anything I thought was fattening – or else I'd just give in and have a binge.

In attempting to alter a cognition or belief, it is important first of all to understand where it might have come from, and the factors which caused the person to arrive at these conclusions. This may also help to reassure her that she is not being completely irrational in thinking this way. Generally clues may be obtained by enquiry into the past history, to see whether the patient has specific experience which is directly relevant to the conclusions reached.

T: So what is it that made you come to believe that everything you eat will go straight to your stomach and stay there?
P: I can just feel that it does – my stomach is so bloated if I eat a proper meal or anything.

149

T: So one source of evidence is the sensations you get from eating – it makes your stomach feel full. What happens then?

P: I make myself sick.

T: What do you think would happen if you didn't make yourself sick?

P: The food would just stay there and make me fat.

There are also likely to be social and cultural factors which have an influence.

T: Was there a time in your past when you thought that you had a big stomach?

P: When I was at school – my stomach always used to stick out.

T: And what was your eating like then – did you eat a lot and make yourself sick afterwards?

P: I used to eat a lot, but I didn't make myself sick.

T: And what else makes you worry about your stomach – did people ever comment on it?

P: Sometimes they used to call me 'fattie' or 'greedy' at school.

T: Did that worry you?

P: It didn't really at the time, but it does more now.

T: What else is it about fat on your stomach that worries you?

P: It's unhealthy to be fat – you get heart disease and things like that. And nobody wants to go out with you.

The patient may then be encouraged to question whether the conclusions she has reached are entirely valid, and if there are alternative ways of looking at the data or factors which she has not taken into consideration. Emphasis should be placed on helping her to introduce doubts as to the validity of her assertions, rather than providing them for her. Otherwise there is a danger of developing a dialogue where the therapist directly contradicts the patient and undermines her confidence.

T: Do you remember the last time you ate a reasonable amount of food without being sick?

P: Yes, it was when I went to visit my mum last week and I couldn't get away to be sick.

T: And what happened that time?

P: I just felt terrible, I couldn't stand it.

T: Did you carry on feeling just as bad, or did it get a bit better eventually?

P: It did get better eventually, but it took ages.

T: What do you think happened to the food in your stomach?

P: I don't know.

T: Is it still there now?

P: I suppose not.

T: What usually happens to food after it reaches the stomach?

P: It goes right through the system, I suppose.

T: That's right – it gets digested, doesn't it. So what would happen if you ate a piece of chocolate now? Would that get digested, or would it stay in your stomach?

P: I'm not sure – I suppose it would get digested.

The main objective of examining alternative explanations is to put across the idea that the thoughts should be seen as beliefs rather than facts. Alternative ways of construing the information should be put forward as potential hypotheses which need to be further investigated, rather than as the correct solution. In order to test out the hypotheses put forward as alternatives to the initial dysfunctional thought, means need to be devised together with the patient. Hypothesis testing might involve direct methods, such as trying out eating a small amount of food in a controlled situation to see whether it leads to bingeing, or asking a sample of people what they typically eat during a day, or finding examples of fat people who are attractive and thin people who are unattractive.

Another useful technique is to ask the patient to take a different perspective, or to imagine how someone else would see the situation from their viewpoint. Choosing a significant person such as a close friend or relative usually allows her to put things into perspective.

T: When people called you fat at school, what did they mean by that?

P: They thought I was fat, I suppose.

T: Didn't you tell me that you've never weighed more than eight and a half stone?

P: I think that was what I used to be.

T: What would your mother say if you asked her if you used to be fat?

P: She'd say I wasn't the smallest, but I was about the same size as most of them. I think she'd say I was just average.

T: Did anyone else ever get called fat when you were at school?

P: I'm not sure, I can't remember really.

T: Did you ever call anyone fat, or call them any other names?

P: Yes, but that was just teasing.

T: Do you think that people might have been teasing you then, when they called you names?

Inherent in the dysfunctional thought there is usually a feared outcome which seems to threaten intolerable consequences if it should turn out to be true, such as getting fat or losing control in some way. Asking the patient to consider the worst which might possibly happen, and see whether it would really be as bad as they imagined, can provide a method to deal with this.

T: Supposing you did have another binge where you couldn't stop eating, then what would happen?

P: I'd eat and eat and get fatter and fatter.

T: And how bad would that be?

P: It would be just awful, I couldn't stand it.

T: Just think about it for a moment – supposing you did manage to keep on eating and put on weight – how would it compare to the way you are now?

P: I'd really hate it.

T: Would you feel as tired and ill as you do now?

P: I don't think I'd feel any worse.

T: Would it be as bad as dying of starvation or coming into hospital?

P: Not really.

T: Would you be able to do your work better than you can now?

P: I suppose I probably could.

T: So how bad would it be compared to the way things are now?

P: It wouldn't be as bad as this.

T: Do you think there would be anything you could do about it?

P: I suppose I could diet.

T: That's right – if your weight was very high, you could cut down just a little bit, couldn't you. Not drastically like you did before, but just enough to get your weight back to normal, and slowly – the same way as we've been working to help you put on weight.

Dealing with other areas of concern

The focus of this chapter has been on dealing with concerns relating to eating and weight. Naturally there are other areas of importance to be dealt with, as in the comprehensive treatment of any disorder, but these will not be discussed here, apart from a discussion of the issue of depression. Self-reported depressed mood is extremely common amongst both anorexic and bulimic patients, and may present difficulties during the course of treatment. Whilst the definitive study of antidepressant treatments for eating disorders remains to be conducted, there is no clear evidence that provision of antidepressant medication adds anything to a psychological treatment in most cases (Garfinkel and Garner 1982). If a patient is considered to present a high suicidal risk, hospitalisation should be considered if necessary to keep her safe. If depressed mood does not lift with improvement in the problems associated with eating and body size, it may need to be dealt with separately in the manner described by Beck *et al.* (1979).

Maintenance and follow-up

Patients should be encouraged to continue to practise the techniques they have learned such as keeping food and thought diaries for as long as they consider these to be useful. They can also be reminded to introduce them again if difficulties recur. After formal treatment sessions have ended, booster sessions may be useful once or twice a year to ensure that progress is maintained.

As in the maintenance of any course of treatment, time should be spent with the patient in considering problems which are likely to arise in the future, and how she will deal with the re-emergence of difficulties which have been dealt with so far. Fairburn's (1985) programme includes a specific maintenance plan which could usefully be given to the patient at the end of treatment. It should be emphasised that progress and maintenance do not usually follow a smooth course, but tend to take small backward steps now and again which do not imply that any previous improvements have been wasted.

Being a therapist with anorexic and bulimic patients

A number of authors (e.g. Cohler 1977; Selvini-Palazzoli 1978) have highlighted the difficulties from the therapist's point of view of working with patients with eating disorders. They suggest that this client group is likely to produce particularly strong emotional reactions in the therapist, which may lead to considerable difficulties during the course of treatment.

These emotional reactions may take several forms. A stubborn refusal to eat in the face of life-threatening emaciation may be interpreted by the therapist as a personal insult. It is important in these circumstances to empathise with the degree of terror which the patient may be experiencing at the prospect of change, and her difficulties in accepting help or trusting people. Another difficulty, described by Garner (1985), is a punitive reaction in the therapist. In the light of current cultural ideals, few therapists are likely to be entirely unconcerned about their own body shape and size. Garner (1985) recommends some specific steps which may be taken to deal with these emotional responses towards these patients.

References

Abraham, S.F., Mira, M., and Llewelyn-Jones, D. (1983) 'Bulimia: a study of outcome', *International Journal of Eating Disorders.* 2: 175–80.
Agras, W.S. (1987) *Eating Disorders: Management of Obesity, Bulimia and Anorexia Nervosa,* New York: Pergamon Press.
American Psychiatric Association (1980) *Diagnostic and Statistical Manual and Mental Disorders* (3rd edn) Washington, DC.
Bachrach, A.J., Erwin, W.J., and Mohr, J.P. (1965) 'The control of eating behaviour in an anorexic by operant conditioning techniques', in L.P. Ullman and J. Krasner (eds) *Case Studies in Behavior Modification,* New York: Holt, Rinehart & Winston.

Beck, A.T. (1976) *Cognitive Therapy and the Emotional Disorders*, New York: International Universities Press.

Beck, A.T., Rush, A.J., Shaw, B.F., and Emery, G. (1979) *Cognitive Therapy of Depression: A Treatment Manual*, New York: Guilford Press.

Beck, A.T., Ward, C.H., Mendelson, M., Mock, J.E., and Erbaugh, J.K. (1961) 'An inventory for measuring depression', *Archives of General Psychiatry* 4: 561–71.

Bo-Linn, G.W., Santa Ana, C.A., Morawski, S.G., and Fordtran, J.S. (1983) 'Purging and calorie absorption in bulimic patients and normal women', *Annals of Internal Medicine* 99: 14–17.

Channon, S. and de Silva, P. (1985) 'Psychological correlates of weight gain in patients with anorexia nervosa', *Journal of Psychiatry Research* 19 (2–3): 267–71.

Channon, S., de Silva, P., Hemsley, D.R., and Perkins, R. (1989) 'A controlled trial of cognitive–behavioural and behavioural treatment of anorexia nervosa', *Behaviour Research and Therapy* (in press).

Channon, S., Hemsley, D.R. and de Silva, P. (1988) 'Selective processing of food cues', *British Journal of Clinical Psychology* 27: 259–60.

Cohler, B.J. (1977) 'The significance of the therapist's feelings in the treatment of anorexia nervosa', in S.C. Fernstein and P. Giouacchini (eds) *Adolescent Psychiatry: Volume V Developmental and Clinical Studies*, New York: James Aronson.

Cooper, P.J. and Fairburn, C.G. (1984) 'Cognitive behavioural therapy for anorexia nervosa: some preliminary findings', *Journal of Psychosomatic Research* 28: 493–9.

Crisp, A.H., Palmer, R.L., and Kalucy, R.S. (1976) 'How common is anorexia nervosa? A prevalence study', *British Journal of Psychiatry* 128: 549–54.

Fairburn, C.G. (1981) 'A cognitive behavioural approach to the management of bulimia', *Psychological Medicine* 11: 697–706.

Fairburn, C.G. (1985) 'Cognitive–behavioural treatment for bulimia', in D.M. Garner and P.E. Garfinkel (eds) *Handbook of Psychotherapy for Anorexia Nervosa and Bulimia*, New York: Guilford Press.

Fairburn, C.G. and Garner, D.M. (1986) 'The diagnosis of bulimia nervosa', *International Journal of Eating Disorders* 5: 403–19.

Fairburn, C.G., Kirk, J., O'Connor, M., and Cooper, P.J. (1986) 'A comparison of two treatments for bulimia nervosa', *Behaviour Research and Therapy* 24 (6): 629–44.

Florey, C.D.V. (1970) 'The use and interpretation of Ponderal Index and other weight/height ratios in epidemiological studies', *Journal of Chronic Diseases* 23: 93–103.

Garfinkel, P.E. and Garner, D.M. (1982) *Anorexia Nervosa: A Multidimensional Perspective*, New York: Brunner Mazel.

Garner, D.M. (1985) 'Iatrogenesis in anorexia nervosa and bulimia nervosa', *International Journal of Eating Disorders* 4: 701–26.

Garner, D.M. (1986) 'Cognitive therapy for anorexia nervosa', in K.D. Brownell and J.P. Foreyt (eds) *Handbook of Eating Disorders,* New York: Basic.

Garner, D.M. and Bemis, K.M. (1982) 'A cognitive–behavioural approach to anorexia nervosa', *Cognitive Therapy and Research* 6 (2): 123–50.

Garner, D.M., Garfinkel, P.E., Schwartz, D., and Thompson, M. (1980) 'The cultural pressure on women for thinness' *Psychological Report* 47: 483–91.

Garner, D.M., Garfinkel, P.E., Stancer, H.C. and Moldofsky, H. (1976) 'Body image disturbances in anorexia nervosa and obesity', *Psychosomatic Medicine* 9: 273–9.

Garner, D.M., Olmsted, M.P., and Polivy, J. (1983) 'Development and validation of a multidimensional eating disorder inventory for anorexia nervosa and bulimia', *International Journal of Eating Disorders* 2: 15–34.

Garner, D.M., Rockert, W., Olmsted, M.P., Johnson, C., and Coscina, D.V. (1985) 'Psychoeducational principles in the treatment of bulimia and anorexia nervosa', in D.M. Garner and P.E. Garfinkel (eds) *Handbook of Psychotherapy for Anorexia Nervosa and Bulimia*, New York: Guilford Press.

Hsu, L.K. (1980) 'Outcome of anorexia nervosa: a review of the literature', *Archives of General Psychiatry* 37 (9): 1041–6.

Hutchinson, M.G. (1985) *Transforming Body Image*, New York: The Crossing Press.

Johnson, W.G., Schlundt, D.G., and Jarrell, M.P. (1986) 'Exposure with response prevention, training in energy balance, and problem solving therapy for bulimia nervosa', *International Journal of Eating Disorders* 5: 35–45.

Keys, A., Brozek, J., Henschel, A., Mickelson, O., and Taylor, H.L. (1950) *The Biology of Human Starvation*, vols 1 and 2, Minneapolis, MN: University of Minnesota Press.

Kirkley, B.G., Schneider, J.A., Agras, W.S., and Bachman, J.A. (1985) 'Comparison of two group treatments for bulimia', *Journal of Consulting and Clinical Psychology* 53 (1): 43–8.

Lacey, J.H. (1983) 'Bulimia nervosa, binge eating and psychogenic vomiting: a controlled treatment study and long term outcome', *British Medical Journal* 286: 1609.

MacLeod, S. (1981) *The Art of Starvation*, London: Virago.

Metropolitan Life Insurance (1983) '1983 Metropolitan height and weight tables', *Statistical Bulletin* January–June: 3–9.

Morgan, H.G. and Russell, G.F.M. (1975) 'Value of family background and clinical features as predictors of long term outcome in anorexia nervosa: 4 year follow-up of 41 patients', *Psychological Medicine* 5: 355–71.

Pearlson, G.D., Flournoy, L.M., Simonson, M., and Slavney, P.R. (1981) 'Body image in obese adults', *Psychological Medicine* 11: 147–54.

Polivy, J. and Herman, C.P. (1984) 'Binge eating: a causal analysis', *American Psychologist* 40: 193–201.

Roche, L. (1984) *Glutton for Punishment*, London: Pan.

Rosenberg, L. (1965) *Society and Adolescent Self Image*, Princeton, NJ: Princeton University Press.

Russell, G.F.M. (1979) 'Bulimia nervosa: an ominous variant of anorexia nervosa', *Psychological Medicine* 9: 429–48.

Russell, G.F.M. (1981) 'The current treatment of anorexia nervosa', *British Journal of Psychiatry* 138: 164–6.

Schwartz, D.M. and Thompson, M.G. (1981) 'Do anorectics get well? Current research and future needs', *American Journal of Psychiatry* 138 (3): 319–23.

Selvini-Palazzoli, M. (1978) *Self-starvation – From Individual to Family Therapy in the Treatment of Anorexia Nervosa*, 2nd edn, New York: Jason Aronson.

Slade, P.D. (1982) 'Towards a functional analysis of anorexia nervosa and bulimia nervosa', *British Journal of Clinical Psychology* 21 (3): 167–79.

Slade, P.D. and Russell, G.F.M. (1973) 'Awareness of body dimension in anorexia nervosa: cross-sectional and longitudinal studies', *Psychological Medicine* 3: 183–99.

Smith, G.R. and Medlik, L. (1983) 'Modification of binge eating in anorexia nervosa: a single case report', *Behavioural Psychotherapy* (3): 249–56.

Swift, W.J., Ritholz, M., Halin, N.H., and Kaslow, N. (1987) 'A follow-up study of thirty hospitalised bulimics', *Psychosomatic Medicine* 49: 45–55.

Toner, B.B., Garfinkel, P.E., and Garner, D.M. (1986) 'Long-term follow-up of anorexia nervosa', *Psychosomatic Medicine* 48 (7): 520–9.

Treasure, J. (1987) 'The biochemical and hormonal sequelae of the eating disorders', *British Journal of Hospital Medicine* 4: 301–3.

Treasure, J., Wheeler, M., Gordon, P., King, E., and Russell, G.F.M. (1987) 'Ultrasound monitoring of endocrine recovery in anorexia nervosa', personal communication.

Van Strien, T., Frijters, J.E.R., Bergers, G.P.A., and Defares, P.B. (1986), 'Dutch eating behaviour questionnaire for assessment of restrained, emotional and external eating behaviour', *International Journal of Eating Disorders* 5: 295–315.

Wardle, J. (1987a) 'Compulsive eating and dietary restraint', *British Journal of Clinical Psychology* 26: 47–55.

Wardle, J. (1987b) 'Disorders of eating and weight: investigation', in S. Lindsay and G. Powell (eds) *Handbook of Adult Clinical Psychology*, Aldershot: Gower.

Wardle, J. and Beinart, H. (1981) 'Binge eating: a theoretical review', *British Journal of Clinical Psychology* 20 (2): 97–109.

Willi, J. and Grossman, S. (1986) 'Epidemiology of anorexia nervosa in a defined region of Switzerland', *American Journal of Psychiatry* 140 (5): 564–7.

Wilson, G.T., Rossiter, E., Kleinfield, E.I., and Lindholm, L. (1986) 'Cognitive–behavioural treatment of bulimia nervosa. A controlled evaluation', *Behaviour Research and Therapy* 24 (3): 277–88.

Wolchik, S.A., Weiss, L., and Katzman, M.A. (1986) 'An empirically validated, short term psychoeducational group treatment program for bulimia', *International Journal of Eating Disorders* 5: 21–32.

Chapter seven

Drug abusers

Stirling Moorey

Over the last 10 years the role of cognitive factors in addiction has been viewed with increasing interest. The old-style disease model, which saw addicts as suffering from an illness which limited their control of their own actions, is being replaced by a self-control model, which emphasises individuals' contribution through their thoughts and actions to their dependence on drugs. One of the features of this theoretical approach is its concern with the factors which various addictions have in common, i.e. the deficits in self-control which can be seen in such widely divergent areas as alcoholism, smoking, and heroin addiction (Levison *et al.* 1983). This chapter will mainly focus on illicit drugs rather than on the physically more damaging but socially condoned drugs such as alcohol and nicotine. Before pursuing the cognitive model of drug abuse further we will look at the conventional forms of treatment.

Treatment of drug abuse

Most workers in the field of addictions would see the problem as multifactorial in its aetiology. Psychological, social, and physiological factors all play a part in producing physical or psychic dependence on a drug. The approach to treatment is similarly eclectic, as far as resources allow, making use of the divergent skills of various disciplines. The modern drug dependence team consists of psychiatrist, nurses, social workers, and psychologists and has more and more a community-oriented approach with good links with local voluntary and self-help organisations.

The treatment of drug dependence falls into two phases: drug withdrawal and general treatment measures.

Drug withdrawal

The aim of all treatment of addicts is to free them from dependence on the drug. Some doctors advocate a period of maintenance on the drug before detoxification. In practice this usually applies only to opiates. The argument for this is that many addicts, particularly polydrug abusers, have an unstable, chaotic life-style, and if they are to overcome their addiction they need to be in as stable a condition as possible. Though plausible, there is little evidence to support this stance. Most doctors would suggest an immediate period of detoxification as an out-patient or in-patient. Before commencing withdrawal an assessment would be carried out over a number of sessions. A psychiatric and drug history is taken, together with details of the extent of present drug use. Physical examination may reveal withdrawal signs or signs of side-effects of drug abuse. If the person is dependent on opiates, three positive urine tests over a period of ten to fourteen days are usually needed to confirm dependence (Gardner and Connell 1970). Methods of detoxification vary depending on the drug used. The basic principle is to replace the drug with another which either has the same effects (e.g. methadone in heroin withdrawal) but can be reduced in a controlled way, or to give a drug which dampens some of the symptoms of withdrawal (e.g. benzodiazepines in alcohol dependence). For more details see Ghodse (1983).

General treatment measures

Getting the addict off the drug is relatively easy. It is prolonging this state of affairs which is difficult. The second phase of treatment will use a variety of measures with the aims of preventing relapse and resocialising the person into a drug-free life-style. The methods used depend on theoretical orientation, the particular problem of the addict, and the resources available. Some units offer a short-term detoxification followed by out-patient treatment with support groups. Others attempt a more radical change and advocate a long admission, often along therapeutic community lines, with the goal of helping the patient to learn more appropriate and mature ways of relating. Social work input to help with accommodation, training for and obtaining jobs, or helping with family problems is frequently used. Psychotherapy is rarely available, though in-patient or out-patient groups run along psychotherapeutic lines are more common. Many of these interventions are influenced by the old disease model, although this influence will not always be acknowledged. Residential treatment centres encourage avoidance of people and places associated with drugs because the addict is not strong enough to cope with them. Unfortunately, the patient in more cases than not will have to return to high-risk areas but does so ill-prepared. The shortcomings of present treatment methods are leading those who treat addictions to consideration of self-control and relapse prevention models. Nevertheless, systematic application of cognitive–behavioural methods is still quite rare.

Cognitive models of drug abuse

Two trends have contributed to the development of cognitive behaviour therapy with addicts: the adoption of a self-control perspective by addictologists coming from a behavioural tradition, and the success of cognitive therapies such as those of Beck, Meichenbaum, and Ellis with clinical populations. Marlatt's work on relapse prevention illustrates the first of these lines of influence on cognitive therapy with addicts. Starting from the fact that most addicts successfully come off the drug for a short time and then resume their drug taking, he argues that attention to factors associated with relapse is vital. In a study of 311 clients with a variety of addictive behaviours (Cummings *et al.* 1980), Marlatt's group found three varieties of high-risk situation. Negative emotional states such as anxiety, frustration, anger, or depression account for 35 per cent of relapses. Interpersonal conflict accounts for 16 per cent, and social pressure (e.g. being offered drugs, being in the presence of other users even if no drugs are offered) 20 per cent of the sample. Marlatt argues that if individuals have a sense of self-efficacy and a coping response, these high-risk situations can be dealt with, but if they do not have a coping response they experience a sense of helplessness. This increases the likelihood of giving in to the temptation to use the drug, which often represents a maladaptive coping response to situations like conflict or feelings of frustration. If the person has positive expectancies about the effects of the substance the probability of using it is further enhanced. Marlatt argues that the movement from a single lapse to a full relapse depends on the attributions the person makes about the cause of the lapse. If a person is committed to complete abstinence a single lapse is a sign of failure. This will lead to feelings of guilt. If the person blames themselves for the lapse this will compound the failure, and lead to a helpless stance ('There's nothing I can do about it, I might as well go on using'). This combination of the cognitive–affective elements of cognitive dissonance and personal attribution are termed the Abstinence Violation Effect. Marlatt has produced a system of relapse prevention which uses cognitive and behavioural methods to maintain abstinence (Marlatt 1978; Marlatt and Gordon 1985).

There have been a number of case reports of cognitive therapy with drug abusers (Weiner and Fox 1982; Collins and Carlin 1983). Woody *et al.* (1983) reported a study of psychotherapy with heroin addicts receiving methadone maintenance. Cognitive therapy and a brief psychodynamic therapy (over a period of 6 months) were compared with a drug-counselling control group. All groups showed improvement, but the psychotherapies proved more effective than the drug-counselling group in reducing symptoms and in allowing the addicts to manage with less prescribed medication. The manual of cognitive therapy used in this study provides a comprehensive introduction to cognitive therapy with drug abusers (Beck and Emery 1977), and will be referred to throughout the course of this chapter.

Other studies which have used cognitive–behavioural packages similar to Beck's therapy have on the whole been with alcoholics rather than drug addicts. Carey and Maisto (1985) reviewed the literature on behavioural self-control methods and covert sensitisation. They felt that research design problems prevented any definite conclusions being drawn at that time, and noted that the researchers rarely conceptualised 'the design and use of self-control procedures on the basis of individual deficits'. Sanchez-Craig (1980), Glantz and McCourt (1983), and Oei and Jackson (1982) have all described cognitive–behavioural programmes for problem drinkers, with encouraging initial results. Brandsma *et al.* (1980), however, reported that 'rational behaviour therapy' was no more effective than insight therapy. Although in one sense outcome measures are very simple in studies with substance abusers, in reality the methodological issues involved are complex. Treatment may improve psychological or social factors without changing the pattern of substance use; is this success or failure? The efficacy of a treatment will also depend on the criterion of 'abstinence' which the researcher defines. For instance, in a study of the application of Marlatt's relapse prevention methods (Chaney *et al.* 1978) there were no overall differences between the treatment and control group at 1 year. When the results for the patients who had taken one or more drinks were analysed, the treated group showed a significant reduction in the amount of alcohol intake.

These considerations are important for the therapist dealing with the individual patient. Criteria for success need to be clearly defined, since it is easy to become demoralised by recidivism. Addiction is by its very nature a relapsing disorder. One of the principles of any self-control model of addiction is that relapse can be an opportunity for further learning and not an indication of total failure. The relapse process may occur several times before individuals acquire the necessary skills to overcome their addiction for good (Prochaska and DiClemente 1983). The therapist and patient need to be aware of this and not get too discouraged if treatment is not successful the first time round. Chaney's results suggest that for many addicts a reduction in drug intake may be a successful outcome in its own right. Cognitive therapy is unlikely to prove a panacea for drug addiction, but there is encouraging evidence from clinical and research studies that it will make a significant contribution to the addictions.

A scheme for cognitive behaviour therapy with drug abusers

The unique problems with which drug abusers present the cognitive therapist require a flexible and eclectic approach. The therapist may wish to choose between a variety of cognitive–behavioural methods when dealing with the individual patient. The scheme of treatment described here is derived largely from the work of Beck and Marlatt. The emphasis on identifying and coping with triggers for drug use as a means of relapse prevention owes much to Marlatt. The techniques described for modifying these triggers and dealing with emotional and interpersonal problems are direct applications of Beck's cognitive therapy. The attempts to address underlying assumptions and self-schemas in the cases described are also applications of Beck's cognitive model. The cases described were all patients attending the Bethlem Royal Hospital Drug Dependency Unit. Most were undergoing in-patient treatment for drug addiction on a unit which adopted a broadly eclectic approach, but which also paid attention to relapse prevention as a new and important contribution to management. The outline of therapy presented here is not by any means a comprehensive or definitive method for treating addictions, but merely suggests a framework which the author personally has found useful. There are five components which roughly correspond to the chronological order of therapy:

1. Engagement.
2. Problem definition and cue analysis.
3. Problem solving and cue modification.
4. Identifying and challenging underlying assumptions.
5. Redefining maladaptive roles.

Successful psychotherapy with any type of patient demands that a relationship of trust is set up as early as possible. This is particularly important when dealing with addicts whose motivation to change fluctuates so easily and whose experience of the 'straight' world often makes them distrustful of professionals. Engaging the patient and maintaining motivation is therefore the first goal of therapy. The next step is to carry out a detailed analysis of the factors which act as triggers for drug taking, and at the same time identify other problem areas. Cognitive and behavioural interventions are then used to reduce the risk imposed by these factors, and to provide strategies for coping with them. This phase will also include other measures such as help with interpersonal difficulties, social skills training, and preparation for work. The final stages of therapy address the deeper cognitive structures which make the person vulnerable to the use of drugs as an ineffective problem-solving strategy.

Engaging the patient

One of the most commonly voiced criticisms of cognitive behaviour therapy with substance abusers concerns the difficulty of working with these clients in a collaborative way. Addicts are 'chaotic', 'deceitful', 'unmotivated', and 'personality disordered', or so the conventional wisdom would have us believe. How is it possible to apply a complex package which requires introspection, self-observation, and a commitment to practising self-management techniques on a regular and ordered basis? It is too simple to answer that the conventional wisdom is wrong. Labelling all addicts as deceitful or psychopathic is certainly an example of a cognitive distortion on the part of the therapist, but neither are such patients an easy group to work with. Many people with anxiety or depression have discrete episodic disorders; in between they are relatively effective problem-solvers. Cognitive therapy makes use of these premorbid skills, bringing the patient's rational self to bear on their present emotional state. There is in fact some evidence to suggest that patients who report the use of self-control strategies even when depressed respond best to cognitive behaviour therapy (Murphy *et al*. 1984). A large number of people who abuse drugs have never developed these problem-solving and self-control skills. Because of these skills deficits they find it harder to understand and work with the cognitive model, while their longstanding patterns of maladaptive behaviour may cause further problems in therapy. These difficulties are by no means limited to this client group, of course: many patients with neurotic disorders have chronic personality problems and prove to be equally hard to engage in cognitive therapy. The challenge in working with this type of patient is to find ways round the personality blocks, and to help them move from a vague, disjointed cognitive style to a more focused, problem-oriented one. Engaging them in therapy is the first, but vital, step in an educative process which goes on throughout the course of treatment.

Establishing a therapeutic relationship

The cognitive therapist needs to have good basic psychotherapeutic skills. Warmth, genuineness, and empathy are just as important as in any other therapy. In fact, these 'non-specific' factors may be more important with addicts. Interpersonal factors may intrude more obviously than in conventional cognitive therapy, requiring constant monitoring. Drug abusers usually elicit a dichotomous reaction from those around them. They either persuade friends and relatives to collude with them as 'sick', or they encounter a totally unsympathetic, rejecting response. A good therapist needs to tread a fine line, showing accurate understanding of the addict's view of their circumstances, while refusing to be dragged into agreeing that the addict is a helpless victim of the drug or the world around them. The therapist must look out both for negative distortions, e.g. 'I've messed everything up for everyone. I'm hopeless' and positive ones such as rationalisation and denial, e.g. 'I can handle this all right myself. It's not a big problem at all'. With more disturbed clients this dichotomy becomes something which is almost forced onto the therapist. The person tries to test out the therapist by manoeuvring them into a totally accepting or rejecting position. If the therapist complies they are then seen as either too weak or unreasonable. In cognitive terms, the patient seems to structure all relationships as totally rejecting or totally accepting, and finds it difficult to establish behaviour patterns in between these two extremes. A similar picture is described by psychodynamic and cognitive therapists who treat patients with borderline personality disorders. This is not to say that addicts necessarily fit all the diagnostic criteria of the borderline personality, but that they sometimes present similar types of within-session behaviour. The key issue here appears to be establishing a relationship that has both trust and limits.

There is not space here to discuss this in depth, but a few guidelines can be outlined.

To establish a trusting relationship which is also therapeutic:

1. avoid moralising;
2. take the patient seriously at all times;
3. show that you are on the patient's side, even if you disagree with the methods they use to get what they want;
4. be flexible about appointment times etc., but not too flexible;
5. be reliable even when the patient isn't;
6. if it turns out that the patient has lied to you, use it as grist for the mill of therapy, don't take it as a personal rejection;
7. but don't let the patient get away with it either.

The collaborative relationship goes a long way towards preventing interpersonal issues becoming too much of a problem in therapy. Once a trusting relationship is established the addiction can be defined as a problem which patient and therapist can work on together. Sometimes the therapeutic alliance is established with surprising ease. The following case example shows how the ideal collaborative relationship is, however, not always achieved.

Ted was a 38-year-old multiple-drug abuser. He came from a family with strict, traditional values, and frequently came into conflict with his father during his adolescence. He left school to work as an apprentice fitter, but became bored with this job after he finished his training. During the 1960s he drifted in and out of jobs, spending some time as a fairly successful rock musician. His occupation on admission to the drug unit was a street trader who worked on the fringes of legality. Ted abused alcohol, cannabis, and opium, on and off, over most of his adult life. His introduction to hard drugs was in an 'opium den' in the Bristol docks, while still in his teens. But he most frequently abused tranquillisers, amphetamines, alcohol, and cannabis. He had two reasons for wanting to give up drugs – threats from his wife that she would leave him, and an impending charge of supplying cannabis.

Ted's behaviour throughout his admission suggested that he was testing out the unit's rules and limits to the full. He would deliberately overstay his pass, coming back perhaps half an hour late. It was quite difficult to confront him on this because of his slightly menacing manner. In therapy this issue of who was in control seemed to be a central one. It interfered with the collaborative relationship since the patient brought very little homework to the session claiming that the problems identified at the beginning of therapy had now disappeared. It later became clear, however, that Ted was in fact operating his own treatment programme, which drew ideas from, but did not directly comply with, that of the unit. He would set himself graded exposure tasks such as going into pubs and visiting old haunts where he knew drugs were in evidence. His argument was, 'I've got to go to these places to do business, so I'd better get used to going unstoned as soon as possible.' Once it was evident that Ted would be 'his own man' to the last, and had to think of himself as 'screwing the system', it became easier for the therapist to redefine the format of therapy. Specific homework tasks were not set. Instead various strategies were discussed and Ted was left to get on with his own treatment programme. This is an example of how it is sometimes necessary to work with rather than against the patient's personality style, even if it is to some extent maladaptive. An alternative approach to psychopathic behaviour is described by Beck and Emery (1977). They assume the patient's goals are legitimate, but the psychopathic behaviour represents a socially inefficient means of achieving them. The therapist sets up a collaborative relationship where alternative methods of reaching the goals are explored and tested out.

Motivation

The person who experiences unpleasant mood states such as anxiety or depression is usually highly motivated to change. Substance abusers are in a very different situation. They are choosing to change an aspect of their behaviour not because it is intrinsically unpleasant, but because its consequences are undesirable. There is inevitably always a state of tension and ambivalence towards the main goal of therapy. For this reason it is not possible to talk of people being motivated or unmotivated to give up drugs. A heroin addict who had been receiving a maintenance prescription of methadone for two years, remained free of illicit drugs and apparently stable, but he still reported frequent cravings for heroin, dreams of using heroin, and an almost daily variation in his determination to abstain. Motivation is always in flux, depending upon external circumstances, mood, and a multitude of other factors. There are those fortunate individuals who begin and remain highly committed to overcome their habit, resolutely forging their path to recovery, but they are the exception.

This is an important point to get over to the patient early in therapy so that a return of craving is not seen as the inevitable forerunner of relapse.

If motivation fluctuates there must still be a point of commitment to change, and it is the therapist's task to bring patients to this commitment and to help them return to it when their spirits are at a low ebb. Prochaska and DiClemente (1983) have described a cyclical model of recovery and relapse. According to this model there are four stages: a precontemplation stage during which the negative aspects of addiction are ignored or denied; a contemplation stage, where awareness of problems sets up conflict; the third stage is one of action to give up the drug; and the final stage involves maintenance of this abstinence. It is during the contemplation stage that most addicts seek help. Miller (1983) has developed a technique called motivational interviewing to help patients move from contemplation to a definite decision and action. The aims of this technique are to increase the person's awareness of their problem, making use of cognitive dissonance, and to aid the decision to change the problem behaviour. At the same time it aims to increase self-esteem and self-efficacy to allow them to feel that they can achieve their new goal.

This approach can easily be incorporated in a cognitive–behavioural therapy since it basically uses a form of guided discovery where patients are gently led towards examining the major disadvantages of their drug taking. The positive and negative sides of drug abuse are examined in detail, the therapist continually asking for clear, detailed information. The therapist attempts to be as empathic as possible to the pressures the person is under from outside influences to change, and also the difficulties that change will entail. Through the interview the therapist summarises and paraphrases the patient's words to highlight the ambivalence. Information is only provided when the patient requests it. It is useful to have in mind, and to explain to the patient, the metaphor of a balance between the advantages and disadvantages of changing the behaviour. This can be written down, but it is best not to do this too soon. Writing it down allows distancing and the exercise can become too intellectual. At this stage the therapist wants to emphasise the patient's emotional involvement in order to get commitment for change. Other cognitive therapy procedures can be used to help motivate the patient. Getting patients to role-play significant others who are affected adversely by their behaviour, or role-playing another addict who has been severely damaged by drug abuse, may be tried (Janis and Mann 1965; Mann and Janis 1968). These types of interventions may play an important part in work with the addictions in the future, even in treatment programmes where cognitive therapy is not the major therapeutic tool.

Table 7.1 shows a female heroin addict's list of pros and cons of drug taking (see the description of Jane, pp. 169–70). Her homework assignment was to list the advantages and disadvantages of her behaviour.

What is immediately striking is the way that all the 'pro' items centre on the pleasure of the total experience, the people, the equipment, the setting, and the effect of the drug. Situational cues would therefore be an important focus for therapy with this patient. Reality testing can be used to assess how realistic the supposed benefits are for the patient. An imagery technique which may also be useful in this context is 'outcome psychodrama' (Janis and Mann 1965). Here clients imagine themselves in the future, and improvise a retrospective account of what has happened as a result of choosing either drug use or abstinence.

Table 7.1 Jane's pros and cons of taking drugs

Pros	Cons
The immediate relief from withdrawal symptoms	Being sick and having to wait for gear
	Getting a dirty hit and being ill
The high: everything is always all right	Having no money for other things
Enjoyment of the fixing ritual	Rows with Tom over who had a better deal
Pleasure of seeing the blood in the syringe	Fear of dying
Pre-fixing ritual	Waiting for Tom to score, wondering if he will bring me any
Going to score, talking about drugs	Being overly preoccupied with drugs

Table 7.2 shows a similar exercise performed by her husband who was also a heroin addict. He was given a slightly more complicated task where the advantages of using and not using are listed separately. This table could be further subdivided into short-term and long-term effects, producing

Table 7.2 Tom's list of advantages and disadvantages of drugs

Not using heroin	
Advantages	Disadvantages
Being physically fit and healthy	Having to be aware that I am always at risk for the rest of my life
Being able to make long-term achievements	Knowing it will always be there
Liking myself as I really am	

Using heroin	
Advantages	Disadvantages
Enjoying the physical effects of the drug	Becoming physically addicted
Feeling incredibly self-confident and secure	Being always at risk health-wise
Having more energy and being able to do things when normally I couldn't be bothered	Being a slave to the drug and having no time for anything else
	Never being able to achieve ambitions, being concerned only with today and drugs

what has been termed a decision matrix. With some clients this further subdivision may be useful since they often have difficulty in thinking of longer-term consequences of their actions.

Rationale

An integral part of any self-control therapy is the explanation of the rationale to the patient. Explaining the connection between thoughts, feelings, and behaviour is much the same as with cognitive therapy (see Beck *et al.* 1979). Booklets can be given to patients, e.g. 'Coping with substance dependency problems' (Beck and Emery 1977). It may take longer to socialise the addict into the model and the therapist may need to reiterate continually the basic concepts and make use of examples from the addict's behaviour within and between sessions. Beck and Emery suggest that the first three sessions are devoted to engagement, orientation, and instruction, but with many addicts this may take much longer.

The role of negative cognitions in the process of engagement and commitment

Once the patient's personal balance sheet becomes evident it is possible to look at how distorted thinking may be unfairly weighting it in favour of maintaining the use of drugs. Two common types of negative cognitions involve helpless/hopeless views of the situations and denial/rationalisation responses. Both of these can be addressed using cognitive therapy. Addicts who are depressed will talk of feelings of worthlessness, the hopelessness of their position, etc. Others who are not clinically depressed may still have maladaptive beliefs which interfere with their ability to work on the problem. For instance Simon, a 23-year-old heroin addict, felt himself to be in the grip of strong cravings which he had no power over. Exploration of his view of the situation showed that he believed that he could not stand strong craving, and that the only way to solve the problem was to remove craving completely. The dichotomous thinking of addicts has been described already. This seems to be one of the major distortions standing in the way of effective cognitive therapy.

John was a 28-year-old man who had been making a successful living as a carpet fitter. He began using alcohol and heroin as a way of winding down after a hard day's work. His personal life suffered greatly and he nearly lost his wife. He experienced great remorse over this and determined to give up heroin. His determination relied so heavily on willpower that he could not allow himself to contemplate being unsuccessful in this. The dichotomy of addiction versus abstinence prevented him from looking at the middle ground of risk situations, trigger factors, and coping strategies, and meant that he went out of the unit without addressing these issues.

With patients like this, part of the problem lies in their use of the all or nothing thinking as a way of motivating themselves to give up. The therapist may want them to examine ways of preventing a lapse turning into a full relapse, but they say that if they let themselves even consider this they might use it as an excuse for trying the drug again.

Rationalisation and denial are commonly encountered defences in drug abusers. They are not character traits but genuinely seem to vary with the general motivation of the client. The therapist can deal with the excuses the patients make to themselves by enlisting the help of their rational self when they are in a state of high motivation. The patient is instructed to look out for habitual self-deceptions, e.g. 'I'll just try it to see what it's like'; 'One little drink won't hurt me'. This can initially take the form of self-monitoring of excuses using a wrist counter, and move on to challenging the distorted cognitions. When a strong urge to take the drug is felt it may be difficult to counter the excuses. The patient can rehearse self-statements which can be used at times of stress. One patient found it difficult to remember the bad things about cocaine. He wrote down his reasons for giving it up and read them out to his wife every morning before breakfast. This had the effect of orienting him to the negative consequences of cocaine abuse and making a 'public' commitment to his wife that he was determined to give up.

Cue analysis

A variety of stimuli act as triggers for drug taking. The cognitive–behavioural model sees these as factors which lead to relapse and maintain drug abuse. Eliciting these triggers is easiest with people who are not physically addicted, and who are in their natural setting, because their drug use will vary in response to them. Addicts in a hospital in-patient setting, particularly those who have completed a detoxification programme, find it much harder to identify cues. It may be that physical addiction swamps most other cues with the overriding impact of withdrawal symptoms as the major cue for further intake of a drug. Once addicts are detoxified and removed from their usual setting they find it hard to remember.

Simon's difficulties in coping with craving were mentioned earlier. He found it immensely difficult to identify any cues, and initially believed that his craving while going through withdrawal was constant and all-pervasive. His life before admission was a blur of drugs. Monitoring craving on a daily basis just produced a blank sheet. It required several sessions of painstaking reconstruction of events before the therapist got an impression of what factors might be significant. Even then this was based heavily on interpretation of the patient's report, with very little in the way of identified thoughts or images. The four major cues seemed to be:

1. boredom,
2. depressed mood,
3. meeting new people, and
4. seeing someone with drugs.

Situations in which he felt unable to cope, or burdened with responsibility, caused depression, and drug taking seemed to be an escape route. The same theme of escape appeared in social settings, where a craving occurred if he was with new people. The cues and the hypothesis of drug taking as a means of escaping unpleasant situations fitted well with other facts about him. He was a rather empty young man with little in the way of initiative or motivation. He objectively overestimated the amount of responsibility he was expected to take by people, but he accurately assessed his own lack of coping skills. It proved difficult to engage him and he left the unit shortly after completing his withdrawal. Fortunately, not all clients have such difficulty in monitoring the internal and external cues for craving.

Jane was a 38-year-old heroin addict. She was an identical twin who came from a stable middle-class family. Her drug abuse started at the age of 21 when she worked as a volunteer in a drug rehabilitation unit. She found the idea of heroin attractive and romantic. It seemed to fit her view of herself as a tragic and vulnerable figure. She quickly became addicted and was a long-term user. Her life varied from episodes of illicit drug use to periods on maintenance prescriptions, with occasional attempts to come off drugs. Despite her addiction she was able to contribute to the rearing of her two sons. Her husband Tom was an addict whom she met in the unit during a previous admission.

Jane presented many of the triggers for an urge to take drugs in the initial interview where she listed the advantages of drugs for her. She seemed to be very sensitive to situational cues. This was further borne out when she monitored her craving between sessions. Programmes on television about drugs or times when other patients talked about drugs all produced a craving.

She was also able to identify her relationship with her husband as a potential risk factor. When he acted towards her in a cold way she became clinging and dependent. She had thoughts such as 'He's going to leave me . . . He doesn't love me'. She would respond by seeking reassurance which resulted in her husband acting in a more withdrawn fashion. When this cycle reached a certain pitch she started to get an urge to take more heroin to relieve the 'pain'. The only other cue she was able to identify was money: it represented drug availability.

There are several methods of identifying cues, which depend to a large extent on the psychological sophistication of the patient. Some will be able

Table 7.3 Methods of identifying cues

1. Circumstances of last relapse
2. Recent experiences of craving
3. Monitoring craving of drug use
4. Producing craving in a session and eliciting cognitions
5. Interviewing significant others

to introspect and give an account of the circumstances of their last relapse. Others will find this more difficult and will need to practise self-monitoring before the factors emerge. For those few people who are unable to offer any cues it may be necessary to interview friends or family members to obtain the relevant information (see Table 7.3).

Problem solving and cue modification

The distinction between general problem-solving strategies as used in cognitive therapy with other disorders and interventions to prevent relapse is an artificial one. In practice many of the problems in the addict's life link in with the risk of relapse in some way. We will therefore concentrate on how the common problems associated with internal and external trigger factors can be dealt with. The aims of cognitive therapy in this context are twofold: first, to teach the person effective problem-solving skills and coping strategies to deal with addiction, and second, to alter, wherever possible, the underlying predisposition to use drugs or engage in other maladaptive behaviour.

Modifying situational factors

Cue exposure and aversion

Situational factors come up frequently as cues for drug taking. The ideal course of action would be to make individuals invulnerable to the effects of visiting places where they have used drugs before, been with other addicts, seen people intoxicated, etc. This is rarely possible, and so strategies of avoidance and coping with craving need to be taught. There are, however, some behavioural methods which can be used to weaken the power that situational factors exert over the individual. These were initially developed out of classical conditioning theories of addiction, and involve variations of either aversion or exposure. Aversion therapy, which used punishments such as electric shocks or emetics, is less fashionable than in the past, and there is evidence to suggest it is less effective than cognitive–behavioural methods (Marlatt and George 1983). One form of aversion therapy, which uses imagery, may be suitable for selected patients. Cautela's covert sensitisation (Cautela 1966, 1967) requires the

Table 7.4 Hierarchy of stimuli producing craving

Stimulus	Estimated craving %
Picture of doctor's surgery	50
Tourniquet and spoon	60
Empty syringe	65
Syringe and needle	70
Syringe and needle containing physeptone	80
Drawing up drug from an ampoule	85
Sitting with syringe and needle against arm	90

patient to visualise in detail a scene where the drug is being consumed, making sure that the cues which have been identified are part of the picture. During this imagery the therapist checks regularly that there is an affective response to the cognitive manipulation, i.e. anticipation and craving. At the point of injection, inhalation, or ingestion, when the addict would experience the effect of the drug, they are instructed to switch the image to an unpleasant one. One of the keys to the successful use of this technique seems to be selecting the most appropriately aversive image. Unpleasant physical experiences such vomiting are often effective, but for others social punishments might be aversive and therefore have more effect, e.g. being discovered intoxicated by your mother. This pairing of images is repeated several times within the session and then the addict practises it several times a day.

In Jane's case we chose to use a form of cue exposure rather than covert conditioning. Her sensitivity to the ritualistic aspects of her drug use made it suitable to use an *in vivo* procedure where the stimuli were the materials of drug taking. Table 7.4 is the hierarchy of stimuli arranged in order of

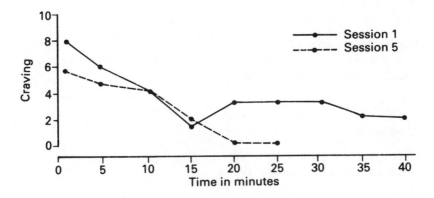

Figure 7.1 Change in craving during exposure to stimulus (tourniquet)

increasing importance. It can be seen that the more closely the situation approximated to actually taking the drug the greater the expected craving. Some of the data from the exposure sessions are presented in Figure 7.1. Within each session there was a reduction in both craving and anxiety over time. Across sessions the level of craving at the beginning of each session reduced, while the time taken for the craving to reduce became progressively shorter. This patient was one of the subjects for a pilot study of cue exposure with addicts (Bradley and Moorey 1987). The method and results presented so far are no different from any purely behavioural exposure task, but the technique was used as part of a cognitive–behavioural programme. There were a number of ways in which this intervention was cognitive as well as behavioural. First, the exposure was presented as a behavioural experiment in which the subject tested out her prior belief that in the presence of the stimulus the craving would not reduce. Emphasis was placed on the way that Jane was actively engaged in the process of coping with her craving. The whole exercise became a form of graded task assignment to increase her self-efficacy. Second, at 5-minute intervals Jane recorded her automatic thoughts and images, reinforcing the relevance of cognitive factors in her understanding of the problem. Third, the exercise was used to teach Jane two cognitive strategies, distraction and challenging cognitions, which she could use to cope if exposed to difficult situations in the future.

Thought monitoring during exposure   The exposure task provided the therapist with valuable information about the cognitions which Jane experienced when she was craving. These thoughts seemed to be grouped into four main categories which are listed with examples:

Pleasant aspects of drug use
I'd enjoy a fix.
The heroin looks familiar and comforting.

Unpleasant aspects of drug use
I'm not even sure I would enjoy how this drug would make me feel.
Having a fix of heroin would be a hassle.

Intent to use the drug
I'd like to risk taking this linctus.
I want a fix.

Intent not to use the drug
I'm sure I wouldn't fix this heroin.
I can't wait to throw this heroin away.

As might be expected the cognitions which were more positive towards drug abuse were reported at the beginning of the sessions when craving was high. As craving reduced, the cognitions focused more on the negative aspects of the experience or the wish to give up drugs. This suggests a correlation between craving and cognitions and raises interesting questions about which changes first in the exposure, thoughts or urges. There may well be an interaction between cognitions and craving such as is found in other feeling states like anxiety and depression. This is a fruitful area for research which has, as yet, hardly begun to be explored. The experience of Jane and other addicts with whom this method has been tried is that over time they experience less and less craving in the face of the stimulus, and develop a sense of mastery over their craving. This method may be associated with high levels of craving at the beginning and it should be used with caution if a patient is already experiencing high craving.

Predicting and avoiding high-risk situations

Situational factors are often so powerful that it is a wise strategy to avoid them unless absolutely necessary. Most addicts are only too aware of this, but some have very rigid and absolute beliefs about the strength of volition, e.g. 'I have to test myself out', 'If I'm strong enough to give up I will be strong enough to face any temptation'. Cognitive techniques can be used to challenge the validity and usefulness of these beliefs. The therapist can ask patients to look at the advantages and disadvantages of this way of thinking, look for evidence about how successful other people have been who have used this method, or weigh up the possible gains versus losses of putting themselves in high-risk situations.

A thorough cue analysis will allow therapist and client to predict which situations might be risky. At each session the week ahead can be previewed and any occasions when the person will be at risk identified and strategies for coping rehearsed. In the early stages of therapy, avoidance of high-risk situations is essential. As therapy progresses exposure to these situations may be programmed as part of an exercise in learning to cope with the cues for drug use.

It may be helpful to introduce the client to the concept of Apparently Irrelevant Decisions (Marlatt and Gordon 1985). People find themselves in high-risk situations through a series of decisions which at first seem perfectly innocent but on further inspection may not be so straightforward. A 28-year-old ex-nurse irregularly abused amphetamines. She described one lapse where she found herself at a loose end on a Sunday afternoon and decided to visit a friend. Since most of her friends were out of town she got on the train to visit a girlfriend who lived a few miles away. This sequence of events led her to the friend who supplied most of her amphetamines.

Coping with high-risk situations

If these situations cannot be avoided the person needs to find ways of preparing for and coping with them. The first step is to get some distance from any urges they may have. Clients can practise observing their craving, using what Emery (Beck, Emery and Greenberg 1985) refers to as the observing self. Another technique is to ride the swells and ebbs of craving like a surfer, a method which Marlatt calls 'urge surfing' (Marlatt and Gordon 1985). Whatever metaphor is used the principle is the same, i.e. being able to stand back sufficiently not to be engulfed by the feelings. The next step is to look for more active strategies to use in the face of craving. Distraction may be a useful short-term strategy, and similar methods can be applied to those used for anxiety. Since cognitions play an important part in maintaining craving, challenging craving-related cognitions will also be helpful. The usual methods of monitoring and answering back automatic thoughts apply equally to drug addicts, but addicts probably need to practise recording and challenging thoughts related to lesser degrees of craving as a homework assignment before exposing themselves to high-risk situations.

Because of the difficulties people have in thinking of rational responses when they are craving, it may be necessary to rehearse self-statements which they can use. A form of stress inoculation can be employed in which the patient induces a craving within the session and practises controlling it using self-statements. Coping imagery can be employed in a similar manner. Anti-craving thoughts can be encouraged and reminder cards can be written out to help the patient remember them when in a tight spot.

Interpersonal factors should not be overlooked. Social pressure, whether direct or indirect, accounts for 20 per cent of relapses (Cummings et al. 1980). Assertiveness training may be needed to help the patient say 'no'. Social support can play a part, just as social pressure can. A simple but highly effective way of preparing for a high-risk situation is for the patient to arrange for a non-using friend to go with them. The cocaine user who made the daily assertion of the ills of drug abuse to his wife (see p. 168) worked in the music business. He found that he could not say no if he was offered cocaine at a concert, but if he took his wife with him he was easily able to resist.

Modifying emotional factors

The decision to take a drug in a high-risk situation is often made in a state of strong emotion. Depression, anxiety, and anger are negative emotions which can act as triggers, and cognitive therapy offers unique methods for dealing with them. The basic techniques of thought monitoring, identifying distortions, and challenging negative cognitions are described adequately elsewhere (Beck et al. 1979; Beck et al. 1985). We will illustrate how some of these can be applied with the negative emotions experienced by drug abusers.

During the initial weeks of her stay on the unit Jane experienced a great deal of anxiety. This was related to her withdrawal from valium as well as heroin. She was taught to monitor and challenge her negative automatic thoughts. She also had patterns of depressive thinking associated with a poor self-image. Both anxiety and depression seemed to occur when Jane felt herself to be under criticism or facing the possibility of rejection by other people. This was particularly evident in the drug unit where she was one of the few females and was also older than most of the patients. She found herself thinking 'They think I'm old and unattractive'. She also found her stance as one of the more mature people in the unit working for her recovery a difficult one, since it brought her up against the subculture of rebellion which existed in the unit at the time. Cognitive techniques focused on her fear of rejection and disapproval. She reassessed her own strengths and began to challenge her belief that she needed to be valued and approved by everyone. Role-play helped her to develop new assertive skills. She responded well to these interventions and the frequency of episodes where she became sensitive to supposed criticism reduced.

The interpersonal factors associated with relapse usually involve some form of heightened affect. There are frequently cognitive distortions to be found in situations of conflict. The repeated cycle of reassurance seeking and rejection between Jane and Tom demonstrates this well. Jane's feeling of rejection was a result of arbitrary inferences she made about Tom's behaviour. He was by nature a solitary and independent person, but she interpreted this as a sign that he no longer cared for her. Tom's difficulty in responding to the demands people made of him led him to magnify the degree of Jane's seeking of reassurance. Therapy with the couple required them to identify the distorted thinking in these situations and to role-play alternative ways of behaving. The high-risk emotions in this couple's relationship were not only negative. Pleasant feelings of closeness and positive expectancies about drug use also contributed to their decisions to use.

Interviewing Jane and Tom together showed that Tom was the one who usually made the final decision which led to relapse. They described a scenario in which they received their giro cheque, and both knew they had the money to 'go and score'. There would follow a subtle non-verbal interaction, which was both pleasant and sensual, where they both had the same images in their minds of getting drugs. Without admitting what they were thinking they worked themselves into a state of craving. It was usually Tom who came out with the final statement: 'Shall we get some then?' He would then go and procure drugs. In the meantime Jane would stay at home thinking, 'Will I get my fair share or will he cheat me?' She would make a scene when he returned and the conflict would only be resolved by the mutual enjoyment of the fix. I worked with a social worker as cotherapist to help the couple handle this situation. We got them to role-play this scene in the session. Jane and Tom identified their distorted cognitions and worked hard at reinterpreting them. When they first started role-playing this scenario they both ended up agreeing to have a fix, but as they practised further it slowly became possible for them to resist.

Underlying assumptions

As therapy progresses it is often possible to recognise recurrent themes in the way patients understand themselves and their problems. The cognitive responses to different situations point to the rules by which they integrate experience and organise their world. These rules are often not verbalised directly but can be inferred by patients' habitual reactions. They act as silent assumptions about drug use, the self, or relations with significant others. Individuals with drug problems describe assumptions concerning their ability to control their feelings and behaviour:

'If I get a craving I have no control over myself.'

'I'm too weak to control myself.'

'Getting over drugs is something I have to do without any help from anyone.'

The section on dealing with negative cognitions related to motivation (pp. 164 ff.) contains some ideas on how to deal with these assumptions.

Other themes in high-risk situations are connected with the emotional or interpersonal aspects of the situation rather than the drug itself. The analysis of one of Ted's risk factors shows how it arises out of maladaptive beliefs about himself in relation to other people. He found that he very easily got into arguments and fights; the tension and anger he felt when this happened was only really relieved by alcohol. Conflict was sparked off by Ted thinking that he was being conned, ripped off, or treated unfairly in some way. If he was to retain his self-respect he thought it essential to come off best, resisting unjust treatment with violence if necessary. Since the arguments usually took place in pubs his judgement was already impaired by alcohol, and the scene was set for misinterpretation followed by further excessive alcohol intake. The assumption on which his reaction was based seemed to be 'I cannot let anyone treat me unjustly and get away with it'.

When Ted was with his family he also got into lots of rows, which ended with him slamming the door and heading straight for the pub. The cognitions in these situations centred on how his wife was acting unreasonably towards him or his 21-year-old step-son. As the man of the house Ted felt compelled to intervene. He had to 'step in and keep them in line' or his position would be threatened. In addition to the assumption that he should not let injustice go unpunished, he also believed that he had to be in charge of his family at all times.

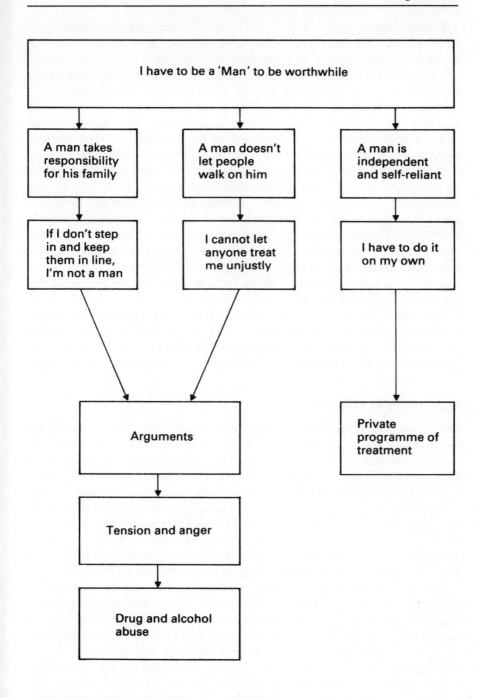

Figure 7.2 Ted's underlying assumptions

Ted was able to say to himself that his difficulty in complying with treatment reflected his distrust of the world in general. He often demonstrated his anxiety about misuse by professionals by saying 'I don't want any of this analysis, I don't want you to shrink me'. His reluctance to come along for treatment in the first place and the compliance problems were clearly related to his belief that 'Given half a chance people will rip you off'. He also had a strong sense of self-reliance. A common cognition was 'I have to do it on my own', which again led to him creating his own therapy programme rather than following that laid down by the drug unit.

Ted's beliefs that he had to do it alone, had to stand up for himself at all costs, and had to be in charge of his family were linked to a deeper assumption: 'I have to be a "Man" in order to be worthwhile.' He had a very stereotyped view of what 'real men' were like. They were rugged, tough individualists, the macho heads of submissive families. They were also constantly vigilant in a hostile world for any personal affronts and responded violently if necessary. Much of Ted's drug abuse and maladaptive behaviour can be seen to spring from attempts on his part to retain his self-esteem through his stereotyped masculine role (Figure 7.2). Despite the difficulties in engaging him in formal cognitive therapy, it was possible to identify these assumptions. He responded favourably to the idea of discussing how these beliefs might be doing him more harm than good, though he did not admit to any structured attempts to change them.

Self-schemas in addiction

With Ted and several other drug abusers the underlying assumptions seemed to form a 'cognitive constellation' (Beck 1985) for which the self-schema was the integrating construct. For Ted the meaning of 'being a man' was the integrating factor. For some patients the concept of 'junkie' served a similar function. Jane described how she gradually built an image of herself through her adolescence as a sensitive young woman who could not stand the traumas of the real world. She had always been 'special' as one of a pair of identical twins. They looked alike, dressed alike, and were treated identically through childhood. As she grew up she still felt special but no longer had her twinship to provide her with that status. Like many people in this situation she developed beliefs about her value based on approval. As mentioned earlier, she believed she could only be happy if she had people's approval. Heroin provided a convenient way of integrating these assumptions about herself into a stable schema. The myth went: 'I am a sensitive, intelligent, and romantic individual who cannot stand the harsh real world without heroin to deaden the pain.' Another young addict described an unhappy adolescence where he became the family scapegoat. He had an enduring self-schema of being stupid, bad, unreliable, and self-destructive. The role of junkie integrated all these negative self-concepts, and also allowed him entry into a subculture where he could turn them on their head and use them as a badge of defiance.

Modifying cognitive structures

Challenging assumptions is a process which follows a similar course to that with other disorders such as depression and anxiety. Once the assumption has been identified the therapist can help the patient list the advantages and disadvantages of holding this belief, challenge it through logical reasoning, and test it out by means of behavioural experiments. If the clinical observations presented here hold true for other drug abusers there may be some value in targeting the self-schemas or role constructs which organise individual assumptions. While the addictive self-schema operates the patient may still remain vulnerable to drug use. Some workers suggest that the addict needs to go through a period of mourning for the loss of the old 'junkie' self, and it certainly seems to be important for the person to talk about and experience how things may be lost as well as gained from their recovery. Not all of the aspects of the old self need to be relinquished. An example of this is the addict's love of risk, excitement, and being different. Rather than challenging these goals and self-concepts it is sometimes possible to find ways of attaining them with more acceptable behaviours. Taking up adventurous sports like mountaineering or parachuting is one method. The therapist might explore with the patient how the patient can avoid becoming 'straight' without resuming drug taking. This involves creating an alternative but drug-free life-style. Marlatt suggests various means of 'life-style modification', e.g. the development of positive addictions such as jogging or meditation.

There are several ways in which the self-schema can be challenged directly. Jane wrote a life history of how her view of herself developed which she called 'My distorted self-image'. Putting the beliefs in a developmental context demonstrates that they are learned and opens up the possibility that they can be unlearned. Whether the account is true or not, it represents the patient's causal theories (Guidano and Liotti 1983) about themselves and their problems, and may generate ideas about strategies for change. Work can also be done on past experiences by getting individuals to go back to the original experience in fantasy and deal with it as if they were handling it now, i.e. to bring the rational, mature self to bear on occurrences which were processed through a child's eyes (see Dryden 1984). Kelly's fixed role therapy is another intervention which can be applied when working with the self-schema. Here the person writes an outline of the new self and 'tries on' this role for a fixed time period as an experiment.

As I have already suggested, the implications of changing the old drug-oriented self must be explored in some detail. What will be lost? Are there ways in which this can be lessened or replaced? What will the new drug-free self actually do? Graded tasks for developing new skills and testing out new ways of perceiving the self can be tried as homework assignments, while other members of the multidisciplinary team may have expertise relevant to the process of restructuring. Change of role obviously has implications for new friends and acquaintances and this aspect of therapy thus links with more socially oriented approaches to treating the drug abuser. There is ample scope for creative intervention strategies based on the cognitive conceptualisation of the problem.

Conclusion

Cognitive behaviour therapy is still in its infancy as a treatment for substance abuse, but there are encouraging indications that it may prove a useful method with this group of patients. This chapter describes experiences with several addicts who were treated with cognitive–behavioural methods modelled on the work of Beck and Marlatt. The importance of engaging the patient in therapy is stressed, and ideas on how to increase motivation are outlined. The therapy described initially deals with the specific environmental and psychological factors of cues and cognitions and then moves on to the more general aspects of beliefs and roles, which are hypothesised to be significant in the maintenance of drug abuse. The contribution of these underlying cognitive structures to addiction has yet to be explored in any systematic manner. In the next few years it is likely that the efficacy of cognitive therapies in addiction will be investigated more thoroughly. Until more definite evidence is obtained on which techniques are most effective, the field remains open for the clinician to draw on and experiment with a wide variety of cognitive and behavioural interventions with individual patients.

One of the major advantages of the cognitive model over other psychological models of addiction, including behavioural and psychoanalytic, is its use as a means of conceptualising problems. Cognitions stand at the interface between physiological, affective, and social processes; thoughts, beliefs, and expectancies are all concepts which can be readily understood by the patient and other professionals. The complexity of addiction demands that treatment programmes are 'multi-modal' and cognitive theories may help to provide a framework within which the various disciplines treating the addict may work towards a common goal.

References

Beck, A.T. and Emery, G. (1977) 'Coping with substance dependency problems', in their 'Cognitive therapy of substance abuse', unpublished manuscript, Philadelphia, PA: Center for Cognitive Therapy.

Beck, A.T., Emery, G.D., and Greenberg, R.L. (1985) *Anxiety Disorders and Phobias: A Cognitive Perspective*, New York: Basic.

Beck, A.T., Rush, A.J., Shaw, B.F., and Emery, G. (1979) *Cognitive Therapy of Depression*, New York: Guilford Press.

Blackburn, I.M., Bishop, S., Glen, I.M., Whalley, L.J., and Christie, J.E. (1981) 'The efficacy of cognitive therapy in depression: a treatment trial using cognitive therapy and pharmacotherapy, each alone and in combination', *British Journal of Psychiatry* 139: 181–9.

Blackburn, I.M., Eunson, K.M., and Bishop, S. (1987) 'A two-year naturalistic follow-up of depressed patients treated with cognitive therapy, pharmacotherapy and a combination of both', *Journal of Affective Disorders* 10: 67–75.

Bradley, B.P. and Moorey, S. (1988) 'Extinction of craving during exposure to drug-related cues: three simple case reports', *Behavioural Psychotherapy* 16: 45–56.

Brandsma, J.M., Maultsby, M.C. and Welsh, R.J. (1980) *Outpatient Treatment of Alcoholism: A Review and Comparative Study*, Baltimore, MD: University Park Press.

Carey, K.B. and Maisto, S.A. (1985) 'A review of the use of self-control techniques in the treatment of alcohol abuse', *Cognitive Therapy and Research* 9: 235–51.

Cautela, J.R. (1966) 'Treatment of compulsive behaviour by covert sensitisation', *Psychological Record* 16: 33–41.

Cautela, J.R. (1967) 'Covert sensitisation', *Psychological Reports* 20: 459–68.

Chaney, E.F., O'Leary, M.R., and Marlatt, G.A. (1978) 'Skill training with alcoholics', *Journal of Consulting and Clinical Psychology* 46: 1092–104.

Collins, R.L. and Carlin, A.S. (1983) 'Case study: the cognitive behavioural treatment of a multiple drug abuser', *Psychotherapy: Theory, Research and Practice* 20: 101–6.

Cummings, C., Gordon, J.R. and Marlatt, A.G. (1980) 'Relapse: prevention and prediction', in W.R. Miller (ed.) *The Addictive Behaviours*, New York: Pergamon Press.

Dryden, W. (1984) *Rational–emotive Therapy: Fundamentals and Innovations*, London and Canberra: Croom Helm.

Gardner, R. and Connell, P.H. (1970) 'One year's experience in a drug dependence clinic', *Lancet* ii: 455–9.

Ghodse, A.H. (1983) 'Drug dependence and intoxication', in M.H. Lader (ed.) *Handbook of Psychiatry, 2, Mental Disorders and Somatic Illness*, Cambridge: Cambridge University Press.

Glantz, M.D. and McCourt, W. (1983) 'Cognitive therapy in groups with alcoholics', in A. Freeman (ed.) *Cognitive Therapy with Couples and Groups*, New York and London: Plenum.

Guidano, V.F. and Liotti, G. (1983) *Cognitive Processes and Emotional Disorders*, New York and London: Guilford Press.

Janis, I.L. and Mann, L. (1965) 'Effectiveness of emotional role-playing in modifying smoking habits and attitudes', *Journal of Experimental Research in Personality* 1: 84–90.

Janis, I.L. and Mann, L. (1977) *Decision Making*, New York: Free Press.

Levison, P.K., Gerstein, D.R., and Maloff, D.R. (eds) (1983) *Commonalities in Substance Abuse and Habitual Behaviours*, Lexington, MA: Lexington.

Mann, L. and Janis, I.L. (1968) 'A follow-up study on the long-term effects of emotional role-playing', *Journal of Personality and Social Psychology* 8: 339–42.

Marlatt, G.A. (1978) 'Craving for alcohol, loss of control, and relapse: a cognitive behavioural analysis', in P.E. Nathan, G.A. Marlatt, and T. Loberg (eds)

Alcoholism: New Directions in Behavioural Research and Treatment, New York: Plenum.

Marlatt, G.A. and George, W.G. (1983) 'Relapse prevention: introduction and overview of the model', *British Journal of Addiction* 79: 261–73.

Marlatt, G.A. and Gordon, J.R. (1980) 'Determinants of relapse: implications for the maintenance of behaviour change', in P.O. Davidson and S.M. Davidson (eds) *Behavioural Medicine: Changing Health Lifestyles*, New York: Brunner Mazel.

Marlatt, G.A. and Gordon, J.R. (eds) (1985) *Relapse Prevention: Maintenance in the Treatment of Addictive Behaviour*. New York and London: Guilford Press.

Miller, W. (1983) 'Motivational interviewing with problem drinkers', *Behavioural Psychotherapy* 11: 147–72.

Murphy, G.E., Simons, A., Wetzel, R.D., and Lustman, P.J. (1984) 'Cognitive therapy and pharmacotherapy, singly and together in the treatment of depression', *Archives of General Psychiatry* 41: 33–41.

Oei, T.P.S. and Jackson, P.R. (1982) 'Social skills and cognitive behavioural approaches to the treatment of problem drinking', *Journal of Studies on Alcohol* 43: 532–47.

Prochaska, J.O. and DiClemente, C.C. (1983) 'Stages and processes of self-change of smoking: toward an integrative model of change', *Journal of Consulting and Clinical Psychology* 51: 390–5.

Rush, A.J., Beck, A.T., Kovacs, M., and Hollon, S.D. (1977) 'Comparative efficacy of cognitive therapy and imipramine in the treatment of depressed outpatients', *Cognitive Therapy and Research* 1: 17–37.

Sanchez-Craig, M. (1980) 'Random assignment to abstinence or controlled drinking in a cognitive behavioural program: short term effects on drinking behaviour', *Addictive Behaviours* 5: 35–9.

Sanchez-Craig, M., Annis, H., Bronet, A.R., and Macdonald, K.R. (1984) 'Random assignment to abstinence and controlled drinking: evaluation of a cognitive–behavioural program for problem drinkers', *Journal of Consulting and Clinical Psychology* 52: 390–403.

Simons, A.D., Murphy, G.E., Levine, J.E., and Wetzel, R.D. (1986) 'Cognitive therapy and pharmacotherapy for depression', *Archives of General Psychiatry* 43: 43–8.

Weiner, H. and Fox, S. (1982) 'Cognitive–behavioural therapy with substance abusers', *Social Casework* 63: 564–7.

Woody, G.E., Luborsky, L., McLellan, A.T., O'Brien, C.P., Beck, A.T., Blaine, J., Herman, I., and Hole, A. (1983) 'Psychotherapy for opiate addicts', *Archives of General Psychiatry* 40: 639–45.

Chapter eight

Offenders

Amanda Cole

Introduction

A number of calls have been made for cognitive processes to be considered in the assessment, analysis, and treatment of offenders (Crawford 1979; Howells 1982; Gudjonsson 1986; Segal and Marshall 1986). Some cognitive theorists have developed models and therapies for particular types of offending behaviour (e.g. Bandura 1971; Novaco 1978; Ellis 1979). Beck's cognitive model and system of therapeutic intervention adopts a problem-oriented approach, focusing on the emotions, cognitions, and behaviours which the client (and others) experience as problems (Beck 1976; Beck et al. 1979; 1985). From this viewpoint, where the problem is not seen as a mere symptom of illness or personality defect, but is conceptualised in the context of a full individual functional analysis, Beck's approach to cognitive therapy has been applied to a whole range of emotional disorders as this book illustrates. Increasingly, these developments are being tested empirically through outcome trials and, thereby, are gaining validity and popularity (e.g. Rush et al. 1977; Blackburn et al. 1981; Murphy et al. 1984).

This model of cognitive behaviour therapy may therefore lend itself to working with offenders whether they are violent offenders, sex offenders, or offenders as a consequence of more primary overt affective disorder or social or behavioural problems. Some guidelines and techniques for working with psychopathic offenders have been described by Beck and Emery (1977) and this chapter will look at extending these to other forms of offence, and other levels of intervention.

Other clinical approaches with the offender

Much effort has been directed at treating deviant behaviour in non-cognitive ways (e.g. Craft and Craft 1984b). Howells (1982) has published a review of clinical approaches to the treatment of aggression. Many reviews exist of work with sexual offenders (e.g. Ellis 1979; Craft and Craft 1984a; Perkins 1986; Gudjonsson 1986). In the cognitive field, perhaps the most comprehensive model to emerge has been Novaco's model of anger and aggression (Novaco 1975; 1977; 1978). His stress inoculation training programme involves teaching clients to monitor bouts of anger, to observe the relationship of these to previously occurring cognitions and environmental events, and to control experiences of anger when they arise, including the use of self-instructional techniques (Meichenbaum 1975). A number of outcome studies have reported use of this approach with a variety of groups suffering anger problems (Schlichter and Horan 1981; Nomellini and Katz 1983; Feindler et al. 1984) and further empirical support for the model has been provided by Lopez and Thurman (1986).

Ellis (1979) has described the successful treatment of an exhibitionist with rational–emotive therapy, as an example of use of a cognitive–affective–behavioural treatment.

Problems of working with offenders

An initial issue in work with offenders, but one that is helped by use of a problem-oriented as opposed to an illness model, is that of whether the offenders construe their behaviour as a 'problem' or not. Therapists familiar with the group often consider those who say their behaviour is not problematic to be inappropriate for treatment. The question of motivation and consent to treatment is, however, a complex one. Pressures may exist from the family or from society at large for the offender to consent to treatment. The offender's incentive to enter treatment may be primarily in order to influence the outcome of a court appearance or the length of stay in an institution. The setting for therapy is also an important question. The artificiality of an institution may constrain therapy and its evaluation to such an extent that the likelihood of effective and lasting change is minimised. Community work with offenders is affected by different problems such as the length of time therapeutic contact may need to be maintained, and the reliability of detection of future offending. These ethical issues and others are considered in detail by both Crawford (1984) and Perkins (1984).

Given these considerations, however, few therapists would regard 'lack of motivation' in clients suffering from emotional disorder or behavioural problems as sufficient reason for not entering into therapy or for termination of therapy. Indeed, depressed clients often present with this as a primary problem. It is not usual to leave unquestioned such statements as 'I didn't feel anything' or 'I've already changed'. Conversely, the incentive for the client to embark on the process of change is carefully assessed and considered. 'Of course I want to change!' is usually not enough. Cognitive behaviour therapy utilises procedures to facilitate engagement in therapy, and also involves techniques to help in conceptualisation of clients' presentation, including their motivation to change. It would therefore seem to have particular usefulness when considering the issues of consent and motivation with offenders. This will be illustrated later in the chapter.

Cognitive–behavioural techniques with offenders

General strategies

Explaining the role of cognitions

An integral part of cognitive behaviour therapy is the description of the cognitive model which the practitioner gives to the client. The connection between feeling and thinking is explained didactically, or by using handouts or metaphor. Examples of the client's own thoughts and feelings are sought. The aim is to make the model explicit and unambiguous to the client. One effect of this may be to help in the identification of the client's own idiosyncratic thought patterns. Should the intervention go on to include active therapy, the rationale for treatment can be described.

Developing trust

When working with offenders, sometimes more than with some other populations, it is essential for the practitioner to develop the client's trust. The client is likely to view the practitioner with suspicion and to assume their perspectives are opposed. In order to gain access to the client's intimate and personal cognitive processes, the practitioner must be seen by the client as credible and trustworthy. Practitioners may achieve this by aligning themselves as closely as possible with the client's views and goals, without at the same time appearing to condone the behaviour. This is a process which should begin in the first contact with the client, and continue throughout intervention. Bancroft (1979) has provided useful guidelines for facilitation of the therapist–offender relationship.

Collaboration

The practitioner should engender a spirit of collaboration with the client from the outset. The emphasis is on a team approach to understanding and perhaps changing the client's behaviour. The practitioner relies on the client to supply accurate raw data, as the client relies on the practitioner to use their expertise to act on the client's behalf or to help bring about change. Mutual feedback becomes a standard element of each contact.

Common cognitive patterns in interaction with offenders

There are a number of patterns of interaction which commonly occur in the relationship between practitioner and offender. These patterns can be understood in terms of the offenders' tendency to think and behave in particular ways. It may be helpful to be aware of these patterns as typical cognitive distortions at the start of the interaction, in order for sessions to be less likely to be sabotaged by them.

Self-defeat

Offenders often seem to be immovably determined to keep behaving in ways that are destructive to their own best interests. They seem predisposed to repeat the same vicious circle of offending, often in the face of punishment, and confrontation or insightful 'therapeutic' observation from professionals or others. Ellis (1979) describes these people as rebellious and treatment-resistant. He suggests that the immediate gratification gained by their behaviour overrules any motivation to change. Although this is undoubtedly true in some cases, an alternative approach can be taken. This focuses on distortions prevalent in thought patterns, and then on specific behaviours linked to these which prevent the client from achieving self-fulfilment. It may be that by defining and correcting these blocks to the client's own goals, the practitioner and client can collaborate towards enduring change of these resistant patterns. The following are examples of such self-defeating cognitions:

1. A 22-year-old man on charges of theft and deception: 'I've got nothing to lose, my lover meant more to me than anything and now he's gone.'
2. A 20-year-old man on charges of conspiracy to rob: 'What's the point? I'm not going to be able to get a job anyway.'
3. A 52-year-old man convicted of indecent assault on teenage females: 'I can't say what I felt. I didn't think I'd done anything wrong.'

Dependency

Some clients believe that they simply cannot get through life without continuing with the offence behaviour. For example, an indecent exposer: 'Things got dull. I felt I needed to do it again.' Or another exhibitionist: 'I'm over-sexed. I have stronger feelings than other boys so I have to do something about it.'

Ellis (1979) postulates that this dependency reaches the level of demand in sexual offenders. He suggests that they demand excessively of themselves, of others, and of the world.

In some offenders this dependency may extend to the relationship with the therapist. Not only does the client believe he cannot get through life without continuing with offence behaviour, but he believes he cannot get through life without the help of others. This may become particularly clear when the question of stopping the offence behaviour arises. The desire for help exceeds any realistic requirements the client may have, and can jeopardise the formation of reasonable goals and maintenance of any degree of change which is achieved during therapy. Indeed, should therapy begin without the cognitive basis of this destructive type of dependency being addressed and changed, temporary relief from the problem only serves to reinforce the notion that the offender needs help and is not capable of change without outsider involvement. Moreover, if they have tended to conclude that they are inadequate or a failure as a result of previous failed attempts at change, this distortion may also be reinforced by such a process. For example, an exhibitionist had received various forms of therapy over the course of sixteen years. The client described to the therapist his reasons for requesting help again as follows:

C: I've always gone to the doctor afterwards.
T: Why do you do that?
C: To get some help to stop me doing it.
T: What sort of help do you want?
C: Any treatment that works. I need something new.

Emery (1980) has developed a procedure for enhancing self-reliance in cases such as this, using cognitive methods.

Misattribution

Another common cognitive pattern involves clients attributing all blame or responsibility to themselves, or to others. These clients are unable to consider the various contributions to the picture made by their circumstances, their learning history, and by chance. It is particularly useful with offenders who hold the second type of misattribution, i.e. blaming others, to address and question this early in the involvement of the practitioner. Once again, a distorted attribution of this kind left unchanged may interfere with the offender's motivation for therapy and their potential to discontinue a repeated offence pattern. Examples from one client of such misattribution are:

'It's the way I was brought up.'
'I'm stuck with a personality I don't accept.'
'She ought to realise when I've started doing it again.'

Howells (1982) has discussed the possible role of attributing negative events to others in mediating aggressive behaviour.

Levels of involvement

There are three main levels of involvement in work with offenders at which cognitive techniques may be of use.

1. Analysis of the offence behaviour; conceptualising the problem.
2. Assessing degree of change and the need for therapy.
3. Therapy itself.

Practitioners with offenders will recognise these levels of intervention with which they may have some involvement. The issue of the stage of involvement in the offence history is a separate one. Offenders may present for help without any involvement of the law. They may present prior to a court appearance. The practitioner may become involved subsequent to a criminal trial, and in a penal or other institution, or in the community. The involvement may be voluntary or statutory. It is possible at any of these stages for the practitioner to be involved at one or more of the levels described.

Analysis of the offence

Conceptualisation is one of the most important steps in completing an analysis of the client's offence behaviour. This means putting the problem in context. The most useful cognitive techniques to aid in this process are those involving the identification of automatic thoughts, meanings, and images before, during, and after the offence. There are a number of basic methods for eliciting these cognitions – the raw material for cognitive therapy. They may be obtained by asking for them during the therapy session. For example, on observing the client suddenly drop his head and look despondent:

T: What's running through your head right now?
C: I'm a freak. People like me should be locked up.

Alternatively, the client may be asked to write down what they were telling themselves between sessions, if the relevant emotion or behaviour arises, or if they find themselves able to recall an incident clearly. For example, concerning a burglary:

Before: 'They shouldn't be allowed so much money.'
During: 'No one will ever see me.'
After: 'At least I'm good at something.'

Imagery can be used to help a client recall a past situation and emotion during a session, and they may then be asked to pinpoint the automatic thoughts 'as if they were happening right now'. Inductive questioning can be used to establish what something means to a client. For example, a client awaiting trial for indecent assault on male teenagers is helped to recall one of the incidents.

T: And what do you notice about him?
C: He's smiling at me.
T: How are you feeling right now?

C: Sort of friendly and affectionate.

T: What are you saying to yourself?

C: I can't snub a child. He'd be hurt.

T: What does it mean that he's smiling at you?

C: Children are attracted to me. They come straight towards me. I'm popular.

This cognitive material can be considered along with situational, emotional and behavioural data in order to formulate the most comprehensive hypothesis possible about the determinants and maintenance of the offence behaviour and the surrounding problems. The practitioner can then go on to test the hypothesis by behavioural experiment within or between sessions, even if therapy is not being considered.

Assessing change; deciding on the need for therapy

Clearly, whatever the level of involvement is to be, an analysis and conceptualisation of the offence behaviour must be completed. In addition, the practitioner may be asked to consider the need for therapy or to provide therapy, either before or after a trial. Alternatively, therapy may be requested without the courts being involved.

There are two basic considerations to be made in reaching this decision:

1. Are any of the situations, cognitions, emotions, or behaviours which played a part in the aetiology and occurrence of the offence behaviour, according to the functional analysis hypothesis, open to change? Are the means available to facilitate this? Is therapist involvement the best, most efficient, effective, and least damaging way to achieve the required changes?

2. Have the necessary changes according to the analysis already begun? Or are they completed? If the client reports that this is the case, can this be substantiated?

Many behavioural strategies have been identified which have been successful in achieving behaviour change for a variety of problems. These strategies may be adopted naturally by an offender to help himself, or he may have been advised of them. Examples of such strategies are self-monitoring, stimulus control procedures, contingency management, developement of alternative behaviours, self-control procedures, learning of new skills.

The effective use of these strategies must be assessed in order to help in treatment decision making, and cognitive techniques can be of assistance in this process. As with offence analysis, techniques for identification of thoughts, images, and meanings may be most helpful first where behavioural change is reported to have occurred through non-cognitive means, but is reflected in cognitive change. For example, a client who had been convicted for underwear theft and voyeurism:

C: I'm confident I won't do it again.

T: How can you be sure?

C: I've proved I can ignore it.

T: OK. But what if a better opportunity presents itself? [*Imagery.*] Imagine you are coming home from the pub after a few beers. It's a warm night. There's no one around. You know you are going to pass the woman's house you've been to before. Here it is. There's washing on the line. You can see some underwear. It's only a couple of yards away. What's running through your mind right now?

C: It doesn't excite me now – the idea of it. I've caused upset and worry to myself and others. It would split me up from my friends who have stood by me. I've tested myself. I've been out to look and I still don't feel tempted.

Second, the offender may have changed their own thinking patterns and attitudes, and in this instance it is most substantive if thoughts can be identified retrospectively, for situations both before and after the reported changes. For example, a man convicted of burglary:

C: I wanted to draw attention to myself. I wanted to make people feel sorry for me. I was obviously the centre of attraction. But I didn't fit into the community. I've never had anyone to go to, but no one was going to care about me like that. I've got a lot to offer other people, but I don't know whether to for fear of rejection. I've come so far I can't stop now. I can't afford another failure – I've done enough failing for one life.

Third, techniques for identifying automatic thoughts have been found to be useful if inconsistencies in thought patterns can be detected. A client may say that his behaviour has changed but indicate that his automatic thoughts remain the same. Alternatively he may report one aspect of his thinking to be different, but overlook another which appeared to be important in the analysis of the offence. For example, a man convicted of indecent assault on teenage girls:

C: If there had been sex in the marriage it wouldn't have happened. Trouble with the wife built it up.

T: How did that make you feel?

C: I was being rejected. I've never been good enough for her. But *she'd* never say sorry if she was wrong – not once in ten years.

This man claimed that he was no longer at risk of committing further offences because he had made a new relationship with a woman. However, he was unable to consider what might happen should she 'reject' him also. The thought that this might be a possibility was in itself too frightening.

Another young man, convicted of indecent exposure, had changed one theme in his automatic thinking – from: 'They wear tight jeans to turn men on. It means they want sex', to: 'They're not after sex. They've got other things to do. Maybe it's because *they* want to look nice'. Another theme remained unchanged along the following lines:

C: They appreciate me exposing myself. They like it. It excites them.
T: What does that make you feel?
C: I'm important and powerful if they have a reaction to me. It's no good if they show no sign of excitement.
T: What do you mean?
C: Well, if they stay calm or ignore me; ignoring's the worst.
T: And what does it mean if they don't ignore you?
C: They like me. It shows they care about me. I make them feel better. I'm useful.

A further cognitive behavioural technique is helpful at this level of intervention, when some degree of change has been reported. Clients are encouraged to take a scientific approach to their problems, whereby changes are considered to be hypotheses until they are reality tested. Behavioural experiments can be designed in collaboration with the client to test the changes reported to have taken place. Such experiments can be suggested as advantageous to the client rather than putting them under pressure to succeed, since they also need to know if the changes are not as effective or durable as they had thought. By presenting this rationale, and relating the desirability of firm evidence of change to the client's own targets and goals, it is possible to encourage the client to test their new behaviours and/or cognitions in situations they previously avoided, or indeed to create new situations purely as a test.

Cognitive therapy

The use of cognitive therapy itself will be illustrated by a full case description. The example covers the use of general cognitive therapy strategies, and specific techniques. It illustrates some of the particular cognitive themes in offender–therapist interaction. An analysis is formed, a treatment decision is made, and hypotheses are tested and modified. Therapy consists of the identification and challenging of a variety of automatic thoughts, and includes periods of experiment and consolidation of change.

Case example

Presentation

The client was a 36-year-old man, who had referred himself via his wife to the general practitioner, and thence to the consultant psychiatrist, who had referred him to the psychological service asking about his suitability for treatment. His problem was one of recidivist exhibitionism, which had begun 20 years before at the age of 16 years.

At the time of referral to his GP, he had been exposing himself on a regular basis as often as three times a week, with some periods of up to 1 month without an incident, for about 14 months. He had not been caught during this time. When I saw him, he had not exposed himself for the 2½ months since he had made contact with the GP, but was experiencing urges to expose two or three times a week.

He presented as a reserved, reasonably articulate man who did not show undue signs of nervousness.

He was seen on three occasions, to complete an assessment of his problems and conduct a functional analysis. Material of interest from these sessions is as follows.

Sessions one to three

Background

The client was born in the West Midlands, and had a sister seven years older than himself. He said he always felt second best to her, and felt he was an unwanted child. He described his mother as irresponsible. She was often not in when he returned from school, and would leave her cigarettes burning, and not pay the bills. He thought she may have been in hospital, and got the impression she may have had an illness through him. He said he thought a lot of his father who was away in the army a good deal. He remembered his parents arguing and said he was not particularly happy at home. He said he was a difficult child. He was weak, and spent some periods of time in hospital. His ill-health included hearing problems which led to some difficulties at school. He used to feign illness in order to avoid school. Although naughty, he could not recall being punished by either parent. He was teased at school and did not have many friends.

He left school at 15 years, and worked for a local builder. He had three girlfriends from the ages of 17 to 21 years, and married the third as she became pregnant. There were two children from this marriage. The client began having affairs at age 26 years, and was sometimes violent towards his wife. The couple began to be involved in partner swapping with other couples, and a decision was made to swap permanently with one couple. He was remarried at age 30 years, his own children staying with his first wife, his second wife bringing with her the two children from her first marriage.

Exposure history

The client began masturbating at 13 years old. At 16 years he says he was trying to find some way to increase his arousal levels. He was not having much luck with girls and was shy. The idea came to him to expose himself through his bedroom window to passing females. This became a regular pattern.

At 17 years old he was reported and convicted. He was fined. He says his family's reaction was to feel sorry for him, and to want to help him. The exposures stopped for a short time when he got his first girlfriend. He failed a get an erection with her, or with his second girlfriend, during sexual activity. His second conviction was at age 18½ years, when he was given a probation order. At 19 years, he met his future wife and experienced his first successful and enjoyable sexual intercourse. At 20 years, he was convicted again, and given a fine and probation order with conditional psychiatric treatment. He was prescribed stilboestrol which removed his sexual feelings, but had a distressing side-effect in that he developed breasts. He stopped seeing his girlfriend. After stopping the treatment, he began seeing her again, and was married at 21 years. After this time he began exposing himself from his works van, rather than the house. He still masturbated to fantasies of exposure, though having regular intercourse with his wife. His fourth and fifth convictions resulted in fines and probation orders, with further psychiatric treatment.

The therapy this time consisted of electrical aversion therapy. He described himself as having 'a confused mind' as a result of this treatment. He said he wanted to expose himself, but did not actually do it. He recalls thinking he ought to try to make the treatment work, but although it felt unpleasant to think about exposure, he was still experiencing urges.

His sixth conviction, at age 25 years, resulted in him being required to have treatment at the Maudsley Hospital in London. Again it consisted of psychotherapy, medication, and aversion therapy. When the behaviour recommenced, he began exposing himself outside, in parks and woods. He says he was afraid of the van being identified. After his seventh conviction, he was given a probation order and fine, without treatment.

At age 29 years, he had begun his relationship with his second wife and for twelve months experienced complete relief from the problem or urges to expose. The problem gradually started again, to women in an age group of approximately 15 to 30 years, and he was convicted again at age 32 years, being given a probation order. He began at this time to indulge in alternative sexual activities, such as displaying pornographic pictures at his car window to passing women. He was hoping to avoid further convictions by these variations, but became conscious that it was not really substituting for exposure, rather that it was keeping him highly sexually aware. He was convicted for a ninth time at age 34 years and fined, this time for his use of pornographic pictures.

A consistent pattern throughout this history was that the client never exposed himself while on a probation order or receiving treatment. The only time he was without urges to expose, apart from when taking stilboestrol, was for the twelve months after his second marriage.

Analysis

A number of hypotheses emerged from material gained from the first three sessions. These will be listed with examples of quotes on which the hypotheses were based. The quotes emerged in the course of the assessment sessions, either in response to direct interviewing questions or through use of automatic thought identification techniques described earlier in the chapter.

1. The client was demonstrating a pattern of destructive dependency. His history showed that the only reliable periods of no offending were while professionals were involved, whether or not they were actively helping, and whatever the nature of the help.

    When asked why he was seeking help even though previous therapy had had no lasting effect:

    'I've always gone to the doctor after I've started doing it again.'
    'I need something new to stop me doing it.'
    'I know if I keep doing it I'll get caught. If I get caught I'll always stop doing it.'

2. There was inconsistency between the client's belief about his ability to control his exhibitionism, and his control of the behaviour itself, which had been for periods as long as 2 years.

    'I know I'll do it again.'
    'I haven't got the willpower.'

3. The client appeared to use no deterrents to recommencing the behaviour once there were no professionals involved. The consequences of starting to expose himself again were to tell his wife, to seek professional involvement, or to gain this through getting caught.

    'My wife stood by me. I couldn't have a better one. I don't tell her until it's all come to light. I don't want to worry her. Then I tell her everything eventually. When I'm exposing, we don't communicate as well. I'm more selfish.'

The treatment decision

Although the client had a history of failed therapies, and the exposure behaviour ceased when he was in therapy, there was no indication that any of the therapies had been successful in reducing urges to expose, other than the stilboestrol which had had distressing side-effects. The incidence of urges to expose had remained undetected during some of the therapies.

Importantly, although no lasting effect had ever been achieved, the client was dependent on therapy, as he saw it, to stop the behaviour in the short term.

'If you can't help, I'll take the tablets again.'

It is significant, however, that when asked about his goals for therapy, he was not aiming at a temporary cessation of the exhibitionist behaviour.

'I want to get rid of the urge and all elements of the problem.'

'I know what it's like not to have the problem at all – for that 12 months.'

'It's the pressure of having it on my mind. It makes me moody and confused. I just want a peaceful mind.'

It was decided to offer the man treatment, while remaining closely aware of the role of his dependency in this.

Session four

The aim of this first therapy session was to test the hypotheses outlined. If the hypotheses were confirmed by eliciting the same automatic thoughts again, and possibly adding to them, a number of strategies could be used. First, the dependency issue should remain of prime importance. Should some cognitive changes occur in the session, the plan for therapy and future sessions should be such that the client maintains the changes alone, and is enabled to perceive that they are not therapist-dependent. A self-help model is obviously an asset in this instance.

Second, the control issue could be questioned and challenged, and more realistic thoughts generated as alternatives.

Third, some aversive cognitions concerning re-offending might be generated by inductive questioning, and if so, suggested to the client for use as deterrents to future exhibitionism.

Fourth, if some cognitive changes are achieved, the cognitive model, including the role of thoughts and feelings in the behaviour chain, can be explained in order for the client to be as aware as possible of the potential benefits to them of maintaining cognitive changes. If they appreciate the rationale for this and agree with it, it is more likely that maintenance of the changes will be successful.

Fifth, a self-help task for use between sessions may be agreed.

These main strategies can be illustrated by extracts of dialogue which occurred during this session:

The issue of control

T: You say you know you will do it again and you haven't got the willpower to stop.

C: Yes, I know the pattern now.

T: So is it possible to say how you've managed to stop since February?

C: Well, I told the wife and the doctor. I knew I needed help.
T: And you've carried on having urges –
C: Yes.
T: But you haven't exposed yourself –
C: Yes, that's right.
T: [*Inductive question.*] So how have you managed that?
C: Well, I've avoided some places. I've been working hard . . .
T: Anything else?
C: I've had less opportunities. I've avoided being alone.
T: And when you have still had the urge?
C: I've controlled it. Like on the way here – I got the urge but I didn't do it. And yesterday, I just carried on working.
T: [*Challenge.*] OK. It seems to me as if you are saying two things here – on the one hand you know you'll do it again, you haven't got the willpower. On the other hand, you say you controlled the urges, sometimes two or three times a week, for 4 months. Which one is nearer the reality?
C: Well I have controlled it – I've said so.
T: [*Challenge.*] So you have got the willpower?
C: Yes, I suppose so.
T: [*Challenge.*] So is it really true to say you *need* to do it when things get dull?
C: No – because I'm not doing it now.

The issue of deterrents

T: Do you say anything to yourself to try and help with the control?
C: I must tell someone.
T: And after you have told someone?
C: I feel better. This time I told my employer, who's a friend, and then I told my wife. I tell her everything and it really helps us to communicate. If we stop talking about the problem it's difficult to start talking about other things.
T: And what happens after that to help you with control?
C: My wife told the doctor. Then I went to him to get some help to stop me doing it. That's why I'm here.
T: [*Inductive question.*] Do you ever think what would happen if you carried on doing it?
C: I know I'll get caught if I keep doing it. It starts off as just the once, but then it builds up.
T: [*Inductive question.*] What would happen to you after all your convictions, if you got caught again?
C: I'm very worried I'd go to prison this time.
T: [*Inductive question.*] And if you didn't, are there any other bad consequences?

C: I'd feel terrible.

T: [*Inductive question.*] Anything else?

C: Well it would be in the papers. People would know all about me and I hoped that wouldn't happen since we moved. I'd lose my friends. I might even lose my job.

Explaining the role of cognitions

At this point, it was explained to the client how what had emerged from the session so far could go on to help him with his problems. In summary, the explanation was something like this, including checks with the client periodically that he understood and was in agreement.

T: Most people think that it's what happens to them that makes them feel and do things. You've said that when things get dull you feel like exposing yourself, and when you see someone and are in suitable circumstances, you end up doing it. I want to suggest to you that there is something else that makes you more likely to feel like doing it, and end up doing it, and that is your thoughts, what goes through your head both at the time and about the whole problem. [*Check with client.*]

It seems to me that if you think you can't control your problem, if you tell yourself you can't control it, it's less likely that you will control it. Also if you don't think of any bad effects of doing it, you are likely only to think of wanting to do it and that will make it more likely. [*Check with client.*]

We've just discovered together that you actually can control the problem better than you realised. You've started to think of whether you actually *need* to do it. Also you've told me all sorts of bad things that could happen if you start up again, which you normally avoid thinking about, but which might just help in your efforts at control. [*Check with client.*]

The client reported understanding the model, and that it made some sense to him, agreeing that his thinking was not quite consistent with his reality.

The self-help task

A prompt card was discussed and agreed upon, as a good way to enable the client to remind himself of his new thinking strategies. The client wrote out his alternative, more realistic thoughts on the card as follows:

SELF HELP CARD

1. I can control my problem.
2. I can control it without having treatment.

3. I don't really need to do it, even when life
    is dull.
4. There are likely to be bad consequences if
    I start again and get caught:
    >   prison
    >   lose my friends
    >   lose my job
    >   feel terrible

It was suggested that during the two weeks before the next session the client should remind himself of his new thoughts and why they were more accurate than his old ones, as a matter of routine. In addition he should use the card to help him resist urges, or to combat any automatic thoughts he experienced about exposing himself, whether triggered by an outside event (e.g. seeing a woman walking past work when he was alone) or not.

Session five

The aim of this session was to evaluate how effective the cognitive changes made in the previous session, and the use of the prompt card to maintain these changes, have been in helping the client control or reduce urges to expose. A decision should then be reached by mutual agreement as to what and when the next therapy involvement should be. The following extract from the session illustrates what was said.

C: The card has been a help as a reminder. I realise I am in control and I don't really need to do it. The pleasure side is a big problem though. I really like doing it.

T: Have you reminded yourself of the deterrents?

C: Yes, I've been trying to think of the law, and what people would think of me if they found out, and how I'd feel.

T: How do you feel about a gap now? Trying for a longer time with these reminders?

C: It's given me a lot of confidence. I hope I'll cope better. In a way I was expecting something like this. It's very clear to me now what's been happening. You've been very straight with me.

Therapist and client collaborated over the length of time to extend the behavioural experiment. It was important that the client experienced long enough away from professional contact not only to control urges, but to test his strategies when he faced actual temptation to expose. A period of three months was agreed, and the rationale for this made fully explicit. The time allowed was for experimentation, not necessarily for success.

Session six

The three-month behavioural experiment was reviewed. What transpired will be illustrated with quotes and thoughts identified from the session.

The client had experienced urges about two or three times a week for the first month and resisted the temptation to expose, using the card and cognitive methods to help him.

'The first month was OK. There were lots of triggers and opportunities and I thought of things to put me off.'

He had then started exposing himself for a period of two weeks, beginning by masturbating while able to see women but without being seen, the behaviour gradually becoming more visible and more frequent until exposure was happening daily at work.

'I decided to expose myself. I was still thinking of the card but I put it to the back of my mind.'

The exposure period stopped again and, along with this, urges to expose ceased. The client was aware that over this ensuing six-week period, urges to expose were gradually coming back, about once a week for the previous two weeks.

'I woke up to what I was doing and stopped. I thought of the consequences again, and this set me off on the right track again.'

In discussion over what he felt had happened over the 3 months, what his opinion was about how he had managed, what his views were about what had gone wrong and why, the following quotes emerged:

'It's difficult to overcome what you really want. I'm not sleeping, I'm worrying about work. It's putting pressure on me again – it's not fair. All I want is peace of mind.'

'I've let people down: you for your help, myself, my family.'

'I don't think I can cope on my own. I'm not trying hard enough. I need to see you more often. I could get my wife to help me – she's around. If I was to tell her, she'd ask me to stop and I'd stick to it.'

'I thought I could cope on my own. I'm not normal. This is a stupid thing that normal people don't have. I can't control it over a long period.'

Re-analysis

As a result of this review, three main points emerged, to be considered at the next session.

1. The dependency issue. There was some evidence that the client had changed his belief about his self-reliance, his ability to help himself. He had utilised the strategies but they had not proved sufficient to maintain lasting control. He had returned to the session indicating renewed dependency on the therapist as a result, but still somewhat altered in his attitude in that he was taking responsibility for his failure

to cope over an extended period. This latter was clearly not a good thing on the surface, since he was showing signs of being more depressed than before. However, one hypothesis was that this may have been a reflection of some enduring change in his thoughts about his responsibility for the problem.

2. The automatic thoughts 'I need to do it' and 'I really want it' appeared not to have changed as a consequence of challenging thoughts about control in session four. Indeed the client had identified the issue of pleasure and 'liking it' as being a problem in session five.

3. A new group of thoughts concerning dissatisfactions the client had about his wife, and a resulting sense of life being dull, had not been confirmed and challenged. The client had suggested in earlier sessions that his need for excitement was met by his exposure behaviour. Thoughts which had been identified were as follows.

Why he had begun exposing after a twelve-month gap following his second marriage? 'Things got dull again. Just the general way of life. I felt I wanted to do it.'

And what did he feel about his wife?

'She's not as attractive as I'd like her to be.'
'Sex is normal. We experiment. We both have a wide outlook, but I think I'm missing out. It's not fair.'
'I just want someone different.'
'She's not really what I want. I'd like her to have more confidence.'
'If she was brighter in herself, I'd rather be seen with her.'

At the same time, the client said about his wife that he could not have a better one, that she loved him completely, that they enjoyed their sex life, and he could not want for more.

Session seven

The aim of the session was to test the three main points emerging from the re-analysis and, if confirmed, to challenge the second two, which are groups of automatic thoughts, and generate alternatives. The process can be illustrated by dialogue:

Dependency

C: It did me good to come and see you. I've lost some of the urges.
T: How has that happened?
C: I know I can cope because I've coped with this latest episode.
T: [*Inductive question.*] How do you make yourself believe you can cope? What evidence do you have about coping?
C: Once I get to a certain pitch, once another pressure comes in, I stop.

What I hadn't realised was that if I get worried enough about the situation, the problem disappears on its own.

T: It's good that you've realised that. But that means you have to start exposing yourself in order to worry about it before you can stop.

C: Mmm.

T: And the worry is what you want to be rid of anyway.

C: Yes, I'm quite low again now. It's just getting into the habit of reminding myself I can cope.

It seemed from this exchange that the hypothesis was confirmed. The client was still taking some responsibility for helping himself, but was not confident he could do it without further sessions.

The issues of wanting to expose and pleasure

T: What's your view about your ability to cope now?

C: I know I can cope, but not over a longer period. It's difficult to overcome what you really want.

T: [*Inductive question.*] So you really want to do it?

C: Not really. I believe I can let it go if I really want to.

T: What would help you to let go of it?

C: If I'm in the right circumstances, things are going well at work, going well with the wife . . . If I'm happy and not looking for excitement.

T: So what happens if you haven't got enough excitement and are not happy?

C: I give in to it as a substitute.

T: [*Inductive question.*] If you didn't do it, what would happen then?

C: I'd have to accept things the way they are and not expect too much out of life.

T: [*Inductive question.*] And how would you feel then, compared to when you were doing it?

C: When I'm not doing it I'm happier anyway.

T: Do you have any evidence of that?

C: After I've done it I feel worse anyway. It's only then that it torments me, I don't sleep . . .

T: [*Challenge.*] So is it really a substitute for not being happy?

C: No, because I don't get any permanent pleasure out of it. Nothing's any different in the long run.

T: [*Challenge.*] So going back to your original thought, is it true that you really want to do it to make you happier if circumstances are not ideal?

C: No. It makes me unhappy.

The issue of dissatisfactions

T: Going back to thoughts about your circumstances. You've said there are dissatisfactions with your wife – she's not attractive enough. She's not as bright and exciting as you want her to be [*Challenge.*] What's so bad about that?

C: It's not that bad. I shall have to make do, and accept things as they are. I'm pretty lucky with what I've got.

T: [*Inductive question.*] And what's the worst that can happen if you never expose again?

C: I'll feel frustrated.

T: Can you cope with that?

C: Sure.

T: What evidence do you have that you can?

C: I've been for more than two years without doing it in the past, and nothing happened.

The cognitive changes concerning pleasure and dissatisfactions were summarised with the client at the end of the session. He said that he felt quite different. It was suggested that he keep thinking these ideas through, and that he monitor urges to expose himself.

Session eight

This session, a fortnight later, aimed to review the tenacity of the cognitive changes over this period, and their effect on urges to expose and frequency of exposure.

The client's following quotes illustrate the content of the review:

'It's given me confidence. I've told my wife all about it – and feel a lot closer to her too. I've been a lot happier.'

'I'm now accepting things I'm dissatisfied with – previously I never did this. I was always wishing I was better than I am. Now I accept how I am. I don't really need to try and be different.'

'I accept my wife the way she is – although she's not perfect. I've appreciated her more.'

'I don't believe I have to do it ever again – because it doesn't give me any permanent pleasure, only unhappiness. The worst I'll feel is frustrated.'

Given that for this client dependency on therapy has been an important part of his presentation, the matter of future contact was discussed at length.

The client felt that there was no need for further sessions. It was agreed that he should have direct access to the therapist should he require it during a six-month period, and that he attend a follow-up session after this time.

The cognitive changes that had taken place during therapy sessions with this client had not been supplemented by keeping formal records of automatic thoughts and written accounts of efforts at changing them to functional, reality-based ones. However, evidence that at this point enduring cognitive, emotional, and behavioural change was likely to have begun was available in the form of the client's reports of his thinking patterns and overall new attitudes, his reports of feeling much better emotionally, and the beneficial effects on urges to expose. Further evidence was provided by his rejection of the offer of future sessions, and by his realistic predictions about how he would continue to cope when future pressures and trigger situations were anticipated. It seems likely that the dysfunctional assumptions underlying the client's original negative automatic thoughts had also been altered fundamentally, and that an extended period of maintenance of the differences achieved would serve to consolidate this.

Session nine

At six-month follow-up, the client reported a lasting effect of his changes in automatic thoughts and underlying assumptions, and on his feelings and behaviour. He had had no urges to expose or incidents of exposure over this period.

Interestingly, in the light of some comments he had made about 'bettering himself', he had begun adult literacy classes and elocution lessons.

He expressed no wish for further appointments.

Conclusion

It has long been acknowledged that there are cultural influences on the incidence of criminal behaviour. Certain values such as 'toughness' and 'masculinity' are reinforced by our society and may actually invite a higher percentage of crimes than in a society which does not prize these values (Toch 1969).

Within the individual such values have an influence on the formation of dysfunctional assumptions, which this chapter has shown can play a major part in negative automatic thinking and the committing of offences.

There are obvious implications for the assessment and treatment of offenders, and indeed for legislation. Cognitive therapy techniques can contribute greatly to the assessment and management of interaction with offenders. Cognitive theory can aid in the understanding and analysis of offence behaviour. Cognitive therapy would seem to be an approach to emotional and behavioural change, which adds fundamentally to the approaches available to date for the treatment of offenders with a general or a specific psychological problem.

The development of the approach with this group, along with controlled treatment trials, process studies, and single case reports, is awaited with interest.

References

Bancroft, J. (1979) 'The nature of the patient therapist relationship: its relevance to behaviour modification for offenders', *British Journal of Criminology* 19: 416.

Bandura, A. (1971) *Aggression: A Social Learning Analysis*, New York: Prentice-Hall.

Beck, A.T. (1976) *Cognitive Therapy and the Emotional Disorders*, New York: International Universities Press.

Beck, A.T. and Emery, G. (1977) 'Cognitive therapy of substance abuse', unpublished manuscript, Philadelphia, PA: Center for Cognitive Therapy.

Beck, A.T., Emery, G. and Greenberg, R. (1985), *Anxiety Disorders and Phobias: A Cognitive Perspective*, New York: Basic.

Beck, A.T., Rush, A.J., Shaw, B.F., and Emery, G. (1979) *Cognitive Therapy of Depression, A Treatment Manual*, New York: Guilford Press.

Blackburn, I.M., Bishop, S., Glen, A.I.M., Whalley, L.J., and Christie, J.E. (1981) 'The efficacy of cognitive therapy in depression: a treatment trial using cognitive therapy and pharmacotherapy, each alone and in combination', *British Journal of Psychiatry* 139: 181–9.

Craft, A. and Craft, M. (1984a) 'Treatment of sexual offenders', in M. Craft and A. Craft (eds) *Mentally Abnormal Offenders*, London: Bailliere Tindall.

Craft, M. and Craft, A. (1984b) *Mentally Abnormal Offenders*, London: Bailliere Tindall.

Crawford, D.S. (1979) 'Modification of deviant sexual behaviour: the need for a comprehensive approach', *British Journal of Medical Psychology* 52: 151.

Crawford, D. (1984) 'Behaviour therapy', in M. Craft and A. Craft (eds) *Mentally Abnormal Offenders*, London: Bailliere Tindall.

Ellis, A. (1979) 'The sex offender', in H. Toch (ed.) *The Psychology of Crime and Criminal Justice,* New York: Holt, Rinehart & Winston.

Emery, G. (1980) 'Self reliance training in depression', in D.P. Rathjen and J.P. Foreyt (eds) *Social Competence: Interventions for Children and Adults*, New York: Pergamon Press.

Feindler, E.L., Marriott, S.A., and Iwata, M. (1984) 'Group anger control training for high school delinquents', *Cognitive Therapy and Research* 8: 299.

Gudjonsson, G. (1986) 'Sexual variations: assessment and treatment in clinical practice', *Sexual and Marital Therapy* 1: 191.

Howells, K. (1982) 'Aggression: clinical approaches to treatment', in D.A. Black (ed.) *Issues in Criminological and Legal Psychology*, No. 2, Leicester: British Psychological Society.

Lopez, F.G. and Thurman, C.W. (1986) 'A cognitive behavioural investigation of anger among college students', *Cognitive Therapy and Research* 10: 245.

Meichenbaum, D. (1975) 'Self-instructional methods', in F. Kanfer and A. Goldstein (eds) *Helping People Change*, New York: Pergamon Press.

Murphy, G.E., Simons, A., Wetzel, R.D., and Lustman, P.J. (1984) 'Cognitive therapy and pharmacotherapy, singly and together in the treatment of depression', *Archives of General Psychiatry* 41: 33–41.

Nomellini, S. and Katz, R.C. (1983) 'Effects of anger control training on abusive patients', *Cognitive Research and Therapy* 7: 57.

Novaco, R. (1975) *Anger Control: The Development and Evaluation of an Experimental Treatment*, Lexington, MA: Heath.

Novaco, R. (1977) 'Stress inoculation: a cognitive therapy for anger and its application to a case of depression', *Journal of Consulting and Clinical Psychology* 45: 600.

Novaco, R. (1978) 'Anger and coping with stress: cognitive behavioural interventions', in J. Foreyt and D. Rathjen (eds) *Cognitive Behaviour Therapy: Research and Application*, New York: Plenum.

Perkins, D. (1984) 'Psychological treatment of offenders in prison and the community', in T.A. Williams and J. Shapland (eds) *Options for the Mentally Abnormal Offender: Issues in Criminological and Legal Psychology*, No. 6, Leicester: British Psychological Society.

Perkins, D. (1986) 'Sex offending: a psychological approach', in C. Hollin and K. Howells (eds) *Clinical Approaches to Criminal Behaviour: Issues in Criminological and Legal Psychology*, No. 9, Leicester: British Psychological Society.

Rush, A.J., Beck, A.T., Kovacs, M., and Hollon, S.D. (1977) 'Comparative efficacy of cognitive therapy and pharmacotherapy in the treatment of depressed outpatients', *Cognitive Therapy and Research* 1: 17–37.

Schlichter, K.J. and Horan, J.J. (1981) 'Effects of stress inoculation on the anger and aggression management of institutionalized juvenile delinquents', *Cognitive Therapy and Research* 5: 359.

Segal, Z.V. and Marshall, W.L. (1986) 'Discrepancies between self efficacy predictions and actual performance in a population of rapists and child molesters', *Cognitive Therapy and Research* 10: 363.

Toch, H. (1969) *Violent Men*, Harmondsworth: Penguin.

Chapter nine

Suicidal patients

J. Mark G. Williams and Jonathan Wells

Introduction

In this chapter, we will consider some of the skills required and issues raised in cognitive therapy with suicidal patients, both those under treatment for depression, and those referred following a suicide attempt. Case examples from our clinical practice will be used to illustrate approaches that we have found useful and some problems in applying them.

The degree to which they express suicidal thoughts needs to be routinely assessed when depressed patients start their treatment. However, there are two contexts in which a therapist will most commonly have to deal with the theme of suicide. First, when a patient expresses suicidal thoughts during the course of therapy, whether or not they have exhibited suicidal behaviour before, these thoughts must be taken seriously. One in ten depressed patients attempts suicide within a year of entering treatment (Paykel and Dienelt 1971). Second, cognitive therapy is increasingly being explored as a means of secondary prevention – the prevention of a new suicide attempt when the client has been referred immediately following an attempt. Such exploration seems timely since no psychological treatment has yet been found which affects the repetition of such behaviours (Hirsch *et al.* 1982; Williams 1985; Hawton and Catalan 1987). To date, no research trial has evaluated cognitive–behavioural therapy interventions with this population, though Fraser's (1987) study of group cognitive therapy (which lasted eight sessions) has given encouraging results. Until more work is done, however, we need to rely on clinical judgement to decide which approaches are likely to prove most effective.

Suicidal thoughts during therapy for depression

Beck *et al.* (1979) emphasise the importance of assessing suicidal risk in depressed patients. If someone expresses suicidal ideas, it is important to determine what method is contemplated, how familiar the patient is with the lethality of medicines, and the availability of methods (e.g. firearms). Assessing the environmental resources for intervention will also be important (i.e. how likely is it that serious suicidal intent would be detected, how likely is it that intervention would be made in time, and how likely is it that adequate medical help could be secured). The therapist will need to be vigilant for verbal or mood cues which might indirectly signal suicidal intent. Verbal expressions of hopelessness provide the best clue. Not all depressed patients are hopeless, and there is an accumulating body of evidence to suggest that hopelessness is the factor which mediates between depression and suicidal intent (e.g. Dyer and Kreitman 1984). Sudden changes in affect in either direction may also signal impending suicidal behaviour.

An assumption of cognitive therapy with these patients is that suicidal intent is a continuum. There is a balance between the intention to live and the intention to die, and even relatively insignificant chance factors may tip the balance. Beck *et al.* (1979) also assume that there are two dimensions along which the motivation of the suicidal patient may vary: *the desire for escape* or surcease; and *the desire to communicate*. People vary in the extent to which either or both of these motivations are present, but the assumption is that the more hopeless patients are those for whom the desire for escape predominates.

Finally, Beck *et al.* (1979) describe in broad terms the stages in helping the suicidal patient: stepping into the patient's world, viewing it through their lens, and attempting to tip the balance against suicide. If *escape* is the main motivation, then the therapist concentrates on the patient's hopelessness and lack of positive expectation. (If hopelessness is due largely to real social problems, then social intervention may be necessary.) If *communication* is the main motivation, the therapist concentrates on determining what is being communicated to whom, and how it can be done more adaptively.

Tipping the balance against suicide also involves building a bridge to the next session, if possible, by getting the patient to see the next episode of suicidal feelings as an opportunity to note in detail how they feel, in order to bring the data to the next session. The therapist might encourage the patient to agree to make explicit what are the pros and cons of living and dying. Dealing with hopelessness will involve careful assessment of the contribution of the reality of the life situation of the patient and of the interpretative schemata which the patient uses to evaluate that life situation. For many there will have been real failures and/or real rejection experiences which must not be minimised by the therapist. But the patient's depression may also have made them select the most catastrophic interpretation of these life situations and of their implication for the future. In this case the question is: what erroneous conclusions are blocking out hope? What alternative behaviours and choices are realistically available to the patient? Stress inoculation can be used, in which the patient uses their imagination of a crisis situation to generate within the session some of the same hopelessness and despair that is typically felt outside the therapy situation. Under these conditions, the patient attempts to generate some alternative coping responses.

Secondary prevention immediately following deliberate self-harm

One of the tasks for a therapist following an attempted suicide episode is to assess suicidal intent and the probability of repetition. Assessment of suicidal intent is best made on the basis of the circumstances surrounding the episode. As a crude guideline, the more the behaviour approximates to suicide, the greater the assumed intent. This has been spelt out in more detail by Beck *et al.* (1974). Critical issues to assess are:

1. How isolated was the person at the time?
2. Was it timed so that intervention was likely or unlikely?
3. Were there any precautions taken against discovery?
4. Did the patient do anything to gain help during or after the attempt?
5. Did the patient make any final acts anticipating they would die?
6. Did they write a suicide note?

The patient's own self-report is also important to take into account:

1. Did they believe what they did would kill them?
2. Do they say they wanted to die?
3. How premeditated was the act? (Two-thirds of patients have not thought about it for more than an hour beforehand. The longer the idea of suicide had been in the mind the greater the suicidal intent.)
4. Is the patient glad or sorry that they have recovered?

Whether the actual medical risk should be taken into account remains a controversial issue. Over a large number of cases there is a significant correlation between actual lethality and suicidal intent (Power *et al.* 1985) but it may be difficult to infer intent from the medical lethality in an individual case. This is because some patients (especially those who are not used to taking pills) may believe that relatively few pills are lethal. In such cases actual physical risk would be no guide to what may in fact be a very serious suicidal attempt. Note, however, the obvious but often overlooked point that the correlation between actual physical lethality and intent is much stronger in cases where the patient is knowledgeable about the lethality of drugs available to them.

Repetition probabilities can be judged through assessment of hopelessness and of suicidal intent for the current episode, and through observing how many of Buglass and Horton's (1974) six vulnerability factors a patient has:

1. Does the patient have problems in the use of alcohol?
2. Have they ever been diagnosed sociopathic or personality disordered?
3. Have they ever had in-patient psychiatric treatment?
4. Have they ever had out-patient psychiatric treatment?
5. Are they living with relatives? (If not, they are more vulnerable.)
6. Have they ever attempted suicide before?

(Buglass and Horton (1974) found that these six items predicted repetition of suicide attempt in an additive fashion. The more vulnerability characteristics, the greater the repetition probability. Even so, the predictive value is limited, for, of those with five or six of the characteristics, only 48 per cent repeated within 1 year.)

Outline for therapy

As noted above, although depression is often associated with suicidal thoughts, not all depressed people are suicidal: it is when depressed people also become hopeless that they are most likely to feel suicidal. Therefore a primary goal of cognitive therapy with suicidal patients, whether the aim is primary or secondary prevention, must be (1) accurate assessment of their state of hopelessness; (2) vigilance for further changes in level of hopelessness; (3) reduction of current state of hopelessness and (4) reduction of vulnerability for future states of hopelessness. Two other important factors must also be assessed: (5) how stable is the patient's life situation (both objectively and subjectively to the client), especially their interpersonal relationships (by far the most common precipitant)? (6) How impulsive is the client? Given the fact that two-thirds of parasuicide episodes are contemplated for less than an hour beforehand, impulsiveness may be considered an important vulnerability factor.

Vigilance for suicidal expression

Patients will often not volunteer direct information that they have thought of suicide. Rather, a number of indirect references may be made, e.g. 'Sometimes I just don't know why I bother'; 'Everything seems so pointless and futile'; 'I don't know that I can carry on much longer like this'; 'I can't see any point any more'. At such points, therapists should pursue the possibility that suicidal thoughts are present: e.g. 'Has it sometimes been so bad you've thought of ending it all?' or 'Have you had any thoughts of suicide running through your mind?'

The patient may arrive at the conclusion that life is intolerable through combinations of the errors in reasoning which have been described in depression – selective abstraction, arbitrary inference, catastrophisation, or overgeneralisation. For example, someone may decide that their life situation is intolerable so they have no alternative but to commit suicide (dichotomous thinking). It may well be that alternative strategies have been too quickly rejected, perhaps because the patient holds a fundamental belief that their life will never be changed or that they cannot be helped. These basic assumptions may prevent the patient from following options that will lead away from the suicidal state.

Many of these errors of logic which underlie beliefs and assumptions are exactly those found in depression. *The particular danger with suicidal patients is that they act so decisively and violently on their beliefs.* A process takes place, often in only a few minutes. First, their thinking about their problems is dominated by the distortions described above; then, they react to these thoughts as inescapable facts, and take proportionately drastic action.

Because this is a process – however swift – intervention to prevent acts of deliberate self-harm may be aimed at different stages of the process:

1. Undermining the beliefs and making the errors in logic explicit.
2. Breaking the link between thought and action. This intervention will use the same core techniques which are used to treat non-suicidal depressives: especially thought monitoring, distraction, task assignment, reality testing, cognitive rehearsal, and alternative therapy. Since these techniques are described in detail elsewhere (Beck *et al.* 1979; Williams 1984) we shall not illustrate their use here. Rather we shall focus on issues that arise in applying them to suicidal patients.

Case transcripts

In the sections that follow, we have selected transcripts from therapy sessions from a number of patients to illustrate particular points. We have preferred this method, since a single session (or even a series of sessions with a single patient) rarely contains all the elements which our clinical experience tells us are important. We begin with an illustration of attempts to consider reasons for living versus reasons for dying. This transcript reveals issues which are then taken up in two further transcripts: (1) the need to deal directly with negative thoughts and (2) inability to imagine possible futures.

Reasons for living and reasons for dying

The following transcript illustrates a possible approach to the 'reasons for dying' versus 'reasons for living' balance. The aim of this procedure is to make explicit what the reasons for living and for dying are for the patient. It assumes that suicidal wishes are the outcome of the balance between the two. Note that patients might not readily find reasons for living. They may be too hopeless or, if they have just attempted suicide, generating reasons for living might produce too much cognitive dissonance. Two ways around this are commonly used. The therapist may ask about reasons for dying first. This takes the patient's predominant impulses seriously, increases rapport, and can enable the patient to be more ready to consider some less pessimistic material. Second, when it comes to asking about reasons for living, the therapist ought not to expect the patient to see *current* reasons for living. The therapist may rather ask what used to be the reasons for living before the patient became depressed, or what would be their reasons for living if they were not so depressed now, if so many things were not going wrong, or if they were ever to overcome their current problems. (It is this option which is used in the following transcript.) Alternatively, the therapist may ask the patient, 'What things have kept you going despite your problems?' The emphasis in the part of the session that remains would normally be to focus on what is blocking the potential incentives to continue living. In the transcript that follows, however, the patient expresses further feelings of hopelessness, and the therapist moves directly to consider the reasons why the patient's attempts to cope, though momentarily successful, do not appear to last very long.

Daphne, a woman in her early thirties, was undergoing cognitive therapy for depression. She had been depressed, on and off, for 13 years and had received a range of antidepressant medication and psychological counselling over this period.

She had married her husband when they were both 24 years, and had two children: Michael (aged 7) and Marion (aged 5). She had continued to work in the clothing trade after the children were born, a decision which had been a point of contention between her and her husband. She had contemplated killing herself many times before and was considered to be a significant suicide risk despite not having ever made an attempt.

P: I'm just a burden on everyone – John, the children, the people at work. Everyone would be better off if I were dead. [*Crying.*]
T: (*Pause.*) When you say 'They'd be better off' it upsets you a great deal.
P: They'd be better off without me.
T: When you feel as bad as you do now, the reasons for dying seem overwhelming. Is that what happens at home too?
P: It happens all the time. When I'm on my own is the worst, after the children have gone to school.
T: Then you feel worse?
P: Yes, terrified.
T: And when you feel terrified, the reasons for dying seem very real, very true?
P: Yes.

T: When you feel so depressed, what are some of the other reasons why you want to die?

P: Pardon?

T: You said just now that you felt a burden – that they'd be better off if you were dead. When you're feeling low, are there other things that make you see advantages in dying?

P: [*Pause.*] Well I'd escape this black despair.

T: Yes.

P: The children wouldn't have to put up with my moods. I hit one of them last week. I felt bad afterwards.

T: The children wouldn't have to put up with being punished so severely. [*Pause.*] Is there anything else that goes through your mind?

P: Sometimes I think John doesn't realise how depressed I feel. He's so wrapped up in his work. I suppose if I died he would see things had really been bad.

Here it is necessary for the therapist to note the possible communicative component to the suicidal thoughts that will need separate investigation. Meanwhile, however, it is important not to be too easily distracted from the agenda currently being worked through – to elicit all the patient's reasons for dying.

T: Are there any other reasons for dying?

P: I just feel I'm wasting everyone's time. No one can help me. I've been like this since I was a child. [*Pause.*]

T: Some reasons for dying are that you would escape from your despair, the children would not have to put up with you, that John would realise how bad you've been feeling, that you wouldn't be wasting people's time any more. Is there anything else?

P: [*Pause.*] I don't think so, no.

T: Can you think of any disadvantages there might be to attempting to kill yourself?

P: Disadvantages?

T: Yes.

P: [*Long pause.*] I think I might fail – end up with brain damage or worse and be more of a burden.

T: Any other disadvantage?

P: Sometimes, when things are going a bit better, I realise how upset the children would be. Michael and Marion climbed into bed last Saturday morning and gave me a big kiss. They'd tried making some toast. The marmalade got everywhere. [*Smiles, then tearful.*]

T: Anything else?

P: Well, I don't know what's on the other side – of death, I mean. I don't have any religious beliefs, but I sort of think, well, it scares me. It might not be peaceful.

T: So sometimes you see there may be disadvantages to dying, or to attempting to die: that you could end up worse off – physically damaged in some way; that the children would miss you; that the other side might not be peaceful. Are these the main things that stop you from killing yourself?

P: I think I'm just scared. I've always been weak. That's my problem. Never able to stand up for myself.

Note again the possibility of picking up this point later when considering this patient's difficulties in communicating, and also notice the fact that she seems to equate taking an overdose with being strong and assertive in some way. At this point, however, the therapist wants to move to reasons for living. This is a difficult transition to make. Although the therapist might see reasons for dying and reasons for living as two sides of a balance sheet, to the patient these reasons for dying can seem overpowering. It will not help if the therapist appears to be minimising their seriousness. One approach is to return to the question, 'When you feel bad this is how you feel; how does it feel on the days when you feel a bit better?' The aim of this would be to get across the message that her thoughts and feelings are correlated with her moods. In fact, the therapist does not take this option.

T: If you were able to stand up for yourself, if you did not feel weak, how do you think things would be different?

Note the therapist has taken another option, to pick up the last point the patient made rather than try and identify good times in the patient's current life. In other words, the therapist is attempting to focus on a possible future if she were able to overcome some of her problems.

P: I'd be a different person. I'd be happier than I am now, anyway.

T: What are some of the things you would do?

P: I might change the way John and I run the house and organise the children and so on. I'd spend more time with the children, take them out more like other mums do, help them with their hobbies.

T: Is there anything else?

P: I think I could enjoy work more. I turned down a promotion last year because I felt I wouldn't be able to cope. Maybe if I could overcome my problems things would seem possible.

T: I was going to ask you about your reasons for living, reasons for staying alive and giving it a go. Could it be that these are some of the reasons for living, the things that you've just told me?

P: But if they're so good, why do I keep thinking of killing myself?

T: This depression makes you lose perspective – that's one of the first things it does. It takes all the nasty things it can find in your life –

past and present – and persuades you that that's all there is. It's very persuasive. Not only that, it tells you that nothing will ever get better.

P: I feel so confused, life is just too much for me. [*Pause.*]

Note this new expression of hopelessness. Having gone through reasons for living and reasons for dying she feels confused. Her reaction to such confusion is expression of her hopelessness. One possible approach at this point would be to take up this particular issue: 'Do you often feel confused by things around you?' or 'Do feelings of confusion often lead to the feeling that life is too much?' An alternative is to identify 'life is too much for me' as a negative thought and test it out. For example, 'When you say "Life is too much for me", how does that make you feel?' – and talk as if it were a good example of the propaganda that depression uses to persuade people that death is the only way out. In this case, the therapist decided to move towards analysis of coping skills in real-life settings. The probable reason for selecting this option is that the session would be soon drawing to a close, so links needed to be drawn between the within-session discussion and between-session behaviour.

T: When life feels too much to bear, what are some of the things that you've done in the past to try and cope?
P: I haven't coped.
T: I'm not just thinking of the events of the past few days. If we go back a few months when things were beginning to go wrong but hadn't yet reached a crisis.
P: I suppose I threw myself into my work, shoved the children off onto John, went for a few long walks. But it didn't help, did it, or I wouldn't be here?
T: You told me once that some things had helped for a little while but they didn't last.
P: They didn't last, no.
T: Can you give me an example of some time when you got really low and managed to cope, even if it didn't last?

There then followed a long description of a time when the patient thought of driving out to a lonely place and 'just disappearing'. She coped by phoning a friend. It helped for a day or two, then she became low again.

Note the emphasis on describing a specific example rather than staying at the general level.

T: Do you think it would be useful to spend some time examining why these things didn't last? If the things you tried had lasted – had made a difference which lasted – would you feel you might have avoided getting so low?
P: I might.
T: Perhaps next week we could look at these things in more detail. Do

you find the same thing happening now, that you try and do something to cope but it only lasts for a while?

P: Yes, it happens almost every day. I try to carry on but I just run out of steam.

T: If we look at your activity scale, what do you expect to try and do tomorrow, for example, that you feel might help but may help only temporarily? [Patient gives details of some activities – walking the dog, washing clothes, talking to customers at work.] To help us discuss this next time we meet, I wonder if you would be able to note exactly how each of them affects you – how much it lifts your mood and for how long. Perhaps you could especially write down what it is that brings you down again. Could we make this the homework for the week?

P: What do you want me to do?

Note the patient's assumption that the therapist decides the homework and the patient has to comply. Alternatively, the therapist might have asked the patient what sort of evidence it would be helpful to gather to help them discuss it. This might have made the patient feel more that she was responsible for the homework. The session ends with the therapist reviewing the session, asking the patient about the homework, what the advantages are of trying to specify why previous coping mechanisms have brought only temporary relief, what some of the difficulties with the homework might be, etc.

If we look carefully at the above transcript we can see that there are some elements lacking in the therapy session. Most obviously the therapist did not complete the reasons for living versus reasons for dying technique. That is, the therapist did not explicitly summarise the patient's view of the advantages and disadvantages of dying versus staying alive. The session was diverted from this by the patient's expression of confusion and hopelessness. In this, the session is fairly typical of day-to-day clinical practice in which a therapist aspires to follow a pattern which is often not actually realised. It may not be that the therapy session was poor: however, there may have been a missed opportunity to make the patient more explicitly aware that there were actual reasons for staying alive, but that these would sometimes be undermined by depression. The therapist might have been able to discuss more explicitly the idea of balance and ask the patient to record some data for homework.

Why did the session move away from the reasons for living versus reasons for dying? The answer may lie in the fact that the agenda item was not explicitly set. At no point did the therapist say something like 'I wonder if we could try to list . . . and then review each to see how true they seem to you now'. The more explicitly the therapist is able to share with the patient what the aims of the current discussion are, the easier it is to give structure to the interchange. This in turn enables closure to take place. Of course, the structure should not be over-rigid or too salient. Cognitive therapy is not a series of mechanical techniques. Nevertheless, some skeleton structure and explicit movement through an explicit agenda can sometimes be a useful aid to the therapist in preventing the hopelessness of the patient from overwhelming the session. Incidentally, it can also provide a role model for a structured, actively problem-solving approach to the patient's problems.

One final point should perhaps be made about the whole notion of a 'balance' between reasons for living and reasons for dying. People who are not depressed or suicidal do not remain hopeful or non-depressed by regularly calculating whether there are more reasons to live than to die. The fact is that no calculation at all is made – positive and negative events are not constantly evaluated on the dimension of whether they constitute a reason to stay alive. This should remind us that there are two aims in treating the suicidal patient. The first is to tip the balance in favour of living rather than dying. The second is to reduce the salience of the living/dying dimension in its entirety.

Evaluating negative thoughts within a session

The transcript we have considered showed how, even while using one therapeutic strategy, the patient may make further expressions of hopelessness. Such expressions may have to be dealt with rapidly, since there may not be much time before such feelings become overwhelming. One technique is to examine, with the patient, the extent to which the belief in a hopeless thought changes over time. This approach is illustrated in the following case.

Marjorie was a 25-year-old single woman admitted to hospital after an overdose of 25 paracetamol. She lived alone, and had taken the tablets when alone at home, only getting help when she began to vomit and guessed that she was not going to die. Her action was seen as demonstrating significant suicidal intent. She was assessed briefly by a psychiatrist who found her to be no longer suicidal, and not suffering from any psychiatric disorder, and she was discharged after 2 days, to stay with friends.

She came to see the therapist within a week of discharge from hospital. In the course of this interview, she talked at length about her family background; she described how as a child she had resented regular visits to her mother in hospital with an unspecified illness, and then, when her mother died when she was 11, she had felt guilty at her own lack of sympathy, and angry with her father for keeping her in ignorance. As a teenager, she had an antagonistic relationship with her father, and during this time she had come to believe that, whilst her sister 'did everything right', 'no one took me seriously'.

Given her evident distress and continuing suicidal ideation at times, it was clear that she needed supportive counselling at the very least. Because it was difficult to specify a particular therapeutic approach at this stage, four exploratory sessions were agreed upon.

During one of these sessions she became very tearful and distraught. Her overdose had been precipitated by the breakdown of a relationship with a man, and she had concluded that she was never going to be able to have a successful relationship. She had not yet felt able to return to work (she was a sales manager), she was still sleeping poorly and volatile in her moods, and she sometimes found herself wondering what was the point of surviving since 'nothing has changed' since the time of her overdose. The aim of the therapist in the transcript that follows was to investigate the belief 'nothing has changed'.

T: Since we've been meeting, we've noticed that there's a number of things you repeatedly say to yourself that really upset you. For example, do you remember last time, what point it was when you started to cry?

P: Yes, it was when I said the same old thing – 'nothing has changed'.

T: When that comes into your mind, it obviously makes you very distressed. Let's try to see why it has such an impact, and how we might reduce that.

P: But it's true, I can't hide from the truth –

T: Well, I'd still like to know what it means to you. I mean, if I had a comfortable, happy life, and I thought 'nothing has changed', I wouldn't expect to be plunged into depression, would I?

P: No, OK.

T: Do you mean 'nothing has changed since October when I tried to kill myself'?

P: Yes, I suppose so.

T: And so does that lead on to the thought, 'If nothing's any different, then I might as well try again and do it properly this time'?

Note that the therapist is here suggesting to the patient what she believes on the basis of his previous impressions of her.

P: Yes, of course it does. That's what's so hopeless.

T: OK, well at least now we're both clear about why that statement has so much impact. It's bound to remind you of when you felt suicidal, and arouse some of those feelings again. What about at other times in your life, though? Have you always thought 'nothing has changed'?

P: Well, no. When I say that to myself I mean 'since the overdose'. Before then, I suppose when I came to this area and started my job, I thought that things were changing and changing for the better.

T: So at least we know that this statement is not equally true over a number of years. I wonder if there are times even now when you believe this statement to a greater or lesser extent.

P: It's not a thought that comes into my mind all the time. I suppose when I'm with Keith [her boyfriend], I don't really believe that idea so much, because I know my life has changed in that I've met him and I'm hoping for a future with him.

T: So when you're with Keith that sort of thought doesn't really have so much impact on you. Is there any particular time of the week when you can absolutely guarantee that this thought will occur to you and you will entirely believe it?

P: I suppose the two worst times of each day are when I get up in the morning, and when I get in after work. Those are the times when I always seem to take stock of myself; in the mornings I feel like an automaton being wound up and marching off to my meaningless job, and in the evenings, when I get in I just see an empty evening ahead of me and I feel just as lonely as I did last year.

It will be useful for the therapist to return at a later point to discussion of these bad periods; to gather more information about them within and between sessions, and to schedule some homework to begin to deal with them. Meanwhile, the therapist wishes to pursue further the way in which this thought is relative to the mood.

T: So in fact, this thought comes along as part of a whole reflective, melancholy mood that you get into at particular times. When you're in that mood, I think big, negative, generalised statements seem especially attractive, but the trouble is that these 'big truths' feed into the depressed mood and tend to make it worse. But anyway, we're not too sure, are we, how true this statement is. We've already seen that it's not absolutely true all the time. But to say 'nothing has changed' is a very devastating comment in itself, isn't it?

P: Yes it is, but that's how I feel.

T: When you say 'nothing', do you mean to include things like your home, and your job, and your friendships?

P: Well, I include my friends, because I hadn't any friends last year, and I haven't got any now. But I don't include my house, because as you know I'm moving soon; and I don't include my job, because I got promotion a couple of months ago, even though that's just put me under more pressure.

T: That's good to hear about some things that *have* changed for you – your house and your job. You'd better remind me about the things that haven't changed.

P: Well, I really mean that the way I feel so low sometimes, that hasn't changed. And that's because the situation with Keith hasn't changed, because I still don't know if I'm going to have a future with him or not.

T: We've divided up your life a bit, into those areas which have changed and those which haven't. So how much do you think you should really pay attention to the general statement 'nothing has changed'?

P: In one way I can see that it's just a thought that seems to fit with my depressed mood, that keeps me depressed, but when I'm down I still believe it.

Note, first, that the therapist has made some progress here in encouraging the patient to see how the belief 'nothing has changed' changes with her mood. Second, the patient has been able to point to things that have changed (house and job). One option would be to use 'alternative therapy' (Williams 1984: 130) to examine a typical situation in which the patient feels despairing and hopeless. The patient would then generate alternative ways of coping, perhaps starting with the attempt to evaluate 'nothing has changed' by bringing to mind the things that have changed. It is likely that this procedure would reveal several obstacles to using such a strategy, which will need to be discussed. They could also become the focus of a homework assignment, the aim of which would be to discover if there are any further obstacles to such coping strategies that have not been anticipated. Note that, as with therapy for depressed patients, setting homework tasks which are aimed at discovering obstacles to be discussed later is more likely to motivate the patient to attempt the homework. The homework which is set with the implicit suggestion that it will make the patient feel better may be *de*motivating if it is not believable, or if the patient feels that the therapist is belittling their problem. Finally, note the hint towards the end of the transcript that it is her relationship with Keith that is the central concern. It is possible that the underlying belief is 'unless things change in that relationship, then nothing has changed'. The therapist might work towards making this belief explicit, and helping the patient to build up or give adequate recognition to alternative sources of satisfaction.

Inability to imagine the future

We have observed that in both primary and secondary prevention the core techniques described in Beck *et al.* (1979) and Williams (1984) may be used. We have suggested that to these should be added a vigilance for expression of hopelessness and a willingness explicitly to discuss reasons for dying and reasons for living. One characteristic of the suicidal patient which often undermines such therapeutic attempts is their difficulty in imagining what the future would be like. Such a difficulty, and one possible technique for dealing with it (time projection), is illustrated in the following case.

Philip, a 40-year-old schoolteacher, was admitted to hospital after an overdose of fifty paracetamol, forty aspirin, and a bottle of whiskey. He had only been found several hours later, when his girlfriend called by chance at the house. He survived without sustaining liver damage, but his overdose clearly showed considerable suicidal intent. He spent several days in hospital, during which time he was assessed by a psychiatrist who did not find him to be suffering from any psychiatric illness.

It emerged that he had made this suicide attempt because of a marital situation that he found intolerable. He had been having an extra-marital affair for the past year, and several times his wife had persuaded him to give up this relationship, only for him to resume it. The day before the overdose his wife had left him, and he had felt that he had failed both his wife and his girlfriend by his indecisiveness.

After discharge from hospital, he stayed with friends 'on neutral ground', and came for weekly appointments with the therapist.

Philip admitted during these sessions that he still felt suicidal at times. For example, he described an incident when he had gone home to visit his wife and 9-year-old son, and had ended up begging her to give him tablets for him to take in overdose. After that evening, he had planned a suicide attempt and played himself melancholy classical music to maintain his depressed state. This mood was only broken when he had news from his girlfriend of a flat which they should be able to move into.

Over a number of sessions, various techniques were used to help Philip gain more control over his suicidal thoughts, which he described as at times suddenly engulfing him and carrying him along with frightening force. He was encouraged to record these thoughts, and the circumstances in which they occurred, in order to achieve more distance from them. As ammunition against these thoughts, he was encouraged to develop a list of 'reasons for living', and together with the therapist he visualised his son, for example, in the present and the future, and in as much detail as possible, so that a very vivid image of his son could then be available to him as a reason for living.

In a similar way, although Philip's crisis was more to do with a perceived intolerable situation in the present than a hopeless future, he was unable to imagine various possible futures for himself that might again act as an argument against suicide. This difficulty in imagining the future became a target for therapy in the transcript which follows. The aim was for him to try and visualise his life as it might be in five hours, five days, five weeks, five months, and five years. It didn't matter with whom he had decided to share his life. What was important was the sense this might give him of progression and continuity, at each stage enhanced by more pictures of his situation, with its possessions, people, activities, and feelings.

T: It seems as if what particularly frightens you is the way a suicidal feeling can sweep over you quite suddenly and almost carry you away.

P: Yes, that's right.

T: We need to understand better, if we can, how this mood develops. Do you think much about the future?

P: No, not really.

T: Can you imagine what life might be like in a year's time?

P: No, it's pretty blank. I don't really know if I'll be around then.

T: It would be very useful if you could visualise your future in concrete terms; I think it would sort of give you something else to hang on to. Would I be right in saying that it's only in the odd black moods that you don't see yourself being around in the future at all?

P: Yes. Most of the time I suppose I'll have some future, but I can't really see what it is.

T: Well, perhaps we could try an exercise to visualise the future in a little more detail. If we sit here and relax, I'll then suggest to you that you picture your life in 5 hours' time, then we'll move on to five days, five weeks, five months, and five years. It doesn't matter if what you imagine actually comes to pass or not. What's important is to see how you can project yourself in a way into the future, perhaps as a way of escaping from the present, and not being engulfed by the problems of the present, but also just to see that it's reasonable for your life to have a progression, a continuity, and to get some encouragement from being able to picture it. Do you see what I mean?

P: I'll try.

T: OK. Let's turn our chairs so that they both face the same way. [*Pause.*]

This was done to avoid distraction of face-to-face visual contact.

T: Right, now, where will you be in 5 hours?

P: I suppose I'll be at home, with Karen busy getting tea!

T: Describe the room to me.

P: I'm sitting in my favourite armchair. I've got my shoes off and my feet up. I'm having a look at the *Evening News*. Karen's behind me in the kitchen area. I often want her to sit down and tell me a bit about her day, but she prefers to get on with the cooking.

T: And what's going through your mind?

P: Well, if it's today, then I expect I'll be worrying a bit to myself about some of the problems at school. There are one or two people in my department who seem particularly unhelpful just now, working to rule and everything.

T: What other things might you be thinking of?

P: Well, I'm always wondering what Deirdre and Alan [wife and son, from whom he is separated] are doing. I miss Alan especially a lot.

T: Can you still get any pleasure from thinking about them?

P: Yes, I'm looking forward to seeing Alan at the weekend.

T: So what might you be thinking about that in 5 hours' time?

P: I might imagine what we'll do. He likes to go and look at the boats, so we might go down to the harbour for an hour or two. It's nice, because we can have some time on our own then, sort of man-to-man.

T: Right, well that sounds as if even tonight there'll be some moments that are quite peaceful, and others, obviously, more traumatic. What about 5 days' time?

There then followed a detailed description of a visit with his son to the harbour.

T: What about in 5 weeks?

P: That'll be the beginning of September, won't it. Well, I will be in the middle of doing some teaching of foreign students then.

T: So what might a Tuesday in September be like?

P: I don't know what might have happened with Deirdre and everything, but let's suppose I'll still be living at the flat. I like the flat, though it's a bit cramped.

T: And what would your day be like?

P: Well, I go off to the school about 9 o'clock. And in fact I look forward to this different sort of teaching. The classes are smaller and it makes a nice change.

T: Do you think you'll be able to concentrate on the lessons all right?

P: Yes, I expect I'll be working pretty hard, and that usually takes my mind off things quite well. I get home about 4 o'clock, and if it's a nice day, I might take the dog round the park for half an hour or so, before Karen gets in.

T: And what about the evening?

P: The evening? Could be anything I suppose.

Note, again, the patient's lack of specificity in imagining the future.

T: Well, tell me about the sort of evening that you might realistically expect.

P: It's possible I could have a pleasant evening, if things are more sorted out by then. I suppose we might spend quite a long time over the evening meal, and hear a bit of the office gossip and everything. Then perhaps, a cup of coffee and one of the classical records that she's got keen on buying recently.

T: And what about 5 years?

P: For all I know I might be Head of Department by then! I think I'd enjoy that actually, and hopefully I'd still be at the same school. Alan would be 16, I suppose, but I like to think I'd have kept in regular contact with him, assuming, that is, that I don't go back to Deirdre. I think we could be pretty good friends by then, Alan and I; with my job and everything, I don't think I'm too bad with teenagers, and I'll look forward to taking Alan out, perhaps fishing. I hope Karen and I will still be together; if we are, we will have come through a lot, and it will have made us very close.

T: OK, let's leave it there. [*Turn chairs back.*] I know that felt artificial in a way, but that's to be expected, because it was a particular exercise we were doing. But I think it showed that you could project yourself into the future, and by the end, you were coming up with quite a lot of things spontaneously, that seemed to hold your attention. Did you find it useful?

P: Well, I'm not sure how much impact all this would have when I was in one of my real 'downers'. Is the idea that I should be able to call on some of these images to keep some of the blacker thoughts at bay?

T: Yes, I think you can look at it as a sort of distraction technique. It's also a way of protecting yourself against the black thoughts of the present that you have when you're depressed. The idea is that if you can be aware of detailed realistic images about the future, you are less likely to feel so hopeless in the present.

Note: (1) It is sometimes preferable to keep the time projection going longer, to try and capture the greater mood of optimism and perspective which the patient may have achieved. Some therapists would therefore instruct the patient to come slowly back in time to the present, while still relaxed, and perhaps to attempt to plan the next few days, before ending the time projection.

(2) The patient expresses some doubt about the ability to use the technique by himself. The therapist might instruct him to practise the technique by himself when he is not feeling so bad in order to become more proficient, and to increase its immunisation effect.

(3) The patient may have been presenting an overly optimistic view of the future. Time projection is likely to be of greater value if the patient is able to visualise some potential problems in detail, but also to imagine being able to cope with them.

Some common problems

Of all the questions that arise when doing cognitive behaviour therapy with suicidal patients, some of the more important may be considered here. First, do not many of these patients have severe real-life problems? Is not their hopelessness understandable? Second, might not consideration of reasons for dying *precipitate* a suicide attempt? Third, how do you know who will benefit from treatment? Which techniques are most appropriate for which patient?

Reality-based hopelessness is indeed often found. Many patients have some real problems that, as we observed, must not be minimised by the therapist. It is worth the therapist bearing in mind, though, that some people appear able to cope with apparently unbearable problems without becoming suicidal. Why? It is possibly because depressive hopelessness is not the same as normal sadness. Financial hardship and interpersonal chaos may reasonably cause a great deal of anger, frustration, and sadness. However, a person becomes depressed and suicidal when their reasonable sadness changes to a situation in which the person tells themselves 'I'm to blame', 'I've never succeeded at anything in my life', 'There is no way things can improve', 'If my love leaves, I am nothing', and so on. When people are under great stress – stress which has understandable consequences on their mood – they need all the coping resources they can muster. What they do not need is a constant stream of negative thoughts and images which convinces them that they are stupid, worthless, and good-for-nothing. Cognitive therapy can be conceived as enabling the person to discriminate between normal frustration and depressive hopelessness, so that the real problems can be faced realistically.

Second, might focusing on reasons for dying precipitate suicidal wishes? In fact, our experience shows that the act of making these factors explicit is more likely to be therapeutic. If the patient believes that there are overwhelming reasons for dying, proceeding with therapy as if these reasons did not exist is not beneficial. Making such reasons explicit encourages the patient to feel that their reasons are being taken seriously. Objective statement of the reasons is only the first step to evaluating the evidence for and against each one and discussing why some reasons are weighted in the patient's mind more heavily than others. This procedure will include evaluating evidence for the reasons for living which may need strengthening. There is no evidence that explicit discussion of reasons for dying actually increases suicidal intent. Indeed, our clinical experience suggests the converse, that if therapists tend to concentrate only on the positive reasons for living their rapport with the patient may be lost and hopelessness increase.

We do not yet know who will benefit most from treatment, or which technique is most suitable for which patient. The evidence from Simons et al. (1984) and Fennell and Teasdale's (1987) outcome trials of cognitive therapy with depressed patients suggests that the patients who naturally tend to adopt an active problem-solving coping style (which has been temporarily obscured by the current crisis) might be most suitable. In the case of depressed patients, this has been assessed using Rosenbaum's self-control scale (Rosenbaum 1980) and by evaluating patients' reactions to the *Coping with Depression* booklet which describes something of cognitive theory and therapy (Beck and Greenberg 1974). No such prospective study has yet been done with suicidal patients.

The question 'Which technique?' is most pressing for the management of post-attempt patients, since the large number of such patients may limit the amount of time available for each. Our clinical experience suggests that evaluating the balance between communication and escape motives is a useful first step, and may be followed by choosing the technique which is most likely to deal with the primary motivating factor. In either case, we suggest that cognitive rehearsal of particularly difficult situations similar to those which have precipitated crises in the past will be helpful (Williams 1984: 127; Hawton and Catalan 1987). During cognitive rehearsal, any or all of the signs of hopelessness which we have illustrated in our transcripts may arise and will need to become the explicit focus of therapy.

Concluding remarks

Because work with suicidal patients uses the same techniques which have been described before in therapy for depressed patients, we have not attempted to illustrate them again in this chapter. Rather, we have focused on the management of suicidal tendencies within the framework which assumes a balance between reasons for living and reasons for dying. In making such a balance explicit, further expression of hopelessness may occur which needs to be dealt with rapidly. Further, it may become apparent that an important factor limiting progress in therapy is the inability to imagine a possible future. We wish to make no claim about which technique is most appropriate for which patient at which point in the development of the depression or suicidal feelings. The research has not yet been done to establish this. However, examination of how to deal in therapy with particular problems that arise in particular individuals, each showing different sorts of cognitive and behavioural difficulties, is an important first step in this endeavour.

Suicidal patients are a highly vulnerable group who naturally arouse considerable anxiety in clinicians. Amongst the range of interventions that may be used to treat this group – hospitalisation, physical treatments, environmental manipulation – cognitive therapy is beginning to show that it has a place. Through careful identification of the depressive thinking that may lead to hopelessness, and through the use of strategies to alter these habits of thinking, our impression is that significant progress can be made in helping such patients overcome their suicidal impulses.

References

Beck, A.T., Rush A.J., Shaw, B.F., and Emery, G. (1979) *Cognitive Therapy of Depression: A Treatment Manual,* New York: Guilford Press.
Beck, A.T., Schuyler, D., and Herman, J. (1974) 'Development of suicidal intent scales', in A.T. Beck, H.L.P. Resnik and D.J. Lettieri (eds) *The Prediction of Suicide,* Bowie, Maryland: Charles Press.

Buglass, D. and Horton, J. (1974) 'A scale for predicting subsequent suicidal behaviour', *British Journal of Psychiatry* 124: 573–8.

Dyer, J.A.T. and Kreitman, N. (1984) 'Hopelessness, depression and suicidal intent in parasuicide', *British Journal of Psychiatry* 144: 127–33.

Fennell, M.J.V. and Teasdale, J.D. (1987) 'Cognitive therapy for depression: individual differences and the process of change', *Cognitive Therapy and Research* 11: 253–72.

Fraser, S. (1987) 'Cognitive and behavioural strategies in the management of suicidal behaviour', unpublished Ph.D. thesis, University of Leicester.

Hawton, K. and Catalan, J. (1987) *Attempted Suicide: A Practical Guide to its Nature and Management*, 2nd edn, Oxford: Oxford University Press.

Hirsch, F.R., Walsh, C., and Draper, R. (1982) 'Parasuicide: a review of treatment interventions', *Journal of Affective Disorders* 4: 299–311.

Paykel, E.S. and Dienelt, N.N. (1971) 'Suicidal attempts following acute depression', *Journal of Nervous and Mental Disease* 153: 234–43.

Pierce, D.W. (1981) 'Predictive validation of a suicide intent scale', *British Journal of Psychiatry* 139: 391–6.

Power, K.G., Cooke, D.J., and Brooks, D.N. (1985) 'Life stress medical lethality and suicidal intent', *British Journal of Psychiatry* 147: 1655–9.

Rosenbaum, M. (1980) 'A schedule for assessing self-control behaviours', *Behaviour Therapy* 11: 109–21.

Simons, A.D., Garfield, F.L., and Murphy, T.E. (1984) 'The process of change in cognitive therapy and pharmacotherapy for depression', *Archives of General Psychiatry* 41: 45–51.

Williams, J.M.G. (1984) *The Psychological Treatment of Depression: A Guide to Theory and Practice of Cognitive Behaviour Therapy*, London: Croom Helm, and New York: Free Press.

Williams, J.M.G. (1985) 'Attempted suicide', in F.N. Watts (ed.) *New Developments in Clinical Psychology*, Leicester: British Psychological Society, and Chichester: John Wiley.

Chapter ten

The wider application of cognitive therapy: the end of the beginning

J. Mark G. Williams and Stirling Moorey

Let us begin this final chapter by picking up a theme which Professor Beck alluded to in the foreword to the book. The application of a novel therapy to an area of clinical work needs to go through certain stages. It is as if the emergent therapy has a developmental history of its own, and is bound to a time course. Such a time course can be observed to have occurred in the application of systematic desensitisation to phobic problems, the application of social skills training to assertiveness problems, and the application of cognitive behaviour therapy to depression. It involves showing, first, that the therapy *can* work with individual case examples; second, that it *does* work with a group of such cases in a clinical series; third, that it works better than control conditions in a properly controlled clinical trial. When this has been achieved, two types of question then follow: (1) *how* does the therapy work in the conditions where it is known to work (e.g. cognitive therapy with depressed patients); and (2) can the therapy be applied to other clinical conditions outside the original domain in which it was developed. It is this second question which has been addressed in this book. Each potential application of the technique will have its own developmental stages to go through, beginning with uncontrolled case studies. Most of the work presented in this book is at this early stage, but this does not prevent us from learning a great deal which can contribute to our work as clinicians or teachers or researchers.

In this final chapter we should like to do four things: (1) to summarise some themes that have emerged from the case material presented in the book; (2) to discuss what other client groups cognitive therapy might be relevant to, and to discuss in more detail its application to people who have learning disabilities; (3) to discern the framework within which cognitive therapists appear to be working and to make it explicit; and (4) to describe some future strategies for research, both fundamental and applied.

Emergent themes

Cross-sectional and longitudinal assessment

Cognitive therapy has often been called a 'here and now' therapy. To a large extent this is true. Session by session, examples of difficult situations are taken from the previous week. Tasks are assigned as homework specifically to create the day by day conditions where more data will be gathered to test out the reality basis of attitudes, thoughts, and images.

But what also emerges from looking at the practice of cognitive therapy is the importance of setting the present in the context of the past. This is especially true in the initial assessment where both long-term developmental issues relating to childhood and adolescence and shorter-term issues surrounding the onset of the current problems are discussed. But how should these data be gathered? Let us look at one or two of the therapists at work in this book to see if any pattern emerges.

Blackburn (Chapter 1) is quick to ask where the problem started. But note that it is not just a series of facts that is being established by the therapist. She takes seriously the opinions, attitudes, and evaluations expressed by the patient about the details they are describing. For example, when the patient describes having been passed over for promotion, the therapist asks how it made the patient feel (p. 6) and then goes on to point out to the patient the distinction between thought and feeling. Similarly, when the patient says of her work arrangements 'I did not know what was going to happen to me', rather than merely concentrating on getting the bare facts (in which case the next question would have been 'And what did happen?'), Blackburn asks 'What did you think could happen to you?' (p. 7). Note that information about the history of cognitive symptoms is here being gathered alongside the 'factual' material. This, of course, appropriately reflects the nature of the development of symptoms: 'fact' is rarely separable from interpretations and feelings that surround events. Interpretations and feelings have consequences for subsequent events and subsequent behaviour. This, then, illustrates an important aspect of assessment in cognitive therapy. As well as cross-sectional (here and now) assessment, there is the need for longitudinal assessment. The development of the current episode and the case history over a longer time period are relevant, but bare 'facts' are of little use. What the cognitive therapist requires are the interpretations and feelings surrounding the autobiography. When this is done, interesting patterns may emerge. Note Greenberg's (Chapter 2) observation of similarities between patients' attitudes towards their symptoms and their outlook on other problems (e.g. 'This means I am defective and can't handle things', 'Problems always get worse and they last for ever' – p. 28). However, also note how she feels that it is very important with the particular patient she discusses not to try to deal with basic attitudes (which have grown up over a lifetime) too early in the therapy.

Engagement in and explanation of cognitive therapy

Our experience of running training workshops in cognitive therapy teaches us that this aspect is one of the most difficult. People ask 'How do you introduce the cognitive model?' How do you begin to get the person to look at their ideas as just that: ideas. Let us look at what the therapists in this book do.

Blackburn (p. 61) in listening to the patient's history asks of an event: 'How did that make you feel?' The patient's reply includes 'I must be inferior'. The therapist responds 'That's what you *thought*, but what were your *feelings*, can you remember?' From early on, Blackburn is making a distinction not didactically, but as part of the questioning and clarification.

Greenberg's patient was nervous when driving into work. He describes 'a nervous state, a feeling of like, "I don't know whether I want to stay here or if I want to go"'. The therapist replies, 'You had automatic thoughts like "I don't know whether I want to go or stay at work"?' Note again, the therapist makes a distinction between feelings and thoughts, not explicitly, but by gradually introducing the distinction into the vocabulary she uses to ask the questions and reflect back what the patient says.

Salkovskis (Chapter 3) describes the engagement of an obsessional patient who began the first session in tears, finding it difficult to start discussing her problem (p. 59).

P: I shouldn't really be wasting your time.
T: It sounds like you had a really upsetting thought just now.
P: Yes.
T: What went through your mind right then?
P: I thought that I must be a very bad patient because I can't tell you about my problems.
T: Well, it's interesting you should say that, because it seems to me that you have just told me one of your problems; I mean that you have a problem talking about your difficulties.
P: Yes, but that's not my *real* problem.

Salkovskis uses the first thing that happens in therapy, the apologies and the crying, as a way of gently introducing the cognitive model. But again this is not done explicitly or didactically.

These examples give us a good indication of how the engagement in this particular form of therapy is achieved. The very style of questioning is the key. When people relate facts, they are asked about their interpretations, their thoughts, their feelings. When they make a statement about themselves, the statement is reflected back but only after having been gently placed within a cognitive framework. The therapist's style thus becomes a model for the patient – a model in which a structured, active, discriminating, questioning approach is substituted for an unstructured, passive, global, declarative approach that many such patients commonly use in their emotional lives. Only when this is under way is the model explicitly and more didactically introduced. Of course, there are exceptions to this sequence, but even so the method of engagement in therapy is similar – questions of clarification which implicitly reflect the cognitive framework.

Techniques for eliciting thoughts and feelings within the session

The variety of techniques for eliciting thoughts and feelings during the session is very large and we can do little more than highlight one or two aspects in this summary. Direct questioning is one approach, and we have illustrated this in talking of the way in which a therapist attempts to engage the patient at the beginning of therapy. The above descriptions also illustrate another approach: using times when the patient appears upset to ask what went through their mind just then. This was a technique that Salkovskis used at the beginning of the therapy session he describes. But a technique which emerges very clearly in some of the case descriptions in this book is the introduction of behavioural experiments within the session to simulate real-life circumstances. For example, Greenberg uses the hyperventilation technique to examine the patient's thoughts and feelings about their own bodily symptoms. After hyperventilation for two minutes the patient reported discomfort: sweating, drowsiness, stinging, apprehension. He also reported the fear that he was going to faint. This in turn reminds him of the feeling that he gets outside the therapeutic situation in which he finds himself asking the question, 'Can I get help?' or 'I'm all alone here, could I get to . . .?' and 'If I died what would happen?' and 'Well, who would care?'

In Channon and Wardle's description of their patient with an eating disorder (Chapter 6), they demonstrate the use of a behavioural experiment (eating a small piece of chocolate) to elicit automatic dysfunctional thoughts. The patient was asked to list her thoughts at four stages: (1) before the food is presented; (2) in the presence of food, before eating; (3) during eating, and (4) after eating. The statements that the patient made were at first fairly specifically related to the chocolate itself: 'Chocolate is unhealthy'; or fairly closely related to the patient's own lack of impulse control: 'If I have one bit I'll go on and on eating'. But these thoughts were able to form the basis of further exploration so that the therapist could ask what the patient meant when she said that chocolate was unhealthy. Once again, the patient's attitude seems unremarkable:

'Everyone knows that chocolate is fattening'. It is not clear that there is very much that is dysfunctional here until the therapist gently pushes a little harder and finds that the patient believes that simply having eaten the small piece of chocolate will make her fat because it just sits in her stomach. The therapist asks about the consequences of this and the person replies, 'It'll just stay there and I'll have a great big stomach and get fat.' Note the therapist's reply to this (once again in the form of a question, and once again using the vocabulary of cognitive therapy so that the point is introduced gently): 'Is that a very frightening idea for you?' Patient: 'Yes – I'd hate myself and look ugly.'

In Moorey's description of the treatment of drug abuse (Chapter 7) we find another example of using exposure to a specific situation to assess the dysfunctional aspects. Tables 7.3 and 7.4 in his chapter reproduce the stimuli that were used in an exposure situation within the session. A picture of a doctor's surgery, a tourniquet and a spoon, an empty syringe, a syringe and needle, syringe and needle containing physeptone, drawing up drug from an ampoule, finally sitting with syringe and needle against the arm. Note how this situation differed from the sort of exposure that might be used in behavioural therapy without a cognitive component. In Moorey's case, the exposure was presented as an *experiment* in which the subject tested out her prediction that in the presence of the stimulus her craving would not reduce. In fact the craving did reduce over time and the therapist was able to point out the extent to which the patient was using active strategies in coping with her craving. As the craving reduced so the automatic thoughts that were recorded changed in nature from 'I'd enjoy a fix' and 'The heroin looks familiar and comforting' at the point at which craving was at the highest, to 'I can't wait to throw this heroin away' at a point when the craving had reduced.

Cole (Chapter 8) gives several examples of the use of imaginal cognitive rehearsal of specific offence situations to elicit the thoughts and feelings of people undergoing cognitive therapy for offending behaviour. A client awaiting trial for indecent assault on male teenagers was helped to recall one of the incidents. The therapist asks what he noticed about a particular imagined young male. When the client replied, 'He's smiling at me', the therapist asked how he was feeling right now. The client replies, 'Sort of friendly and affectionate.' The therapist is then able to ask what it meant that he was smiling at him? The client replies, 'Children are attracted to me. They come straight towards me. I'm popular.' Cole uses this material to derive as comprehensive a hypothesis as possible about the setting conditions in which the offending behaviour occurs and what is maintaining it. Making these issues explicit to the client can then lead to mutual decisions as to what behavioural experiments can be done to test out (within or between sessions) the factors which are involved in their behaviour.

Dealing with dysfunctional attitudes

Making explicit dysfunctional attitudes is a theme common to all the cognitive therapy strategies which have been illustrated in this book. These are sometimes directly related to the 'symptoms'. For example, the exhibitionist mentioned by Cole who said, 'I am over-sexed. I have stronger feelings than other boys so I have to do something about it.' But Cole also points out how closely related this is to a feeling of dependency. This means that the client not only believes that he cannot overcome his propensity to continue with offence behaviour but also believes he cannot cope in life without the help of others. His feeling of need of help may exceed the resources he needs to enable him to stop. This can jeopardise the formation of reasonable goals and maintenance of change as a result of therapy.

A similar self-schema is illustrated by Moorey in his description of drug abusers: 'If I get a craving I have no control over myself'; 'I'm too weak to control myself'. But the other side of the dichotomous thinking is also represented in their assumptions: 'Getting over drugs is something I have to do without any help from anyone.' Moorey's description of the self-schema of Ted on p. 178 shows how a person's attitudes and behaviour can be closely interrelated. Note also the example of Jane on p. 178 to whom heroin provided a way of integrating a number of assumptions she had about herself into a stable schema which ran something like this: 'I am a sensitive, intelligent, and romantic individual who cannot stand the harsh real world without heroin to deaden the pain.'

Cognitive therapists use a variety of methods to assess underlying attitudes. One common method is to use a questionnaire such as the Dysfunctional Attitude Scale (Weissman and Beck 1978). This yields a score, but perhaps more valuable than that, it can form the basis of a discussion with the patient within a session and the basis of patient's own thought catching outside the session. In a second technique to help between-session thought catching, the patient can be asked to look out for the occurrence of 'shoulds', 'musts', and 'oughts' in their daily life. Often when these words occur, there will be a general belief lying 'below the surface'. The patient can then try to practise discerning what these beliefs are, and to what extent they are maladaptive.

A third technique is to use consequential analysis, or the 'inverted arrow' technique, within a therapy session. When a patient expresses an idea and a great deal of affect accompanies it, the therapist sometimes feels that the affect generated is too intense to be due simply to the thought they have expressed. In this case the therapist asks what the consequences would be if that thought were true. A particularly good example of consequential analysis is given by Warwick and Salkovskis (Chapter 4) in discussing their patient who had a problem with her throat. This patient found she needed to 'click' her throat in order to reduce discomfort. If she delayed this 'clicking' then it was very uncomfortable. The therapist then finds an opportunity to ask what it is about the throat that makes it so frightening. At this point the patient replies, 'Because it's so uncomfortable, and I think, where the hell is it all going to end?' The therapist is then able to ask, 'Where do *you* think it's going to end? What is the worst thing that could happen?' This allows the patient to say, 'Well . . . I've got a good imagination. . . .' Still the patient talks about the details of the symptoms rather than answering the questions about the worst that could happen. However, by gentle persistence on the part of the therapist, the patient says, 'In the end I shan't be able to walk, shan't be able to breathe, eat properly, and then I'm afraid I shall be taken away from my family, nobody will look after me, I can see it.' This line of questioning has thus discovered a very significant underlying fear in this patient.

But not all underlying attitudes are so evidently fearful. Sometimes they take the form of assumptions and 'frames of reference' which the patient has learnt from relationships with parents, sibs, and peers from an early age. Because of the developmental stage at which these attitudes were learnt, they become incorporated into the self-schema and are rarely challenged. A very good example of discussion of these issues is given in the tenth session of the case described by Ruth Greenberg (pp. 42–5). The discussion moves from the thought 'I can't do it' through 'I can't handle the responsibilities of a perfect person' to the thought that his mother didn't really care about him, and directly to a discussion of his mother having had perfectionist standards based on her other son who had died when the patient was 3 years old. In the transcript which follows this discussion, the therapist gently reality-tests some of the patient's fixed notions.

Other applications of cognitive therapy

The examples we have chosen in this book have necessarily been selected ones. We decided to examine the use of cognitive therapy with only adult clients, despite the fact that cognitive therapy is being often used with older patients and with adolescents. However, the principles in applying cognitive therapy to these groups do not differ in any way from those which have been illustrated in this book. Cognitive therapy has also been applied to the treatment of relationship problems between partners. Cognitive therapy offers a particularly appropriate range of techniques for the treatment of a couple's problems, since it involves a combination of education, assignments, and uncovering dysfunctional expectations and aspirations which each has about the other and about the relationship.

But there is one particular group of clients which we would like to discuss in more detail: the clients with a learning difficulty. The reason for wishing to illustrate the application of cognitive therapy to this group is partly that their emotional problems are often simply attributed to their handicap. A second reason is that cognitive therapy has often been accused of being only applicable to the 'intellectual' client. Cognitive therapists have just as often repudiated this suggestion, but no clearer demonstration of this repudiation could be given than to illustrate its use with clients who have a mental handicap. In the following section we therefore give some details showing how work with handicapped clients can use the framework to be described later (see Table 10.1), varying the complexity level of the techniques to suit the client, but keeping the cognitive model in mind to guide the formulation and overall strategy for the therapy.

Application of cognitive therapy to clients with a learning difficulty

This section will use illustrative case material from the casebook of one of us (SM).

Case 1

A 23-year-old man who was mildly mentally handicapped and suffered partial hearing difficulties presented with complaints of inability to concentrate and depression, associated with ruminations about various subjects. A psychiatric examination did not reveal symptoms of clinical depression. His depressive feelings centred on his concerns about the way his family were thwarting his independence, the fact that he never knew his real father, and the constraints of this dual handicap. A functional analysis showed that the ruminations occurred most frequently when he was alone, and that he was spending most of his evenings alone in his bedroom. The ruminative themes were a mixture of grandiose fantasies (being a mafioso, robbing a bank, becoming a drug smuggler) and unpleasant preoccupations about who his real father was, how to find him, etc. The therapist conceptualised the problem as a cognitive behavioural trap, in which the ruminations served to raise his self-esteem in the short term by their offer of simple solutions to his problems (becoming a macho man, finding his lost father), but became aversive because of the impossibility of putting them into practice. In addition, they produced a negative spiral in which his activity level decreased, allowing more ruminations and less and less opportunity for rewarding experiences. The option of family work was not available, so an individual treatment plan was devised. A simple intervention proved highly effective. He kept a diary of his daily activities and severity of ruminations. Once the inverse relationship between activity and ruminations was establirhed, he was encouraged to carry out activity scheduling, where high-risk times for ruminations were filled with pleasant activities. The patient chose his own activities which he described as ones which gave him 'spirit', but which had much in common with Beck's concept of mastery experiences (Beck *et al.* 1979: 128–31). He thus not only distracted himself from his negative cognitions but also engaged in behaviour which raised his self-esteem (adult literacy classes, car maintenance classes, trips to the West End on his own without the risk of non-fulfilment of the goal). His ruminations reduced in frequency, but his family difficulties continued and required further counselling.

Note the use of the patient's *own* word 'spirit' in therapy. This is an important aspect of cognitive therapy in general and especially where there is a danger that the patient will misunderstand the therapist's ideas and terminology.

Case 2

Case 1 illustrated the use of behavioural techniques within a cognitive formulation. The second case illustrates the use of *cognitive coping strategies* (see Table 10.1). These strategies require a degree of understanding and participation on the part of the patient since they are essentially self-help procedures. Self-instructional training has been used widely in cognitive behaviour therapy with children (Meichenbaum and Goodman 1971; Kendall and Finch 1976, 1978). Patients are taught to use self-statements to guide them through a task, or help them cope with a stressful situation. The self-statements are, ideally, chosen by patients, but if provided by the therapist should be meaningful for them and appropriate for their developmental level. In the method described by Meichenbaum the therapist first models the technique, then instructs the patients to use self-statements out loud, and then gradually encourages them to make the statements covert.

A 20-year-old girl presented with recurrent episodes of emotional disturbance which occurred twice a month and lasted 1 to 3 days at a time. During these episodes she was tearful and anxious and would talk to herself and shout. Psychometric testing showed that she had an IQ of 70 (Verbal 71, Performance 70). The history and clinical features suggested that these were recurrent anxiety attacks. A functional analysis revealed clear precipitants for these since they occurred whenever there was impending change or preparation for an event. Thoughts and interpretations played an important role in these attacks: any uncertainty triggered a set of anxious thoughts such as 'What am I going to do?', 'I have to get ready in time', etc. She would be heard to say these out loud repetitively when distressed. At domestic chores she would frequently leave her own job and do someone else's, and if she had to get ready for anything she would be distressed and preoccupied for hours or days before. The common theme behind these situations seemed to be her overreaction to the difficulty and importance of a task (due to cognitive distortions) as well as an inability to determine when a task was finished, what its limits were, and how well she was performing at it (due to cognitive deficits in the way she coped with a task; see Figure 10.1).

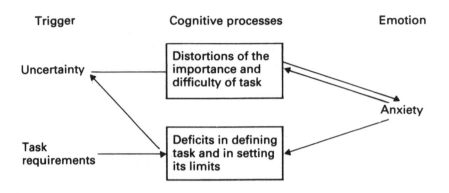

Figure 10.1 The role of cognitive distortions and deficits in mediating anxiety (Case 2)

The problem having been formulated in a cognitive–behavioural way, she was offered six sessions of anxiety management training. She was taught basic relaxation techniques which she employed very well. Attempts at cognitive restructuring were less successful. She found it difficult to recall and identify her anxiety-provoking thoughts, and found it difficult to reality-test her fears. At this point the therapist used a different level of the hierarchy (see Table 10.1), moving to more simple cognitive strategies, applying a combination of problem-solving and self-instructional training. She was taught a simple procedure for approaching a task which involved four steps:

1. 'What do I have to do?'
2. 'Am I doing it?'
3. 'How do I know I've finished?'
4. Once the task was complete (e.g. packing ready for a visit home) she rewarded herself and actively put it out of her mind.

(Self-instructions were deliberately made so that they could be applied to various tasks. Kendall and Wilcox (1980) found that instructions of this kind which could be used across a number of situations produced better results than more restricted ones.)

The problem-solving sequence was rehearsed over several sessions and there was a rapid decrease in the frequency of her anxiety attacks. She was obviously working hard at this, but found it difficult to describe what she was doing, saying 'It just goes out of my head' or 'I just don't think about it'. Another important component of the programme was a change in behaviour of the staff in the institution where she lived. On the basis of the analysis staff sought to increase the consistency in her environment by being clearer and more concrete in their communications with her. Unlike Case 1, this treatment was a complex package involving behavioural, cognitive, and environmental change, which made it difficult to determine which components contributed to the symptom relief.

Case 3: Cognitive Restructuring

While self-instructional training is effective in making up for deficits in cognitive skills, cognitive restructuring focuses on cognitive distortions. The patient is taught to monitor thoughts associated with unpleasant emotions such as anger or depression. Once these 'automatic thoughts' are identified, a variety of techniques are used to demonstrate their distorted nature. For instance, a patient may distort a situation in an 'all or nothing' way by concluding that if his girlfriend is not nice to him she has stopped loving him, and further distort his interpretation of her behaviour by jumping to the conclusion (arbitrary inference) that she will never love him again. The patient practises catching negative thoughts and reinterpreting events in a more realistic way. By therapist and patient working together to test out the validity of the patient's beliefs, much of the conflict which could potentially arise is avoided. An important aspect of these theories is the role given to beliefs and attitudes. The range of assumptions in these patients is no different from those found in other clients. Typical underlying assumptions might be 'I can only be happy if I'm a success'; 'If someone is angry with me it means I'm a terrible person'. It would appear that these represent the most abstract elements of cognitive theory and one would expect a high degree of intellectual ability in order to work with these concepts. However, the following case suggests that patients of borderline normal intelligence can sometimes make therapeutic use of these concepts.

F was a 26-year-old man who suffered brain damage at the age of 9 as a result of a road traffic accident. He was left with global intellectual impairment (IQ 71 WAIS R, Verbal 75, Performance 65). His insight into his disability left him depressed and frustrated. His main problem was with anger control, associated with the normal vicissitudes of life which make most people irritable. The fact that he reacted with excessive irritation suggested he had deficits in the cognitive strategies people normally use to control anger. But in addition to this, F showed cognitive distortions in the way he overreacted to situations. 'He shouldn't have said that', 'He was doing that to wind me up', 'They shouldn't do this to me, I wouldn't behave like that to them' were the thoughts running through his mind at the time. Underlying this was an idiosyncratic belief that all these people were violating a social rule: 'People should behave to me in a way I would behave to them.' Since he always tried to be polite, being rude was breaking this rule and people who did so deserved all they got. When the attitude was formulated in this way he responded immediately with, 'Yes, that's it . . . that is . . . that is the key', and was able to look at the disadvantages of his rather idealistic expectation. From this point on he was able to obtain much greater control of his moods.

These preliminary findings suggest that this model is of use in understanding and treating the emotional problems of adults with learning difficulties. In addition to tailoring treatment strategies to the intellectual level of the patient, there may need to be other changes in the standard cognitive therapy package. The patients described here were all treated in the conventional one-to-one therapeutic relationship, with sessions weekly or fortnightly, lasting half an hour to an hour. This is an effective format for cognitive restructuring with general psychiatric out-patients (Murphy *et al.* 1984; Blackburn *et al.* 1981), but may not be flexible enough for this client group. Problems of maintenance and generalisation might be reduced by increased flexibility. Assessment of the problem was helped by other informants, but this could be taken one step further if direct observation were carried out, and the patient asked to talk themselves through stressful situations. Further information on 'hot' cognitions might be obtained by patients using a tape recorder between sessions, and there is scope for creative use of audiovisual materials with patients with poor literacy skills. Length and frequency of sessions may need to be made more flexible, with shorter and more frequent sessions to maximise learning. All these factors can be explored further to establish which might be the best methods of service delivery.

The cognitive framework

Different cognitive levels

It seems clear, on reading these case descriptions and those in other chapters in this book, that although different problems were being addressed, nevertheless the cognitive therapy techniques used share common assumptions about how cognitive factors interact with affect and behaviour to produce symptoms. The authors are clearly working with assumptions about how cognitions can have their effects at various 'levels'. In this they are following Beck's model in which cognitive events (thoughts and images of loss, negative interpretations of ambiguous events) arise when a stressor activates an underlying cognitive structure (an attitude, belief, or assumption). These assumptions, such as 'My value as a person depends greatly on what others think of me' or 'If a person I love does not love me, it means I am unlovable', are not themselves depressive, but when certain events occur (e.g. negative feedback on one's work in the first case; being jilted by a lover in the second case) they allow a negative inference to be drawn ('I am nothing', 'I am unlovable').

According to this model, the more underlying dysfunctional assumptions a person has, the more vulnerable they will be to becoming disturbed, since there will be a wider range of situations which will activate one of them. The theory assumes that, once activated, the underlying depressive structures cause biases in memory for past events, in perception of current ambiguous situations, and in anticipation of future events. We can see from the case descriptions given in this book that the sources of ambiguity may be both external and internal to the person. An example of a misinterpretation of an external event is a child smiling at one of Cole's clients receiving cognitive therapy for offending, or the drug abuse patient, Ted, who responded to a disagreement in a pub with the thought 'I cannot let anyone treat me unjustly and get away with it'. Examples of ambiguity arising from internal sources occur in Greenberg's patient where panic symptoms are interpreted in terms of having a heart attack: 'You don't really know what is wrong with you and you are just really scared that something could happen, that you could die'. Similarly, the hypochondriacal woman, who feared that she had cancer, found that a number of symptoms would activate this fear: feelings of dryness or pain in her throat, difficulty swallowing, changes in her voice, and lumps or blotches on her skin (Warwick and Salkovskis, Chapter 4).

Finally, by whatever means such negative thoughts, images, and interpretations arise, they have subsequent effects on mood and behaviour. Thus, even in cases where such cognitive phenomena are secondary symptoms, they can still play a causal role in *maintaining* disturbance of emotion and behaviour. We shall discuss later the increasing evidence that the length of episode and the probability of relapse are partly due to a process whereby mild affective disturbance activates a relatively large amount of negative thinking.

In summary, the cognitive model suggests that cognitive structures (beliefs, assumptions) may render a person more *vulnerable* to depression in the face of a stressor; that the combination of assumption and stressor causes a number of cognitive events (ideas of loss) to occur with increased frequency and intensity which helps to *precipitate* a depressive episode; that whether or not this causal sequence occurs, cognitive factors (negative interpretations of ambiguous social situations or ambiguous symptoms) may act to *maintain* depression. Two questions arise. First, what are the implications of this model for the way in which therapy is conducted? Second, is a 'levels' model theoretically cogent?

Implications of a 'levels' model for therapy methods

In this book we have seen something of the range of techniques which therapists have brought to bear upon these vulnerability, precipitation, and maintenance aspects of emotional and behavioural disorders. It is important to note that the cognitive model, as set out above, does not imply that the use only of cognitive restructuring techniques by themselves will be sufficient to bring about permanent changes in thought–affect–behaviour links. The cognitive therapy practised here uses both behavioural *and* cognitive techniques. Figure 10.2 is a diagrammatic representation of this combination which one of us has used (Williams 1984) to illustrate cognitive therapy. This diagram illustrates three points. First, that cognitive therapy consists of both cognitive and behavioural interventions, and not simply techniques dealing with thoughts alone. Second, that in many forms of cognitive therapy, the progression is from the use of a relatively greater proportion of behavioural techniques, at the outset of therapy and/ or when the patient is more seriously disturbed, towards inclusion of more explicitly cognitive techniques. Third, that within both cognitive and behavioural components, therapy progresses from the relatively more simple to the more complex. Within behavioural work, this implies a

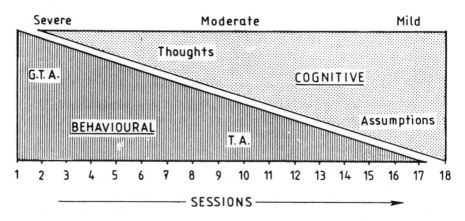

SEVERITY OF DEPRESSION

Note: G.T.A. = graded task assignment
      T.A. = task assignment

Figure 10.2 Relative proportion of cognitive and behavioural techniques used as a function of stage in therapy and/or severity of depression

Table 10.1 A hierarchical arrangement of cognitive and behavioural techniques by complexity

	Techniques	Level of complexity
Behavioural techniques	Contingent reinforcement Activity scheduling Relaxation Role-play; modelling	Low
Cognitive coping strategies	Problem solving Self-instructional training	
		Moderate
Cognitive restructuring: (1) 'Surface'	Thought monitoring Challenging negative thoughts Reality testing Reattribution	
(2) 'Deep'	Making explicit underlying fears, assumptions, 'if–then' rules Distinguish core from peripheral assumptions	High

progression from graded task assignment to assignment of whole tasks. Within the cognitive component, this implies shifting from a discussion of cognitive events (thoughts, images, particular interpretations) to dealing with underlying beliefs, attitudes, and schemata.

The variation in complexity of the different components of cognitive therapy is important. A more detailed outline is presented in Table 10.1.

The important implication of the cognitive model for how these techniques are used in the therapy sessions described in this book is that they are not all simply added together to form a collection of individual cognitive and individual behavioural techniques. We have already pointed out how therapists working within the cognitive model in this book use the cognitive framework right at the outset to guide the questions which elicit information from the client about their long-term and short-term past, and about their current functioning. It is important to make this point lest studies which purport to test cognitive therapy for some client groups be misinterpreted. For example, there have been five outcome studies which have examined some forms of cognitive interventions with anxious patients, summarised by Stravynski and Greenberg (1987). However, each of these studies takes one or two cognitive techniques (e.g. self-instructional training which attempts to change the internal self-talk of a person; or cognitive restructuring which challenges and repeatedly exposes the fallacious thinking of the anxious patient) and either compares these with behavioural exposure or adds them to a package of behavioural methods to see how much they make a difference. It comes as no surprise to find that nothing much is added by 'cognitive' techniques, thus delivered.

According to the cognitive model as developed by Beck, setting out to compare cognitive and behavioural tasks in this way misses the point. The cognitive model used by the therapists in this book suggests that behavioural assignments are themselves a potential way of changing the cognitive biases in patients with emotional and behavioural disorders. The important element of the cognitive model is its assertion that behavioural exposure is not sufficient *unless* it changes these cognitive biases. If behavioural exposure does not produce cognitive change, the model predicts that the patient will relapse. Is such a theory likely to be correct?

Theoretical cogency of a 'levels' model

Two issues arise here. First, is there any evidence for entities such as 'underlying dysfunctional attitudes' in the various client groups described here? Second, do these attitudes play the role the model ascribes to them as factors which outlast any particular episode of a disorder and render a person vulnerable for another episode?

The first question appears easier to answer. The chapters of this book have uncovered much evidence of dysfunctional attitudes in the various types of patients. Just two examples will suffice. Consider the assumptions of Warwick and Salkovskis's patient about her health: 'If I get an illness it will be untreatable'; 'Both sides of the body must be absolutely identical or there is something wrong'; 'Symptoms inside the body are more serious than ones on the outside'; 'Symptoms always mean something or they wouldn't be there'. The predictions of the cognitive model are clear and unambiguous in this case. They suggest that if this patient is treated with a therapy which successfully deals with her anxiety about current symptoms, even if it reduces the frequency and intensity of intrusive thoughts about her health, it will not prevent relapse if she retains these dysfunctional underlying assumptions. Sooner or later they will be activated again, and symptoms will return.

Another example is given by Greenberg's patient who suffers from panic attacks. She was able to identify four levels at which his fears could be represented. First, the fear of the physical effects of panic; second, fear of affect itself; third, the reactions to family and significant others; and fourth, the view of himself as inadequate and incompetent. Once again the cognitive model makes the clear prediction that even if one were able to deal with his fear of the physical effects of panic and thus reduce his symptomatology, nevertheless leaving him with the underlying attitude to himself as 'inadequate and incompetent' would leave him with a continued vulnerability for further breakdown.

Biran (1987) illustrates treatment of a single case of agoraphobia which suggests that the treatment of agoraphobia may need to take dysfunctional attitudes into account. The first stage of the treatment was exposure with some attempt to change surface cognitions. A great deal of progress was made, but careful assessment revealed that at the end of this phase many core dysfunctional attitudes remained which were tackled in a second phase of therapy. Nine-month follow-up revealed no relapse. This result needs to be followed up by the inclusion of specific hypotheses about relapse in future outcome studies.

The answer to the second question is more difficult. Do dysfunctional attitudes, if untreated, act as relatively permanent vulnerability factors, as Biran clearly assumed? Has not the evidence from studies which show normalisation of dysfunctional attitudes on recovery from depression revealed that what we once thought were vulnerability factors have turned out to be merely state-dependent variables (Wilkinson and Blackburn 1981; Lewinsohn *et al.* 1981; Simons *et al.* 1984)? If so, patients will have many permanent-looking dysfunctional attitudes when distressed, but these will disappear when the distress remits.

There are indications that this conclusion is premature, however. According to Teasdale (1983), an important maintaining factor in depression is the extent to which any amount of affective disturbance produces cognitive changes. These assumptions are examined in a further paper by Teasdale and Dent (1987) in which recovered depressives and 'never depressed' controls were given mood induction and the extent of cognitive change examined. They found that for equivalent degrees of mood shift, the recovered (and presumably more vulnerable) group showed greater tendency to rate themselves negatively. Vulnerability for depression may thus be defined in terms of the amount of affective disturbance needed to make people react with global negative self-evaluations. If a relatively *small* affective disturbance causes a *large* cognitive reaction there is a greater likelihood of the negative spiral twisting more deeply. Notice that these notions overcome the problems that arise from the negative findings in the research literature. For example, one would not necessarily be able to measure this vulnerability in the complete absence of current depressed mood, so that testing recovered patients may often show little cognitive differences (Wilkinson and Blackburn 1981; Lewinsohn *et al.* 1981). The vulnerable people may nevertheless be those who react to small mood disturbance with more 'catastrophic' cognitions. To deny that these people are vulnerable is like ignoring a hair-line split in a brake pipe of a car. The pipe may work perfectly well under normal driving conditions, but under extra load of sudden fierce braking, it may give way.

If this is correct, then the time to assess vulnerability is when there is likely to be some small amount of affective disturbance (Teasdale 1988). For example, if two patients, on completing treatment, have the same level of mood disturbance but the mood of the first is associated with greater dysfunctional attitude than is the mood of the second, then the first should be more vulnerable to relapse. There is indeed evidence from outcome

trials of depression (Simons *et al*. 1986) that people who respond equiva-
lently to the acute phase of treatment (in terms of their behavioural and
emotional recovery) have different probabilities of relapse depending on
the level of their dysfunctional attitudes at treatment termination. Whether
a similar point can be made about other disorders is not yet clear.

There are important implications of these findings for how to test the
cogency of any theory which sees dysfunctional attitudes as vulnerability
factors. In testing the model in other clinical disorders, it may prove
insufficient merely to measure such attitudes at the beginning and end of
treatment and during remission. Dysfunctional attitudes may appear
normalised during times of low stress. Vulnerability consists of the
tendency for fast and extensive recruitment of dysfunctional attitudes when
stress levels begin to increase. This predisposition may well be a relatively
permanent aspect in some patients, and future research must work towards
clarifying how such a predisposition is activated.

Future Research

Basic research on cognitive processes

In this section we examine just one example of the way in which basic
research can help our understanding of cognitive processes: research on
depression and autobiographical memory. It has been known for some
time that depressed people are more likely to retrieve negative than
positive events from the past (Lloyd and Lishman 1975). Further research
has shown that this is not due simply to having more negative events in
one's past or to a tendency to misclassify neutral and positive events as
negative (Teasdale and Fogarty 1979). Recently we have found an additional subtle deficit in the memory of depressed people. Their memory for
emotional events (both positive and negative) tends to be less *specific*.
That is, in respose to an instruction to remember a specific episode when
given a cue word (e.g. happy, angry), they are more likely to refer to
categories of events (e.g. 'birthday parties' or 'the times he argued with
me'). Patients are especially poor at recalling specific positive memories –
which reverses the normal tendency in non-depressed control subjects to
be more specific in positive memories (Williams and Broadbent 1986;
Williams and Scott 1988). Why does this occur?

Retrieval from autobiographical memory is a staged process in which a
general description of the memory required is generated, plus mnemonic
cues to help search for specific examples of the general description. For
example, in searching for a happy memory, one is likely first to recall the
sort of activities or people or places that make one happy, then to search
for specific examples. We believe that depressives are particularly likely
to stop at this general stage, partly because it is effortful to be more

specific, but partly because these patients store emotional events in long-term memory (LTM) in overgeneral categories, making it more difficult to retrieve specific instances.

The significance of this difficulty in recalling specific memories can be seen in therapy where a person fails to give specific examples of times when they have been happy. Without such ready recall of concrete examples of coping successfully with life in the past, solving current problems is made even more difficult. The lack of specificity exists even if they are able to report in *general* terms that their lives are happy. They are then in the cognitively confusing position of believing their lives *should* be happy, but having little ready access to specific evidence. The resulting guilt only adds to the depressive's problems.

Neither is it much help that their memory of unhappiness is also more overgeneral (though to a lesser extent than positive memories). Successful problem solving requires an ability to recall relatively detailed pictures of past problems so that possible ways around obstacles can be more easily seen. For example, Wahler and Afton (1980) found that mothers under stress who had relationship problems with their children tended to use global blameful statements to describe their children's behaviour. They found it difficult to retrieve specific examples of the children's bad behaviour. As part of a parent training programme mothers who were able to learn to be more specific to describe their children's behaviour were also those mothers who responded best to the therapy.

What is the importance of these results for cognitive therapy? First, diaries which record activities or thoughts may be of therapeutic benefit in part by encouraging patients to be specific in looking at their problems. Second, Wahler and Afton imply that diary keeping is a *skill* which may take time for patients to learn, since it involves a degree of specificity of description which is particularly hard for such patients to achieve spontaneously. When depressed patients fail to keep diaries, therapists often interpret this to mean that patients are not motivated to use the technique, or, even worse, are trying to undermine the therapy. There may be such patients, of course, but these hypotheses ought not to be considered until one has rejected the skill-deficit hypothesis. One would not blame a dyslexic child for not being able to spell. Neither should one expect a depressed patient to be able to identify, write down, or recall specific examples until this deficit in their cognitive processing has been explicitly addressed as part of treatment.

Future strategies for clinical research

Ultimately the efficacy of cognitive therapy with each of the client groups discussed in this book can only be tested by a properly controlled outcome study. In such studies random assignment of clients to different groups, using clearly defined patient groups diagnosed by internationally recognised criteria, are essential. Good outcome studies are very difficult to do (hence their scarcity) but at least, as a minimum, they need to have the following characteristics. First, there must be an appropriate control condition. Sometimes it is permissible for this control condition to be a treatment-as-usual condition (as, for example, used by Teasdale *et al.* 1984). This is more appropriate where cognitive therapy is being used for the first time specifically for that group. However, the case for using a treatment-as-usual control group must be made on each occasion, for it does not control the quality of the control therapies that are given (e.g. the length of time they spend with a therapist).

A second aspect of cognitive therapy which will need to be taken into account in an outcome trial is the quality of the therapy being delivered. It will be important to make tapes of sessions and to have them assessed by experienced cognitive therapists to check (1) that the therapy format conforms to the cognitive therapy model in general, and (2) that the quality of the particular cognitive therapy being used is adequate. Without these reassurances, any failure to produce the predicted effects may too easily be put down to the poor quality of the therapy. If cognitive therapy does *not* work very well for a particular client group we need to know that sooner rather than later, without escaping into excuses about the quality of the cognitive therapy.

Third, an outcome trial needs comprehensive assessment of behavioural, affective, and cognitive variables. These need to be made not only by self-ratings but by an independent assessor. Ideally they should be combined with some measures which assess self-schema or attention or memory biases which have been derived from experimental cognitive psychology. In a recent book on the application of cognitive psychology to emotional disorders, Williams *et al.* (1988) suggest that the measures of outcome should be matched to the type of psychopathology. Thus, for example, it is more appropriate, for anxiety-based disorders, to use outcome measures which assess biases in automatic aspects of encoding and retrieval. Conversely, it is more appropriate to use, as a measure of outcome in depression-based disorders, procedures which assess strategic or effortful aspects of cognitive processing, as most tests of memory do.

Fourth, there needs to be adequate follow-up for at least one or two years after the initial acute phase of treatment. An important aspect of this follow-up is that it should not merely be a single assessment to see how well each group of patients is still faring. Cognitive therapy claims to be a treatment which will not only be effective in the acute phase but also prevent relapse. The follow-up phase is a crucial aspect of the study and should be built into the design. This means that the numbers of patients in each group should be sufficient so that if the predicted proportion of relapses occur in the cognitive therapy and control groups, then the comparison between the groups will have sufficient power to show the difference to be attributable to the therapy rather than to chance. For example, one might expect a control group to have a relapse rate of 50 per cent. One may be quite happy if the cognitive therapy was able to cut the relapse rate by half to 25 per cent. Indeed, that would seem to be a very good outcome. However, to be able to confirm that this difference did not occur by chance one would need sufficient numbers. If there were forty-eight responders in the trial evenly split between the two groups (twenty-four in each), then in the control group twelve people would relapse, leaving twelve improved. In the cognitive therapy group six people would relapse leaving eighteen improved. Analysis of these data yields a chi-square of 3.2 which has not achieved statistical significance at the 5 per cent level. One could not be sure that this result did not occur by chance. Increasing the number of responders in the trial to sixty (thirty in each group) allows statistical signifi-cance to be achieved at a 5 per cent level (with a similar breakdown of results), with fifteen out of the thirty relapsing in one group and seven out of the thirty relapsing in the other.[1]

Another aspect of building the follow-up into the design at the outset of the study is that one can define relapse *pre* rather than *post hoc*. Many studies which perform naturalistic follow-ups (that is, waiting to see which patients return for treatment) also incur the problem that people may return to treatment for different reasons and at very different levels of symptoms. Some may not return for treatment at all, and yet have very severe symptoms. Others return with very mild worries. Thus it is necessary, if the follow-up is to be adequate, to build in some repeated assessment of the frequency and intensity of signs and symptoms. Such repeated assessment will also take into account the occurrence of further negative life events and chronic difficulties. One would not wish to judge two (otherwise similar) patterns of relapse as being truly equivalent if the first followed an extremely severe life event and the second seemed to occur unprecipitated.

Third, a follow-up which is built into the design at the outset of the study will have some proper hypotheses about which patients are most likely to relapse. For example, as we have seen above, the cognitive model would predict that those people who, despite the fact that they are symptom-free at the end of the treatment, nevertheless continue to express dysfunctional attitudes, are the most likely to relapse.

We have concentrated on outcome studies as being the main strategy for clinical research, not because it is the only strategy, but because it is one of the most difficult strategies to implement well. The main alternative to outcome studies is to look at short-term, within-session changes in specific aspects of cognition and affect in response to specific manipula-tions. The most clear-cut example of using such within-session 'mini-treatments' is a series of studies by Teasdale and his co-workers at Oxford on the use of distraction techniques to reduce the frequency of negative thoughts. Teasdale's research in the 1970s was one of the first to demonstrate experimentally that negative thoughts could maintain negative mood by showing that negative mood was reduced when negative thoughts were reduced (Teasdale and Rezin 1978). Subsequent research has shown that this effect is more likely to occur in patients who are defined towards the neurotic end of the Newcastle Endogeneity Scale (Fennell and Teasdale 1987). For an equivalent degree of reduction in the frequency of negative thoughts, the more endogenous patients show a more attenuated mood response. This research has implications for use of this particular technique when treating depressed patients.

Similar procedures can be used within cognitive therapy for other client groups. A good example of this is the use of exposure to stimuli associated with drug use (Moorey, p. 171). The therapist was able to look at change in craving during exposure, and was therefore able to test out a hypothesis of the client that craving would not recover over time while she was exposed to these stimuli. Additionally, the therapist was able to note the changes in the nature of thoughts and images which came to mind during the exposure session. If a series of standard exposures were to be used with different patients it might be possible to derive very useful clinical guidelines indicating which patients would benefit most from this technique. Cognitive therapy provides a range of techniques which lend themselves very easily to the scientist–practitioner mode of therapy.

Both strategies of clinical research, larger-scale outcome studies, and smaller-scale investigation of the processes underlying treatment have been used for some time in research into depression. They are beginning to be used with research with other client groups. It is a very exciting time to be a cognitive therapist, able to make use of these techniques for new client groups for whom they have not been used in the past. The cases described in this book show that the techniques appear to be able to be used very effectively indeed. Longer series of patients and standardised outcome trials will follow. This volume marks the end of the beginning for the wider application of cognitive therapy.

Note

1. To achieve these numbers of responders, there will need to be more patients in the initial treatment trial, since not all patients will respond to the acute treatment.

References

Beck, A.T., Rush, A.J., Shaw, B.F., and Emery, G. (1979) *Cognitive Therapy of Depression: A Treatment Manual*, New York: Guilford Press.

Biran, N.W. (1987) 'Two stage therapy for agoraphobia', *American Journal of Psychotherapy* 41: 127–36.

Blackburn, I.M., Bishop, S., Glen, I.M., Whalley, L.J., and Christie, J.E. (1981) 'The efficacy of cognitive therapy in depression: a treatment trial using cognitive therapy and pharmacotherapy, each alone and in combination', *British Journal of Psychiatry* 139: 181–9.

Fennell, M.J.V. and Teasdale, J.D. (1987) 'Cognitive therapy for depression: individual differences and the process of change', *Cognitive Therapy and Research* 11: 253–72.

Kendall, P.C. and Finch, A.J. (1976) 'A cognitive behavioural therapy for impulse control: a case study', *Journal of Consulting and Clinical Psychology* 44: 852–7.

Kendall, P.C. and Finch, A.J. (1978) 'A cognitive behavioural therapy for impulsivity: a comparison group study', *Journal of Consulting and Clinical Psychology* 46: 110–18.

Kendall, P.C. and Wilcox, L.E. (1980) 'Cognitive behaviour therapy for impulsivity: concrete versus conceptual training in non-self controlled problem children', *Journal of Consulting and Clinical Psychology* 48: 80–91.

Lewinsohn, P.M., Steinmetz, J.L., Larson, D.W., and Franklin, J. (1981) 'Depression related cognitions: antecedents or consequences?' *Journal of Abnormal Psychology* 90: 213–19.

Lloyd, G.G. and Lishman, W.A. (1975) 'Effect of depression on the speed of recall of pleasant and unpleasant experiences', *Psychological Medicine* 5: 173–80.

Meichenbaum, D. and Goodman, J. (1971) 'Training impulsive children to talk to themselves: a means of developing self control', *Journal of Abnormal Psychology* 77: 115–26.

Murphy, G.E., Simons, K.D., Wetzel, R.D., and Lustman, P.J. (1984) 'Cognitive therapy and pharmacotherapy; singly and together in the treatment of depression', *Archives of General Psychiatry* 41: 33–41.

Simons, A.D., Garfield, F.L., and Murphy, T.E. (1984) 'The process of change in cognitive therapy and pharmacotherapy for depression', *Archives of General Psychiatry* 41: 45–51.

Simons, A.D., Murphy, G.E., Levine, J.E., and Wetzel, R.D. (1986) 'Cognitive therapy and pharmacotherapy for depression', *Archives of General Psychiatry* 43: 43–8.

Stravynski, A. and Greenberg, D. (1987) 'Cognitive therapies with neurotic disorders: clinical utility and related issues', *Comprehensive Psychiatry* 28: 141–50.

Teasdale, J.D. (1983) 'Negative thinking in depression: cause, effect or reciprocal relationship?' *Advances in Behaviour Research and Therapy* 5: 3–25.

Teasdale, J.D. (1988) 'Cognitive vulnerability to persistent depression', *Cognition and Emotion* 2: 247–74.

Teasdale, J.D. and Dent, J. (1987) 'Cognitive vulnerability to depression: an investigation of two hypotheses', *British Journal of Clinical Psychology* 26: 113–26.

Teasdale, J.D., Fennell, M.J.V., Hibbert, G.A., and Amies, P.L. (1984) 'Cognitive therapy for major depressive disorder in primary care' *British Journal of Psychiatry* 144: 400–6.

Teasdale, J.D. and Fogarty, S.J. (1979) 'Differential effects of induced mood on retrieval of pleasant and unpleasant memories from episodic memory', *Journal of Abnormal Psychology* 88: 248–57.

Teasdale, J.D. and Rezin, V. (1978) 'The effects of reducing frequency of negative thoughts on the mood of depressed patients – tests of a cognitive model of depression', *British Journal of Social and Clinical Psychology* 17: 65–74.

Wahler, R.G. and Afton, A.D. (1980) 'Attentional processes in insular and noninsular mothers: some differences in their summary reports about child behavior problems', *Child Behavior Therapy* 2: 25–41.

Weissman, A.N. and Beck, A.T. (1978) 'Development and validation of the Dysfunctional Attitude Scale', paper presented at American Educational Research Association Annual Convention, Toronto. Canada.

Wilkinson, I.M. and Blackburn, I.M. (1981) 'Cognitive style in depressed and recovered depressed patients', *British Journal of Clinical Psychology* 20: 283–92.

Williams, J.M.G. (1984) *The Psychological Treatment of Depression: A Guide to the Theory and Practice of Cognitive Behaviour Therapy*, London: Croom Helm and New York: Free Press.

Williams, J.M.G. and Broadbent, K. (1986) 'Autobiographical memory in attempted suicide patients', *Journal of Abnormal Psychology* 95: 144–9.

Williams, J.M.G. and Scott, J. (1988) 'Autobiographical memory in depression', *Psychological Medicine* 18: 689–95.

Williams, J.M.G., Watts, F.N., MacLeod, C., and Mathews, A. (1988) *Cognitive Psychology and Emotional Disorders*, Chichester: Wiley.

Index

Abraham, S.F. 128
Afton, A.D. 245
agoraphobia *see* panic disorder and
    agoraphobia
Agras, W.S. 128
AIDS 99–101
Alberti, R.E. 123
American Psychiatric Association 78,
    106, 127
anorexia nervosa *see* eating disorders
anxiety: hypochondriasis 79–81, 83–4;
    obsessions and compulsions 50–3;
    panic disorder and agoraphobia 25–8
Anxiety Checklist (ACL) 111
attitudes, dysfunctional *see*
    dysfunctional attitudes
Automatic Thoughts Questionnaire
    (ATQ) 21–2

Bachrach, A.J. 128
Bancroft, J. 185
Bandura, A. 183
Barsky, A.J. 78
Beck, Aaron T. vi; anxiety 25–6, 50,
    103, 174, 178, 183; cognitive model
    161, 183, 238, 242; cognitive therapy
    vii–xv; *Coping with Depression*
    11–12; depression, CT 1, 4, 14, 107,
    152, 183, 206–7, 210, 219, 225; drug
    abuse 160, 164, 167; dysfunctional
    attitudes 20, 147, 232; panic
    disorders 28; suicidal patients 206–8,
    210, 219
Beck Depression Inventory (BDI) 21,
    111, 133, 136
Beech, H.R. 53
behaviour therapy and CT 241;
    obsessions 50–2, 53

Beinart, H. 140
Bemis, K.M. 128, 137, 140, 147
Bethlem Royal Hospital 161
Bianchi, G.N. 78
binge eating 145
Biran, N.W. 242–3
Blackburn, Ivy M. vi; CT for depression
    vi–viii, 23, 72, 103, 183, 238, 243;
    depressed in-patients viii, 1–23, 110,
    228–9
Blanchard, E.B. 103
Bloom, J.R. 106
Bo-Linn, G.W. 146
Bradley, B.P. 172
Bradley, L.A. 103
Brandsma, J.M. 160
Broadbent, K. 244
Bruni, J. 103
Buglass, D. 208–9
bulimia nervosa *see* eating disorders
Burns, D. 18, 123

cancer, fear of 94–6
cancer patients xi, 103–24; case study,
    Margaret 110–23; control loss 107–8;
    coping strategies 109; grief 107; pain
    108–9; physical problems 108;
    problems 109–10; psychological
    problems 104–5; rationale for CT
    105–6
Carey, J.B. 160
Carlin, A.S. 159
Catalan, J. 206, 225
Cautela, J.R. 170–1
Chaney, E.F. 160
Channon, Shelley vi, xii, 127–53, 230
Christensen, H. 72
Clark, D.M. 26, 29

Clarke Institute, Toronto 127
cognitive model 238–44
cognitive therapy vii–xv, 227–48; and
    behaviour therapy 241; cancer
    patients xi, 103–24; depressed in-
    patients viii, 1–23, 228–9; drug
    abusers xii–xiii, 157–80, 231;
    dysfunctional attitudes (q.v.) 232–3;
    eating disorders xii, 127–53, 230–1;
    engagement and explanation 229–30;
    future research 244–8;
    hypochondriasis x–xi, 78–102, 232–3,
    239, 242; and learning difficulties
    233–8; model 238–44; new
    applications vii, 227, 233–4;
    obsessions and compulsions ix–x,
    50–76, 229–30; offenders xiii–xiv,
    183–204, 231–2, 239; panic and
    agoraphobia ix, 25–49, 228–30, 233,
    239, 242; and relationship problems
    233; suicidal patients xiv, 206–25;
    techniques for eliciting thoughts and
    feelings 230–1
Cohler, B.J. 153
Cole, Amanda vi, xiii–xiv, 183–204,
    231–2, 239
Collins, R.L. 159
compulsive behaviour see obsessions
    and compulsions
Connell, P.H. 158
Cooper, P.J. 128
Craft, M. and A. 183
Crawford, D.S. 183–4
Crisp, A.H. 127
Cummings, C. 159, 174

Dean, C. 105
Dent, J. 243
depressed in-patients viii, 1–23, 228–9;
    case study, Anne viii, 5–21;
    problems 3–4, 22–3; rationale 2–3
depression: and eating disorders 152;
    and obsessions and compulsions 72;
    see also suicidal patients
de Silva, P. 53, 62, 130
Devlin, H.B. 104
Dickerson, M. 76
DiClemente, C.C. xiii, 160, 165
Dienelt, N.N. 206
drug abusers xii–xiii, 157–80, 231;
    cognitive models 159–60; CT scheme
    160–1; cue analysis 168–70;
    motivation for treatment 164–7;

negative cognitions 167–8; problem
    solving and cue modification 170–6;
    rationale for treatment 167; self-
    schemas 178–80; therapeutic
    relationship 162–4; treatment 157–8;
    underlying assumptions 176–8
Dryden, W. 179
Dyer, J.A.T. 207
Dysfunctional Attitude Scale (DAS) 20,
    21–2, 111, 123, 232
dysfunctional attitudes 232–3; cancer
    patients 111, 117–24; depression 9,
    16–18; drug abusers 167–8, 176–8,
    232; eating disorders 136, 146–52;
    hypochondriasis x, 79–81, 232–3;
    obsessions and compulsions ix, 50,
    53–6, 71–2; offenders 185–7, 194–7,
    203, 232; panic disorders ix, 25–8,
    29, 233; suicidal patients 216–19;
    techniques for eliciting 230–2

eating disorders xii, 127–53, 230–1;
    assessment 130–6; case study, Carol
    xii, 129–30, 136–52; definition
    127–8; dysfunctional thoughts
    146–52; eating behaviour 144–6;
    education 141–2; motivation for
    treatment 140–7; rationale for
    treatment 140–1; therapists'
    responses 153; treatment 128–9, 137;
    weight restoration 142–3
Edwards, S. 76
electroconvulsive therapy (ECT) 2, 22
Ellis, A. 183, 186
Emery, G.D.: anxiety 25, 174;
    depression 187; drug abuse 160, 164,
    167, 183
Emmelkamp, P.M.G. 76
Emmons, M.L. 123
engaging patients in CT 229–30;
    depression 4, 229; drug abuse xii–xiii,
    161–2; hypochondriasis 84–5;
    obsessions x, 63–9, 229; offenders
    185; panic disorder 229
Espie, C.A. 51

Fairburn, C.G. 127–8, 153
Fazio, A.F. 1
Feighner, J.P. 1
Feindler, E.L. 184
Fennell, M.J.V. 23, 224, 248
Finch, A.J. 235
Florey, C.D.V. 136

Foa, E.B. 51, 72
Fogarty, S.J. 244
Fox, S. 159
Fraser, S. 206

Gardner, R. 158
Garfinkel, P.E. 130, 152
Garner, D.M. 127–30, 134–7, 140–3, 147, 152–3
George, W.G. 170
Ghodse, A.H. 158
Gittleson, N. 72
Glantz, M.D. 160
Goldberg, D. 2
Goldstein, A. 51
Gomez, J. 108
Goodman, J. 235
Gordon, J.R. 159, 173–4
Gordon, W.A. 106
Greenberg, D. 241
Greenberg, Ruth L, vi; depression 11–12; panic and agoraphobia ix, 25–49, 228–30, 233, 239, 242
Greer, S. 104–5, 110
Grossman, S. 127
Gudjonsson, G. 183
Guidano, V.F. 179

Hakstian, A.R. 1
Hamilton, M. 5, 20
Hamilton Rating Scale for Depression (HRSD) 5, 20, 21, 111
Harrison, J. 53, 62
Hawton, K. 206, 225
Herman, C.P. 140
Hibbard, M.R. 110
Hirsch, F.R. 206
Hodgson, R. 53
Holland, J.C. 104–6
Hollon, S.D. 21
hopelessness xiv, 2, 111, 223–4
Hopelessness Scale (HS) 111
Horan, J.J. 184
Horton, J. 208–9
Howells, K. 183, 187
Hsu, L.K. 128
Hughson, A. 104
Hutchinson, M.G. 143
Huxley, P. 2
hyperventilation 26, 29, 33–6, 39, 230
hypochondriasis x–xi, 78–102, 232–3, 239, 242; case studies 86–92, 94–101; cognitive-behavioural hypothesis

79–82; definition 78–9; other hypotheses 93–4; principles of CT 84–6, 101–2 reassurance 83–4

Jackson, P.R. 160
Janis, I.L. 165–6
Johnson, W.G. 128

Katz, R.C. 184
Kendall, P.C. 21, 235–6
Keys, A. 140
Kirk, J.W. 62, 72–3
Kirkley, B.G. 128
Klerman, G.L. 78
Kreitman, N. 207

Lacey, J.H. 128
Larcombe, N.A. 103
learning difficulties 233–8; case studies 234–8
Leith, B. 103
Leonhard, K. 78
'levels' of cognitions 238–44
Levine, P.M. 104, 110
Levison, P.K. 157
Lewinsohn, P.M. 243
Liddell, A. 53
Liotti, G. 179
Lishman, W.A. 244
Lloyd, G.G. 244
Lopez, F.G. 184

McCourt, W. 160
McIntosh, J. 104
McLean, P.D. 1
MacLeod, S. 142
Maguire, P. 103, 105
Maisto, S.A. 160
Mann, L. 165–6
Marks, I.M. 51, 72, 78
Marlatt, G.A. 159–61, 170, 173–4
Marshall, W.L. 1, 183
Massie, M.J. 104, 106
Medlik, L. 128
Meichenbaum, D. 184, 235
Metropolitan Life Insurance 136
Miller, W. 165
Moorey, Stirling, vi, xii–xiii, 157–80, 227–48
Morgan, H.G. 128, 130
Morris, T. 104–5, 107
motivation for treatment: drug abusers

xii–xiii, 164–7; eating disorders
137–40; offenders xiii
Murphy, G.E. 1, 162, 183, 238

negative thoughts *see* dysfunctional
attitudes
Nemiah, J.C. 78
Newcastle Endogeneity Scale 248
Nomellini, S. 184
Novaco, R. 183–4

obsessions and compulsions ix–x,
50–76, 229–30; application of CT
56–8; assessment 58–62; behavioural
model 50–2, 53; cognitive model
52–6; compliance with treatment
63–9; and depression 72;
development of disorder 53–6;
negative automatic thoughts 71–2;
obsession without compulsive
behaviour 72–4; relapse prevention
74–5; treatment 63–75
Oei, T.P.S. 160
offenders xiii–xiv, 183–204, 231–2, 239;
case study 191–203; clinical
approaches 183–4; CT techniques
185–91; problems 184–5

Panic Belief Questionnaire 26–8
panic disorder and agoraphobia ix,
25–49, 228–30, 233, 239, 242; case
study, John 28–49; perceptions of
danger 25–8
Paykel, E.S. 206
Pearce, S. 108
Pearlson, G.D. 134
Perkins, D. 183–4
phobia *see* panic disorder
Pilowsky, I. 78
Polivy, J. 140
Power, K.G. 208
Present State Examination (PSE) 5
Prochaska, J.0. xiii, 160, 165

Rachman, S.J. 51, 53, 62, 72
reassurance 56, 83–4
relationship problems 233
Rezin, V. 248
Richardson, P.H. 108
Roche, L. 142
Roper, G. 53
Rosenbaum, M. 224
Rosenberg, L. 133, 136

Rush, A.J. 1, 103, 183
Russell, G.F.M. 127–8, 130, 134
Ryle, J.A. 78

Salkovskis, Paul M. vi; hyperventilation
26; hypochondriasis x–xi, 78–102,
232–3, 239, 242; obsessions and
compulsions ix–x, 50–76, 229–30
Sanchez-Craig, M. 160
Schlichter, K.J. 184
Schmale, A.H. 105
Schonfield, J. 105
Schwartz, D.M. 128
Schwarz, S.P. 103
Scott, Jan vi, xi, 103–24
Segal, Z.V. 183
Selvini-Palazzoli, M. 153
Shaw, B.F. 1
Shipley, C.R. 1
Silberfarb, P. 104
Simons, A.D. vii, 3, 225, 243–4
Slade, P.D. 134, 140
Smith, G.R. 128
Sobel, H.J. 106
Spielberger, C.D. 21
Spitzer, R.L. 1, 5
State-Trait Anxiety Inventory (STAI)
21
Stern, M.J. 103
Stravynski, A. 241
Suicidal Ideation, Scale of (SSI) 111
suicidal patients xiv, 206–25; case
studies 210–23; and depression (*q.v.*)
206–8; future, inability to imagine
219–23; hopelessness 223–4;
negative thoughts 216–19; prediction
of suicide attempt 208–9; reasons for
living v. dying 210–16, 224; therapy
209; vigilance 209–10
Swift, W.J. 128

Tan, S.Y. 103
Taylor, F.G. 1
Teasdale, J.D. 1, 23, 224, 243–8
Thompson, M.G. 128
thoughts, technique for eliciting 230–1;
see also dysfunctional attitudes
Thurman, C.W. 184
Toch, H. 203
Toner, B.B. 127
Treasure, J. 142

Valliant, P.M. 103

Van Strien, T. 134, 136
vomiting 146

Wahler, R.G. 245
Wardle, Jane vi, xii, 127–53, 230
Warwick, Hilary M.C. vi;
    hypochondriasis x–xi, 78–102, 232–3,
    239, 242; obsessions and
    compulsions 57, 63, 72–3;
    reassurance 56
Watkins, J.T. 1
Weiner, H. 159
Weisman, A.D. 105, 109
Weissman, A.N. 20–1, 232
Wells, Jonathan vi, xiv, 206–25

Westbrook, D. 72–3, 83
Wilcox, L.E. 236
Wilkinson, I.M. 243
Willi, J. 127
Williams, J. Mark G. vi, xiv, 107,
    206–25, 227–48
Wilson, G.T. 128
Wilson, P.H. 1, 103
Wing, J.K. 5
Wolchik, S.A. 128
Woody, G.E. 159
Worden, J.W. 103, 105–6, 109

Zeiss, A.M. 1